# The Archaeology of Greek Colonisation

## Essays dedicated to Sir John Boardman

*edited by*
*Gocha R. Tsetskhladze and Franco De Angelis*

Oxford University School of Archaeology
Monograph 40

*Published by*
Oxford University School of Archaeology
Institute of Archaeology
Beaumont Street
Oxford OX1 2PG

*Distributed by*
Oxbow Books
Park End Place, Oxford OX1 1HN

ISBN 0 947816 61 5

First published 1994
Reprinted with minor corrections and a new preface 2004

*The photograph on the front cover shows the sun setting over
the site of the Greek colony of Panticapaeum (Crimea), seen from Myrmekion.
(Photo: P. Leriche)*

*The photograph on the back shows a war-galley overtaking a merchantman
travelling under shortened sail, on an Athenian black-figure cup of c. 510 BC.
(Photo: British Museum)*

*Printed in Great Britain*
at the Short Run Press, Exeter

# Contents

"The historian who will accept archaeological data only where
they support a text is a phantom that still stalks the subject;
as is the language man who thinks that all pictures illustrate texts."

John Boardman, *Antiquity* 62 (1988), 796

# Preface

The present volume contains lectures given during Hilary Term 1994 at Oxford University, in the Ruskin Lecture Theatre of the Ashmolean Museum. This lecture series was dedicated to Sir John Boardman, Lincoln Professor of Classical Archaeology and Art, to mark his retirement, although he was initially not aware of the organisers' intention to honour him in this way.

The subject of the series was chosen for several reasons. Colonisation is, if not the main, at least one of the most important phenomena of Greek history, since Greeks set up colonies in new environments, establishing themselves in the lands stretching from the Iberian peninsula in the West, North Africa in the South, and the Black Sea in the North-East. In this colonial world Greek and local cultures met, influenced, and enriched each other, resulting in the foundation of modern European culture.

Many generations of scholars have studied Greek colonisation, though their efforts have largely focused on aims narrowly defined, such as the literary traditions of the foundation of the colonies. However, there are major limitations to what may today be said about Greek colonisation from ancient authors alone. Studies have shown that the potential for future advances of the discipline can only come from archaeology. Large-scale archaeological research is yearly producing new evidence, allowing us to look at Greek colonisation from a different angle. The aim of the lecture series was not just to take these new discoveries into account but also to introduce new approaches to handling both the old and new data, pointing out at the same time the gaps and possible future directions for the study of Greek colonisation from the archaeological viewpoint.

These aims were formulated with Professor Boardman's work in mind. There is no doubt about Boardman's leading role in classical archaeology and art; he has written many works of fundamental importance in almost every branch of the discipline. Among these numerous interests, one in particular has been with him from early on, namely the Greeks overseas. Since the beginning of his professional career, Boardman has recognised the importance of archaeological evidence to the study of Greek colonisation, and so it was thought fitting to organise this series of lectures concentrating on one of his prime interests.

It might be seen as odd that we include a chapter by the person being honoured, but we justify this by the fact that there are few specialists in Britain who know better the archaeology of Greeks in North Africa. Furthermore, we think that there is everything to be said for having Boardman as a contributor when, once again, he demonstrates that he deserves to be one. His abilities have been recognised by his having occupied, for many years and with great distinction, the chair of Lincoln Professor of Classical Archaeology and Art in Oxford which, traditionally, has always been held by scholars of the highest world-wide reputation and prestige.

Professor Boardman's colleagues and past and present pupils agreed to participate. From the start our aim was to incorporate all the regions of the ancient world which witnessed Greek activity, as Boardman himself had done in his standard study of this phenomenon. After receiving the texts from the various contributors, we recognised the different character of the essays, and we decided as editors to give the individual authors as much freedom as possible to preserve the original approach of the lectures. This is why each chapter has its own personal method of presentation. Some authors did not feel the need to encumber their texts with many notes and long bibliography (the latter can easily be found in the standard works of reference: for example, *The Cambridge Ancient History*). Other authors, however, owing to the nature of their material and argument felt that the inclusion of such information would be necessary. However, this volume of essays should not at all be considered a new edition of Boardman's great work *The Greeks Overseas: Their Early Colonies and Trade* (London: Thames and Hudson), because only some aspects of the regions studied are treated. All the chapters, moreover, deal with the establishment and early development of the colonies; such subjects as the relationship between Greek colonists and native populations – which in any case was recently studied in a volume edited by Descoeudres (Oxford 1990) – are the editors' aim for a future volume.

Although the present volume chiefly focuses on the archaeological evidence, the historical side was not overlooked by the contributors. We believe that study of Greek colonisation from the historian's point of view is as important as the material remains themselves. The combined study, from all different angles, is what is needed to understand this crucial phenomenon in the history of the ancient world. A major project studying Greek colonisation as history is already under way, a volume edited by Irad Malkin (to be published by Brill in Leiden).

The chapters are organised according to the rules of the *Oxford Journal of Archaeology*, which allows individual bibliographies at the end of each contribution – an arrangement which better suits the regional approach and avoids the confusion of one large bibliography – as well as special abbreviations in addition to the general list we have compiled. There is no introductory chapter because the essays themselves demonstrate in various ways the importance of archaeology in the study of Greek colonisation.

After attending these lectures, Professor B. W. Cunliffe suggested that we should put them together as a single volume. The initial plan was to publish them as a special issue of the *Oxford Journal of Archaeology*, but this quickly grew into a volume in the Committee for Archaeology's Monograph series. We are extremely grateful to him for this suggestion and also for his co-operation and advice in the course of preparing the book. Thanks are also due in this respect to David Brown and his staff at Oxbow for their technical help and prompt publication. We are grateful to Marion Cox for redrawing most of the maps and plans, and also to Bob Wilkins and Jennie Lowe of the Institute of Archaeology's Photographic Department for preparation of the photographs. We would like to extend our gratitude to the British Museum (Department of Greek and Roman Antiquities) and Professor P. Leriche (Director of Research, CNRS, E. N. S., Paris) for permission to reproduce the photographs which appear on the dustjacket. The editors would like to thank personally Jill Drake, Administrative Secretary at the Institute of Archaeology, for organising so well the post-lecture receptions held in the Institute. Finally, we would like to thank warmly the contributors for taking part and our many colleagues, students, and members of the public who attended the lectures.

G. R. Tsetskhladze and F. De Angelis

# Preface
## *to this paperback editon*

We are very pleased to present this paperback edition. The hardback edition had been out of print for several years. We received many communications asking that it be reprinted or a new edition prepared. The editors and authors have been gratified by the evidence of how widely the volume has been used, especially by students.

Initially, we thought of updating each chapter to take account of recent developments, but this proved technically impracticable except at great expense. Thus, here is the text as in 1994, but with a few minor corrections.

1999 saw a new edition of John Boardman's *The Greeks Overseas*, containing an epilogue, at pp. 267–282, which gives a brief account of major developments since the previous edition (1980) and makes extensive use of our *The Archaeology of Greek Colonisation*. In our 1994 Preface we stated that a comprehensive history of Greek colonisation would shortly be published by Brill. John Boardman repeated this at p. 298 in his new edition. Unfortunately, this project has been delayed, but, under new editorship (G. R. Tsetskhladze), it is once more moving forward. It will now appear in two volumes under the title *Greek Colonisation. An Account of Greek Colonies and Other Settlements Overseas*.

More than a dozen reviews, generally very favourable, appeared of the 1994 edition. We would like to thank all the reviewers. We also wish to extend our gratitude to Prof. B. Cunliffe, once again, and, of course, to the individual authors, who made this book such a success. It is our sad task to record that one author, M. Popham, has passed away.

Gocha R. Tsetskhladze and Franco De Angelis
London/Vancouver
March 2004

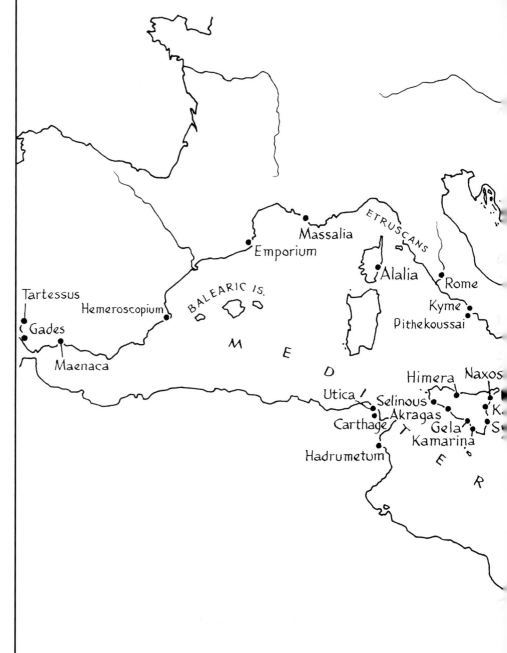

ETRUSCANS

Massalia

Emporium

Alalia

Rome

Kyme

Tartessus

Hemeroscopium

BALEARIC IS.

Pithekoussai

Gades

M   E

Maenaca

D

Himera   Naxos

Utica

Selinous   K.

Akragas

Carthage   T   Gela   S

Kamarina

E

Hadrumetum

R

# GREEK COLONISATION ~

Olbia

Panticapaeum

Tyras

Histria

Theodosia

Chersonesus

Phasis

BLACK SEA

Mesembria

Sinope

Apollonia

Amisus

Trapezus

Epidamnus

Heraclea

taponion

Byzantium

Chalcedon

Corcyra

PHRYGIA

Cyzicus

Chalcis

Phocaea

Corinth

Eretria

LYDIA

Aspendus

CILICIA

ACHAEA

Miletus

Al Mina

se

Mégara

IONIA

PAMPHYLIA

Rhodes

CYPRUS

CRETE

Tyre

PHOENICIA

A   N   E   A   N

Barca  Cyrene

LIBYA

Naucratis

Memphis

E G Y P T

# List of Abbreviations

| | |
|---|---|
| AA | *Archäologischer Anzeiger* |
| AION | *Annali dell'Istituto universitario orientale di Napoli. Seminario di studi del mondo classico. Sezione di archeologia e storia antica* |
| AJA | *American Journal of Archaeology* |
| AJP | *American Journal of Philology* |
| AR | *Archaeological Reports* |
| ASAA | *Annuario della Scuola Archeologica di Atene e delle Missioni Italiane in Oriente* |
| BAR | *British Archaeological Reports* |
| BASOR | *Bulletin of the American Schools of Oriental Research* |
| BCH | *Bulletin de Correspondence Héllenique* |
| BEFAR | *Bibliothèque des Écoles Françaises d'Athènes et de Rome* |
| BIA | *Bulletin of the Institute of Archaeology (London)* |
| BICS | *Bulletin of the Institute of Classical Studies (London)* |
| BSA | *Annual of the British School at Athens* |
| CAH | *The Cambridge Ancient History* |
| CRAI | *Comptes Rendus de l'Académie des Inscriptions et Belles-Lettres* |
| CronASA | *Cronache di archeologia et di storia dell'arte* |
| CQ | *Classical Quarterly* |
| DdA | *Dialoghi di Archeologia* |
| DHA | *Dialogues d'Histoire Ancienne* |
| JDAI | *Jahrbuch des Deutschen Archäologischen Instituts* |
| JHS | *Journal of Hellenic Studies* |
| JbRGZM | *Jahrbuch des römisch-germanischen Zentralmuseums (Mainz)* |
| LIMC | *Lexicon Iconographicum Mythologiae Classicae (Zurich and Stuttgart, 1981– )* |
| MDAI(R) | *Mitteilungen des Deutschen Archäologischen Instituts, Römische Abteilung* |
| MEFRA | *Mélanges de l'École Française de Rome, Antiquité* |
| OJA | *Oxford Journal of Archaeology* |
| PBSR | *Papers of the British School at Rome* |
| RA | *Revue Archéologique* |
| RDAC | *Report of the Department of Antiquities, Cyprus* |
| REA | *Revue des Études Anciennes* |

# Chapter 1

# The Nature and Standing
# of the Early Western Colonies

## A. M. Snodgrass

In an important paper of a decade ago, Jean-Paul Morel identified "the motives for Greek colonisation" as one of a series of "subjects of research that have become less important" (Morel 1984, 123–24). This was one of the reasons why I declined the editors' request to take that as my subject. The rather awkward title that I have chosen reflects an intention to concentrate instead on the immediate *results* of the colonising movement, especially as they affected the colonists themselves. This will be a contribution too partisan to masquerade as a *bilan de recherches:* rather, it is stating a case, against the background of the past ten years of research in this field, in which some of the most important contributions have been made by non-archaeologists.

I begin by drawing particular attention to one of Morel's notable insights, the huge empty gaps in the map of the Greek colonies in the West, and the relatively wide spacing of the colonies that were established (1984, 127–29). We can see the force of this observation most clearly by comparing the western venture with another movement traditionally held to be roughly contemporary, and involving some of the same Greek cities, the settlement of the north coast of the Aegean. Here we have the feeling that every possible niche of settlement is being occupied: in the West, the picture is markedly and permanently different. We shall return to this contrast later. Meanwhile, let us note Morel's own interpretation of the pattern in the West: he concluded that the location of the colonies here was determined with a high degree of caution and hesitation on the part of the Greeks, as if they "had drawn back .... wherever powerful and organised peoples were installed before them" (1984, 128). This may well have been true. I also take this pattern as testifying to what is the main theme of this paper, the unprecedentedly planned, deliberate and calculated nature of the movement to settle in the West. As subsequent history showed, it was, in a way that almost nothing done in Greece before the eighth century BC was, building to last and building for success.

One rather earlier insight into the pattern of Mediterranean colonisation generally is often overlooked today, perhaps because its implications are now uncontested. It appears in the preface to the *Penguin Atlas of Ancient History* (McEvedy 1967, 10–11 with figs. 4–5). Colin McEvedy used a kind of theoretical 'nearest neighbour analysis' to quantify the degree of *indentedness* of a coastline. He showed that one characteristic of indented coasts was that each coastal location was more likely to have, as its nearest neighbours, other coastal locations; and that even an inland settlement might have a majority of such neighbours, rather than other inland settlements. Finally, by superimposing a fine-grained grid of squares on the map of the

Mediterranean, he was able to single out and shade in those stretches of coast where such conditions prevailed. The resultant map is, to all intents and purposes, a map of ancient (Greek and other) Mediterranean colonisation. Coupled with Morel's explanation of where and why the Greek expansion stopped short, it comes close to giving a predictive geographical model for the entire process of overseas settlement in the eighth, seventh and sixth centuries BC.

Another phrase from Morel's paper, his description of the Western Mediterranean as "a fantastic cauldron of expanding cultures", has been quoted with strong approval by Nicholas Purcell (1990, 33). I would not dissent: indeed, I think that today we should be ready to add yet another ingredient to this mixture. We have long since accepted the idea that Greek and non-Greek elements lived side by side on many western sites. I think it is time to admit the likelihood that the Greek element was itself much more of a mixture – and not just in the joint ventures by more than one city – than the ancient historical accounts suggest; that the description of, say, Syracuse as 'a Corinthian colony' need mean little more than that the oikist and his immediate entourage came from Corinth. Does not Archilochos, with his cry that "the ills of all Greece have come together in Thasos", imply just such a picture (fr.102 West)? Only thus, I believe, can we account for the sudden bursts of colonisation, ostensibly by a single city in a short span of years, at a time when the population of Corinth, Chalkis or any other Greek city can hardly have sufficed to man a series of colonising expeditions, let alone be *compelled* by pressure of numbers into undertaking them.

Over-population and land-hunger, as motives for the colonising movement, have always had to confront the objection that, whatever the level of population in the Greek cities in the second half of the eighth century may have been, it was so much higher in the fifth, that supplementary factors must at least be called in to explain the early recourse to colonisation. The strongest of these factors, in my view, must have been the injustices, perceived or real, personal or collective, in the distribution of land and the access to power. Hunger, as we have learned in earnest in recent decades, can exist in a generally well-fed society; the same could easily have been true of the hunger for land in early Greece.

These are, however, not very controversial sentiments with which to overlay my general acceptance of one of the main tenets of recent scholarship on the settlement of the western Mediterranean, namely its cosmopolitanism. If belatedly, we have all come to recognise the degree of integration of indigenous and intrusive populations, and between intruders of different origins. The Phoenicians, in particular, have become as prominent in places – such as Sardinia and southern Spain – where we had not particularly expected to find them prominent, as they remain fugitive in places where Thucydides had expressly led us to look for them (vi.2.6: "all round Sicily"). But now it is time to take issue with another trend of recent scholarship that is on the way to general acceptance: I hope I shall be able to characterise fairly a view with which I am in radical disagreement.

During the 1980s, a new analysis has begun to find favour, which runs along something like the following lines: 'The isolation and backwardness of Greece during the Early Iron Age has been grossly exaggerated: so much so that it is unjustified to talk any longer of a 'dark age'. Greek venturers, with Euboeans to the fore, had been establishing overseas contacts since at least the tenth century' (the word 'commerce' may or may not be used here, but there is sure to be a reference to the finds at Lefkandi at this point). 'Presently permanent settlements began to be established, again with Euboeans to the fore, with Al Mina on the fringes of the eastern continental powers being succeeded by Pithekoussai on its western island site, the latter a forerunner of the new style of overseas expansion which we call colonisation (Euboeans yet again to the fore), but which is nothing more than a continuation of long-standing processes. Throughout this period, Phoenicians and Greeks are engaged in complementary activity, sometimes in rivalry, sometimes in collaboration, sometimes indistinguishable from each other. On the Greek side, these processes result in the linking of the Aegean world to a Mediterranean-wide network with itself at the centre, the colonies remaining firmly tied to the apron-strings of their mother cities'.

I do not wish to reject the entirety of this picture: in particular I accept, as already implied, the reality of early Phoenician activity in the West, though it is well to remember that, for them, the Aegean was itself part of 'the West'. What I wish to question is, first, the degree of Greek participation in all these earlier activities beyond Aegean waters. The evidence, however greatly we may differ in our assessments of its significance, will be agreed to be very much more impressive in respect of the inward movement of artefacts and practices to the Aegean, than of the corresponding outward transmission. On the one hand, we have not just portable objects – some of them of intrinsic value like the Lefkandi jewelry, others with a different significance like the inscribed bowl from Knossos – but also architectural evidence (the apparent Phoenician presence at Kommos), and evidence for the learning of techniques (the foundry deposit at the Lefkandi settlement). Presently there is the suggestion of resident Oriental goldsmiths (and later of bronze-workers) at Knossos, and of a specialised unguent-bottling establishment in the Dodecanese. Behind all this, we have to envisage the likelihood of bulk importation of certain raw materials: most notably, copper and tin, from the time that bronze objects again begin to be plentiful in Greece. The striking features of this evidence are that it suggests a wide range of activities, certainly entailing the movement of people as well as goods; that it is geographically rather restricted – central Euboea, central Crete, Athens and the Dodecanese between them account for nearly all of it; and, no doubt partly as a consequence, that its visible impact on the material culture of Greece as a whole is not very great. Phoenician temple-plans are not generally imitated: Cypriot rod tripods are sparingly imported and, again, not widely imitated, at least in metal; gold jewelry and even cheap imports like faience beads are slow to spread beyond the original close circle of contact-points; resident craftsmen are hard to detect elsewhere; and so on.

Yet this evidence seems imposing indeed when we compare it with that of its counterpart, the outward-going movements from the Aegean. Cyprus may be regarded as a special case because of its already partially Greek-speaking population; but even if we include it, there is little more than a scatter of pottery, thinly if fairly widely spread, to cover the lapse of between two and three centuries, mostly from sites without the least hint of independent evidence for a Greek presence (for Al Mina see below). If it is a residual Hellenocentric prejudice which nevertheless urges us to interpret both sides of this picture as resulting primarily from Greek enterprise, then it has a very thin and unbalanced diet to feed on. A sceptical archaeologist with a different training, innocent of either the Classical or the Orientalist tradition, might even conclude that, between the time of the last major Aegean emigration to Cyprus, probably in the first half of the eleventh century BC, and the settlement of Pithekoussai in the first half of the eighth, there is no *proof* of any Greek having set foot beyond the Greek-speaking world of the Aegean, and perhaps its Cypriot extension.

Except of course at Al Mina, so often and so confidently described as a Greek *emporion* or even a Greek colony. But this foundation-stone in the edifice of early Greek overseas enterprise has been struck by two heavy blows in the past few years. The first was Rosalinde Kearsley's detailed study of the pendent-semicircle skyphos (Kearsley 1989). It was on the chronology of this type of drinking-cup that the traditional date for the first Greek presence at Al Mina ("*c.* 825 BC") partly rested. Her study now proposes a partial revision of that chronology, with 'Type 6' of the pendent-semicircle skyphos, including the great majority of the pieces from Al Mina as well as other far-travelled examples, being assigned to the second half of the eighth century (1989, 101–104, 142–45). The site was in existence earlier, but she concludes that there is no proof of Greek presence or even Greek participation at Al Mina before 750 BC.

I am well aware that her dating, and indeed her classification, have been criticised, not least from the direction of Oxford (Popham and Lemos 1992). But it seems to me that her evidence, particularly that from Eretria and Paphos, strongly suggests that this type of skyphos was still being produced in the later eighth century. Once we acknowledge this extension of the date-range, the Al Mina material begins to wear a different look. It is common ground that the overwhelming preponderance of the early Greek pottery from the site dates to c.750 BC and later; if we can no longer insist on an earlier date for the relatively few pendent-semicircle skyphoi, then they no longer have to support, with the aid of only a handful of sherds of other types, the heavy burden of proving a further 75 years of earlier Greek activity at the site.

The second setback is more fundamental. The axiom of resident Greeks at Al Mina, at any time before the sixth century, has itself been increasingly questioned. That axiom was always based on the pottery, like so much of the accepted picture of early Greek activity in the East: architecture, burial-practices and other aspects of the material culture of Al Mina gave little or no support for it. Even the interpretation of the pottery has been beset by the doubts that arose over the stratification of the early levels at the site. A laudable early attempt to isolate one class of early Greek ware as having been actually made at the site (Boardman 1959) foundered on the rock of scientific analysis, which pointed instead to Cyprus as the place of manufacture (Jones 1986, 694–96). (In passing, the systematic tendency to underrate the role played by Cyprus has from the beginning been a *Leitmotiv* of the study of early Greek expansion). Now, in a new paper, J. Y. Perreault (1993) has concluded that Al Mina cannot by any strict standard pass as a Greek *emporion*. He makes telling use of the discovery of a sizeable collection of early Greek pottery at Tyre, a site which other evidence forbids us to regard as in any sense Greek. Al Mina must presumably carry with it Sukas and Bassit, two nearby sites where the evidence for a Greek presence is either weaker or later. Perhaps I may also mention here the work of Joanna Luke in her Cambridge doctoral dissertation now approaching completion, which has led her to the same conclusion (Luke 1994). Al Mina does not meet certain clear criteria for the presence of a foreign community in a port of trade. Rather, the precise nature of the Greek pottery found – exclusively eating and drinking vessels – together with its inland distribution, points to the site's having functioned as a mere funnel for the transmission of table-ware to the élites of the more important administrative centres that lay inland.

The combined effect of these two lines of argument is to throw grave doubt on the evidence of Al Mina, in respect of both its significance and its claim to a precolonial date. But where does this leave the overall picture of overseas activity in the tenth, ninth and early eighth centuries BC? I am not going to emulate the imaginary archaeologist whom I conjured up just now, and argue that *none* of this activity need have been Greek; that all the goods transported in both directions could have been carried by others. An appropriate illustration may be found in the comparison of two contemporary distribution maps, and in the differing interpretations of them by two different scholars (Fig. 1.1 *overleaf* ). The glass bird beads shown in the first map have a distribution that by-passes the inner Aegean as it extends from the Levant to Italy; the 'Lyre Player seals' shown in the other map have a parallel distribution at both extremities, but this time cover the Aegean as well. For Hans-Georg Niemeyer who drew attention to the comparison (Niemeyer 1984, 29, figs 20–21), it is the *difference* between the two that is significant, and it suggests to him that the former class of objects were carried by Phoenicians, the latter by Greeks. For John Boardman, there is a significant *resemblance* between them, in that both exclude the far western Mediterranean, a finding that seems difficult to reconcile with the view that the Phoenicians were the carriers in either case; in the absence of any evidence for sea-transport on the part of the Aramaeans who actually produced the Lyre Player seals, the implication is that Greeks are the likeliest carriers (Boardman 1990, 10–11, fig. 20). For our purposes, the significant thing is that both interpretations agree in assigning some part of the eighth-century traffic to Greeks.

More generally, one cannot ignore the insistent appearance of the Euboeans, on both sides of the balance of imported and exported objects. This cannot be attributed either to coincidence, or to any superior quality in their pottery. It must mean that they in some way controlled a privileged channel of communication into and out of the Aegean; while the sequel, their primacy in the movement to colonise, hints strongly that they were already well-travelled themselves. My overall response to this recent appraisal of precolonial Greek overseas activity is therefore that it is greatly exaggerated; that it shows a quite disproportionate preoccupation with painted pottery; that it is partly founded on dubious chronology; but that it is nevertheless not entirely imaginary.

We have been looking largely towards the East, because that is the direction in which nearly all the precolonial evidence points. But we should also acknowledge that a revision of the dating of pendent-semicircle skyphoi has repercussions in the West. Kearsley (1989, 101–4) assigned to her 'Type 6' the skyphoi from Veii and Villasmundo, as well as most of those from Al Mina. What this implies is that some of the western "pre-colonial" Greek trade need not be such; rather it is, to adopt a phrase which I first heard used by David Ridgway, "para-colonial". As such, it would cast a different light on our picture of the beginning of western colonisation; especially as, in the West as in the East, we have to accommodate the possibility of Phoenician or other non-Greek carriers taking Greek artefacts with them, a realisation which we owe primarily to the discoveries in the Phoenician sites of southern Spain.

Now I wish to direct attention briefly in another direction, neither East nor West but North. I have already fleetingly referred to the Greek colonies on the northern coast of the Aegean.

Here recent discoveries, which I hope to discuss more fully elsewhere (Snodgrass 1994), have so radically transformed our picture of the sequence of developments that I wish to suggest that it is here, and not in the shadowy appearances of Euboean pottery on western Asiatic sites, that we should be looking for understanding of the precedents for western colonisation. We have learned that settlement from central or southern Greece, of at least a durable and probably a permanent nature, may be found in sites of the Chalkidike peninsula from possibly the twelfth or eleventh, and at the very latest the mid-ninth, centuries BC. A most significant feature is the repeated appearance of pottery of Euboean type, together with local imitations. Partial comparison can be made with the ninth-century settlement, apparently also from Euboea, of certain of the Cycladic island-sites; chronologically, there must even be some overlap with the Ionian Migration. Here then is an episode which links – as indeed the ancient Greeks linked them – the earliest movements across the Aegean with the later *apoikiai* in the West.

The northward movement, unlike those to the Cyclades, involved a continental coast with a potentially or actually hostile indigenous population in close proximity, a feature which links it to both the Ionian and the western settlements. But it differs from the Ionian Migration in bringing the Euboeans to the fore, in the context of durable colonial establishments, many years before the western ventures began. It also throws a discreditable light on the flimsy and mostly late historical evidence, on whose basis we used to assign the northern settlement to a date roughly contemporary with that of the western colonies – if anything (since Euboeans led the way in both and it is hard to imagine their undertaking them simultaneously) a shade later. Twenty-five years after he published *The Greeks Overseas*, John Boardman wrote that the book "was criticised for taking too little notice of texts (it took too much)" (Boardman 1988, 796) – a judgment that some of us might echo about our own and others' writings in that period.

The great difference between northern and western Greek colonisation is of course that of distance. Whereas from the outer coast of Euboea to the tip of the Pallene promontory is a sail of only about a hundred miles, in which one can be in sight of land throughout, the journey to Pithekoussai is about eight times as long, including passages of much greater danger like the rounding of Cape Malea. When we couple this with the contrast, already noted, in the density of colonisation in the two areas, we may see a causal connection. The sites of the western colonies look as if they were chosen with a lot of circumspection, with regard not only (as Morel rightly said) to the "powerful and organised peoples" who were there before them, but also to each other. Of course, the early settlers could not know that their new outposts would become prosperous and powerful; but one way to provide for that eventuality was to allow plenty of space for them to expand. There were exceptions – Megara Hyblaea was a little uncomfortably squeezed in between Syracuse and Leontinoi, and eventually its inhabitants were to pay the price for this – but they are few and far between. With the colonies in the Chalkidike, if overcrowding or any other cause made settlement no longer viable, an oared ship could return to the mother-city for consultation within two or three days and, in the direst emergency, the whole of a small community could be evacuated. In the West, the degree of commitment was so much greater that the founding of a new colony must have seemed more or less irrevocable to all  concerned. We cannot know the strength of the ties which the

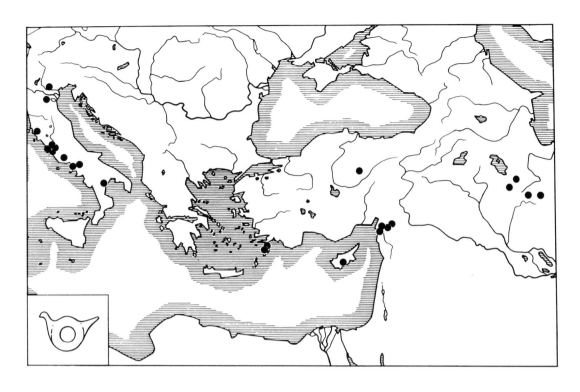

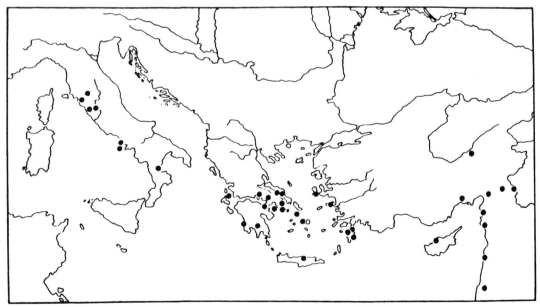

*Figure 1.1   Comparison of distributions of glass bird beads (above, after Niemeyer 1984, 28, fig. 20) and of Lyre-Player seals (below, after Boardman 1990, 10, fig. 20)*

early northern Aegean settlements maintained with their homeland; but with the western colonies we are in a stronger position ... and this brings me to my last argument, the degree of independence of the western colonial cities.

Here once more we broach Morel's list of "subjects of research which have become less important", for "the relations between mother cities and their colonies" were on that list. There has indeed been an apparently inconsequential sequence of swings in the pendulum of opinion on this subject, no doubt because a judicious selection of the evidence can be enlisted to support either side in the argument. Nevertheless I shall risk re-opening that argument, since independence is at the heart of my case, that western colonisation is to be set apart from anything that had preceded it.

One possible way to establish that case is to state, *a priori*, that we are now dealing, both in the Aegean and in the West, with the world of the *polis*, and that this therefore places western colonisation in a fresh category. But this is rather begging the question: one group of sceptics might ask how we can be so sure that institutions were not already in place at the time of the northern Aegean settlements, or even of the Ionian Migration; another (and I would number myself among them) might question whether the establishment of the colonies presupposes that the entire *polis* system was then already in place. There is no doubt that the western colonies rapidly came to exemplify that system in its most clear-cut form; but what of the argument that they may, in many ways, have been the *first* Greek settlements to do so?

Let us turn to rather more specific and empirical arguments. The last component in the 'straw man' case that I set up earlier on was the view that the whole process of early Greek expansion resulted in the creation of a sort of spider's web of contacts with the Aegean at its heart. Whatever the truth about the precolonial period, I maintain that the outcome of western colonisation was nothing of the kind; and I believe that the objectives, as well as the results, of colonisation reflect this fundamental difference. A reading of Irad Malkin's book (1987) provides us with a number of starting-points which are worth enumerating.

The religious and political measures taken when a colonising party set out for the West were far-reaching. Almost from the outset, the key role played by the Delphian Apollo can be documented, even if we choose to take a sceptical view of the very early oracular consultations (which I myself do not). The evidence from Delphi itself suggests that such a role would have been out of the question in periods before the eighth century (Morgan 1990, 106–147). The selection of the oikist was an even more important new feature: in political terms, because of the extraordinary powers with which he was endowed, and in religious terms because of his close linkage with Apollo himself, and also because of his subsequent destiny, to be commemorated with cult at the heart of the city that he had founded. A striking feature of Malkin's book is indeed his closing argument (1987, 261–66) that these cults may have been the very earliest instances of public, communal founder-worship in the Greek world.

The evidence now available for the early incidence of planned settlements in the western colonies also justifies a reappraisal of old assumptions. Politically, this planned element is one of the reflections of the power of the oikist; but culturally it is even more significant, in that it shows the Greek mind grappling with entirely fresh problems. Such at least is Malkin's view (1987, 135–186); and the clearest evidence for it is the demonstration that such planning often dictated religious decisions, by determining the location of the colonial cult-centres according to rational, secular principles. The sanctuaries were placed where they would fit best with the organisation of the settlement. I am not sure that this is necessarily the *first* time that such factors had operated: I think that something of the same kind may have happened with the location of the sanctuary at a site like Zagora on Andros, a century or so earlier. But it is certain that none of the established cities of the Greek homeland can have faced such decisions, or enjoyed such opportunities.

The apportionment of rural land is a topic briefly touched on in Morel's paper (1984, 140–141), but one that lies largely outside the scope of Malkin's book. Here it is difficult to trace any clear picture back to the initial years of western colonisation, though the attempt has been made. But here again we can declare in principle that the colonists were dealing with a fresh problem, for which life in Aegean Greece can have offered no full precedent. As with the lay-out of the main settlement, so in the allocation of rural land an entire community had to be provided for in "a single rationally planned act" (Malkin 1987, 186).

One other area where we have a relatively full body of evidence is that relating, not to colonial life but to colonial death. Gillian Shepherd's study of burial practices in certain of the Sicilian colonies (Shepherd 1993 and forthcoming), in which she reveals a pattern of competition and emulation, not of the practices of the mother cities, but of those of other nearby colonies; some awareness of indigenous burial customs is also detectable. The overall picture is one of a robust independence, which forms early in the lives of the new settlements and increases steadily thereafter. Her thesis also re-interprets certain other features which had hitherto often been seen as indicative of a dependent or nostalgic hankering for the 'old country', such as the use made by colonial cities of the Panhellenic sanctuaries, above all Olympia. It emerges that a better interpretation of the Western Greek policy of conspicuous dedication, and later of the erection of treasuries, is that these activities served less to satisfy provincial longing, than to assert colonial prowess and prosperity, in an arena chosen for its unavoidable impact on the consciousness of the cities of the homeland. It is after all a fact that, after not many generations had elapsed, the early colonies were already in a position to challenge the attainments of the Aegean cities, by a wide range of criteria – populousness, legislative innovation, temple-building, fortification, and almost any indicator of prosperity that one liked to choose. This result could not, as I have already admitted, have been predicted at the time of their foundation, but it was surely one of the long-term aims that dictated the choice of their locations.

This essential separateness of the colonial world is also a theme of Carol Dougherty's (1993) recent and pithily entitled paper, which focuses on the strange correlation between the office of oikist in a colony, and the status of social outcast in the homeland, often on grounds of criminal acts. The theme recurs often enough to reinforce the notion that to found one of the early colonies was to make an irrevocable, indeed an urgent break with the society of the homeland. It reminds me of a sentence, set in a rather different context, from Malkin's book: "It is probable that in certain respects colonization resembled a crime because it took land from someone else; for this reason it was important that the act of colonisation receive moral sanction from Apollo" (Malkin 1987, 90). This time we are confronted with a kind of problem which would have been a commonplace within the world of the Aegean, in the Chalkidike, in Ionia and earlier still no doubt in Cyprus; but which was now for the first time arising in relation to peoples outside the confines of the known Greek world.

The outline of my case will by now be clear enough. The early western colonists may have persuaded themselves that they were following in the footsteps of predecessors in the Heroic Age, but they should not persuade us. They were attempting something without full precedent. By transposing practices rehearsed in the small world of the Aegean coasts and islands to a wider stage and to alien coasts, they were creating a whole new category. If their initial objectives included an element of extending the culture of the Greek world to new shores, this was very soon forgotten in the much greater challenge of founding a new world altogether. For that, in the end, is what they did.

## BIBLIOGRAPHY

BOARDMAN, J. 1959: Greek potters at Al Mina? *Anatolian Studies* 9, 163–69.

BOARDMAN, J. 1988: Classical archaeology: whence and whither? *Antiquity* 62, 795–97.

BOARDMAN, J. 1990: The Lyre-Player group of seals: am encore. *AA*, 1–17.

DOUGHERTY, C. 1993: It's murder to found a colony. In Dougherty, C. and Kurke, L. (edd.), *Cultural Poetics in Archaic Greece* (Cambridge, Cambridge U.P.), 178–98.

JONES, R.E., 1986 *Greek and Cypriot Pottery* (Athens, British School at Athens).

KEARSLEY, R. 1989: *The pendent semicircle skyphos* (London, BICS, Supplement 44).

LUKE, J. 1994: *The nature of Greek contacts with the Levant in the Geometric period (with particular reference to the ceramic evidence)*, Unpublished Ph.D. dissertation, University of Cambridge.

MALKIN, I. 1987: *Religion and Greek colonisation* (Leiden, E. J. Brill).

McEVEDY, C. 1967: *The Penguin Atlas of ancient history* (Harmondsworth, Penguin).

MOREL, J. P. 1984: Greek colonization in Italy and the West. Problems of evidence and interpretation. In Hackens, T., Holloway, N. D. and R. R. (edd.), *Crossroads of the Mediterranean* (Louvain-la-Neuve, Université Catholique de Louvain / Providence, Brown University).

MORGAN, C. A. 1990: *Athletes and Oracles* (Cambridge, Cambridge U.P.).

NIEMEYER, H.-G. 1984: Die Phönizier und die Mittelmeerwelt im Zeitalter Homers, *JbRGZM* 31, 3–94.

PERREAULT, J. Y. 1993: Les *emporia* grecs du Levant: mythe ou réalité? In Bresson, A. and Rouillard, P. (edd.), *L'Emporion* (Paris, E. de Boccard, Publications du Centre Pierre Paris 26), 59–83.

POPHAM, M. R. and LEMOS, I. 1992: review of KEARSLEY 1989, *Gnomon* 64, 152–55.

PURCELL, N. 1990: Mobility and the *polis*. In Murray, O. and Price, S. (edd.), *The Greek city from Homer to Alexander* (Oxford, Oxford U.P.), 29–58

SHEPHERD, G. 1993: *Death and religion in Archaic Greek Sicily: a study in colonial relationships*. Unpublished Ph.D. dissertation, University of Cambridge.

SHEPHERD, G. The Pride of Most Colonials: Burial and Religion in the Sicilian Greek Colonies, *Acta Hyperborea* 6. (Copenhagen).

SNODGRASS, A. M. 1994: A new precedent for westward expansion: the Euboeans in Macedonia. *AION* 16 (volume *dedicato a Giorgio Buchner*).

# Chapter 2

# Precolonization:
# early Greek contact with the East

## Mervyn Popham

My theme is early Greek contacts with the East. By Greece is meant the Mainland, the Aegean and Crete, while the period is the Early Iron Age, following the breakdown of the Late Bronze Age civilization in those regions.

That breakdown did not immediately follow the destruction of the Mycenaean palaces in what, for convenience, may be called the 1200 BC disasters, even though great disruption must have been caused, economically and socially, leading in some cases to peoples uprooting themselves and moving to other regions, some overseas. The picture is a complex one, but with the assistance of Desborough's study of the period in his *Last Days of the Mycenaeans* we can now see that, after a stage of settling down, there was a recovery of sorts, apparent psychologically in a new spirit of optimism visible in their art, and, more concretely, in signs of intercommunications round the Aegean and much further afield. The basis for this revival is unclear but it was not due to the re-establishment of palatially organized economies. Part of the reason must lie in the events which surround the 1200 destructions and what followed soon after, a complicated issue, the strands of which we may never satisfactorily unravel.

One aspect, however, is reasonably certain, and this may have been a basic constituent in the revitalizing of intercommunications – the evident 'diaspora' of the Mainlanders overseas where their arrival can be detected on Crete, southern Asia Minor, Philistia and most of all in Cyprus, where their language was eventually to establish itself alongside the indigenous tongue. Their presence as one element, and it was no more than this, in the new settlements in the Levant, provided a common link or bond with the areas from which they had migrated.

My main reason for these preliminary remarks lies in the belief that the same bond (with the coast of Asia Minor and especially Cyprus), surviving all the troubles then to come, may have been a factor, too, in the Dark Age, the early stage of the Iron Age.

I turn first to the east Aegean at this stage, which brings me immediately to a problem which ought to be a prelude to any discussion of Greek contacts with the East, and to a series such as this on colonization. I mean the settling of Greeks on the coast of Asia Minor – a move linked with the so-called Ionian Migration though it involved Aeolians, Dorians and others as well. This event, tradition seems to place very early in the Iron Age.

However, this is an issue I intend to side-step, partly because it deserves more detailed consideration, but principally because our archaeological knowledge of the area is still too sketchy and incomplete to reach any firmly based conclusions. It *is* a problem in that our present inadequate evidence indicates that it is not until a late stage of Protogeometric, say near 900 BC, that Greek pottery appears there; pottery which, if you want, could be linked with the traditions of such a migration. Much the same, too, is true of the Aegean Islands, through which any such movement must have passed. Here we encounter a serious archaeological difficulty in that it is hard to envisage, say in Attica, conditions, including a sufficient population, at this or an earlier time which would have led to such a movement. On the Dorian side, circumstances seem even less favourable, in the Argolid for instance, while the Dorians of the West, including Laconia, as far as we can see remained in isolation, remote from developments taking place in the Aegean, and remained so for a long time to come.

I suspect, and I put it no firmer than this, that Mainland settlers did migrate to Asia Minor and to some of its neighbouring islands from several regions but that this took place towards the end of the *Late Bronze Age*, and in some cases it was to join Mycenaeans already well established there; there is supporting evidence on Chios and Rhodes. I think that they may have survived the final troubles in small but sufficient numbers to re-establish in time links with their various homelands and later to attract some fresh immigrants from them. Not, however, in large numbers and not on one occasion but rather a trickle and that spread over several centuries.

Such an explanation might find favour with some philologists concerned about the dialects and their distribution. Indeed the existence of these different dialects, and to some extent differing institutions, along the Asia Minor coast might have led the Greeks themselves to wonder how it came about and contributed to the creation of the legends, though they placed them at a later stage than I have suggested.

To turn now to our central theme, early contacts with the Near East, I avoid the term-re-establishment of contacts out of my basic agreement with the opinion of Hector Catling who has suggested that, in the case of Cyprus, communications between that island and the Greek Mainland were never entirely severed even at the very beginning of the Iron Age.

Let us begin in Euboea and, more specifically at Lefkandi, which will play a prominent part in my discussion, as you would expect from one of its excavators (Fig. 2.1.a). But it is not just favouritism, as I hope to show. For much of the evidence at the Greek end, where I shall begin, is concentrated at that site.

The settlement, which I have suggested may have been called Lelanton, where we have excavated only a small part, will not feature in my discussion though it has made its contribution and was the port of entry for the trade we shall be considering. It is much less easy to envisage it now as a thriving harbour town than it was when we first went there in 1965. Then caiques still moored alongside it to collect bricks from the neighbouring factories, which they transported principally to the islands (Fig. 2.1.b). Now the brickworks have closed down and the bay has become a marina for the speed-boats and yachts which are the pastime of the Athenian visitors who have built their summer villas and apartment blocks along the seashore, transforming the little fishing village into an ever expanding town. On the slopes above it were the ancient burial grounds of the Iron Age settlement which will concern us and especially one of the cemeteries now called Toumba, which lies in front of the large Protogeometric building there to which I shall refer later.

Our earliest evidence for long distance contacts comes at the end of Sub-mycenaean and at

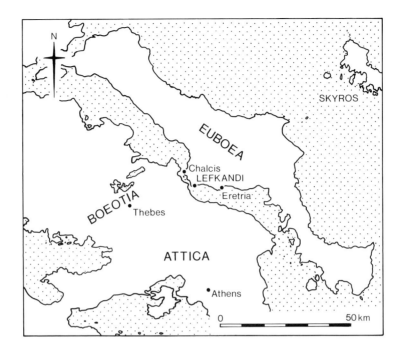

*Figure 2.1  Lefkandi: (a) location map (b) West Bay below Xeropolis in 1965-6*

*Figure 2.2  Near Eastern imports and local adaptions at Lefkandi: (a) S.16,10  (b) P.3,16 (c) S.46,3 (d) S.16,10 (e) P.22,19 (f) P.3,9.*

the beginning of the Protogeometric stage, say around 1000 BC on conventional chronology. As so often, pottery is the indicator. Both at Lefkandi and Athens, two shapes of vase enter the local repertories, the flask and the pyxis; and it seems pretty certain that the prototypes for them came from Cyprus which had retained these forms after they had dropped out on the Mainland. They are followed by a flutter of bird vases, two in the same tomb at Lefkandi, one an import (Fig. 2.2.a), the other a modified local version. Again Cyprus is most likely to have returned them at this stage to their original Mycenaean homeland. There is no ambiguity about another vase, a certain import from yet further afield, from the Syro-Palestinian region (Fig. 2.2.c). Then, apart from a necklace of faience (Fig. 2.2.d), there appears to be a lull – though this may be due to the few tombs of this stage we have excavated – until we arrive near the end of the Middle Protogeometric stage, not later than 950 BC, when we have the burials inside the monumental building at Toumba, which I prefer, despite objections, to call the Heroon, at least in the sense that it is the resting place of a warrior hero.

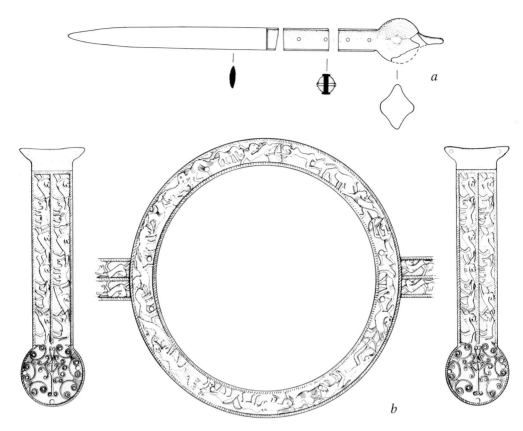

*Figure 2.3 From the 'Heroon' burials at Toumba: (a) iron age dagger with ivory pommel, L. 35cm (b) decorated rim of bronze amphora, D. 41cm.*

Both burials in the central shaft make their contribution, the male cremation and the accompanying female inhumation. The warrior's cremated remains had been placed in a bronze crater, the mouth of which was closed by a bronze bowl (Fig. 2.3.b). Its shape, the decoration of its rim with an animal frieze and hunters armed with bows, and the technique of manufacture generally, all point to Cyprus as its home. It may have been somewhat of a prized heirloom. Certainly this must be so of the necklace of his consort comprising a pendent and beads of gold. Precise parallels for the decoration of the pendent, the minute granulation, and for its bracket, as well as for the beads, are found in Babylonia where they can be dated to around 2000 BC. No wonder it had suffered some damage in its travels over the centuries before it arrived at Lefkandi. By the lady's head, ominously perhaps, lay an iron dagger for which I have yet to find a home, though its elaborate ivory pommel clearly point to some area of the Near East (Fig. 2.3.a).

Iron and the exotic material ivory raise much wider issues since they occur together on the earliest Sub-mycenaean dagger found in Athens, as, too, on another later sword at Lefkandi.

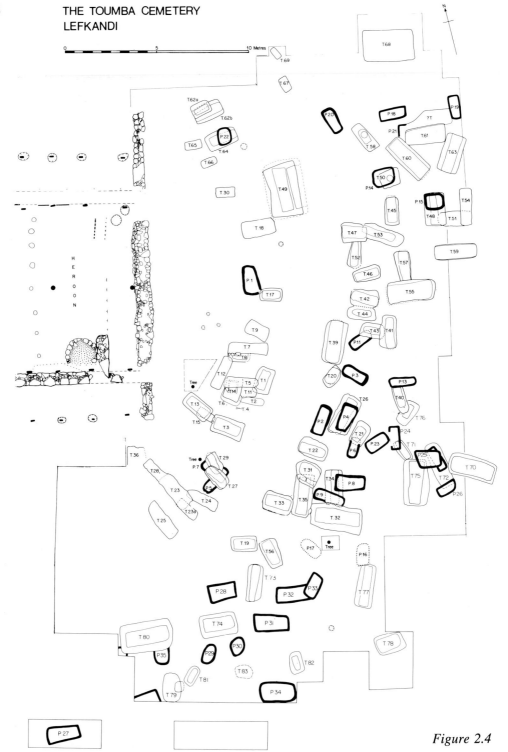

*Figure 2.4*

It is hard to believe in the existence of an ivoryworker in Greece in the Sub-mycenaean stage. So, could it be that the earliest weapons were not made locally but were imported, and that it was their arrival which sparked off a desire in Greece to learn the new technology of ironworking and ultimately led them to manufacture their own weapons? This is just speculation, but it may find some support both in a sword of similar type with ivory hilt in a burial dated near 950 or somewhat earlier in Cyprus (in the Skales cemetery) and is in harmony with the view at present most favoured that the Greeks derived their knowledge of iron technology from that island.

Beyond question, Cyprus was the home of one vase contained in a tomb belonging to the next stage, Late Protogeometric, a bichrome flask decorated in red and black, a type which the local potters imitated (Fig. 2.2.e–f). As they did too another Cypriot shape which they must have seen, a shallow bowl with a stick handle which the Lefkandian potter changed into a spout though retaining the general shape and its characteristic system of rayed decoration (Fig. 2.2.b). A further borrowing accompanied the rich offerings containing the Cypriot flask, a small box, though interestingly in this case the imitator was based in Athens as its fabric clearly shows. There too the flask was copied, as at Lefkandi.

We have now entered the late stage of Protogeometric, say between 950 and 900, a time when the burial ground in front of the Toumba building begins to expand, a cemetery much richer than the others and one which could well contain the descendants and relatives of the nearby hero, who in turn may have been a king (Fig. 2.4). Be that as it may, the burials there have provided us with an extraordinary wealth of Near Eastern imports which make it certain that the Syro-Palestinian region, and even perhaps Egypt are involved.

As a change from pottery, I turn first to bronze vases (Figs. 2.5; 2.6). The plain bowls are the least diagnostic; we now have seven examples, the earliest being that with the Heroon burial where you will recall it was used as a lid for the cremation urn, a practice which occurs too at Athens but not until the Middle Geometric stage. More distinctive is the type of flat-based squat jug with handle in the form of a lotus bud; of these there are now three. The type has a long Egyptian ancestry but also was imitated in Phoenicia. Our two examples of the round-based situla with loop handle has a similar background. One is plain, the other, badly corroded, appears to be engraved in part with an Egyptian or Egyptianizing offering scene. If only its apparent hieroglyphic inscription were legible, its source would have been more easily determined. Similar in general shape, the spouted jug must be related but at present it seems to be unique.

Yet more exciting has been the finding of two engraved bowls. One (Fig. 2.7) has already been illustrated in a preliminary report. Its main frieze depicts in repeated form heraldic helmeted griffins facing an elaborate palmette or Near Eastern 'Tree of Life' as it is sometimes called. The lower frieze is badly corroded but palm trees and animals can be recognized. North Syria has been suggested as its likely place of manufacture but this is far from certain. Similar doubts exist in the case of the second bowl (Fig. 2.8), recently restored and badly corroded in places. It, too, has a tree with what appear to be attendant sphinxes. Its main scene, however, belongs to a known genre in which a row of women, in this case three, carry offerings towards a table with vases on it; beyond it further offerings are made to an altar, on the other side of which is a seated goddess or priestess, while a group of musicians

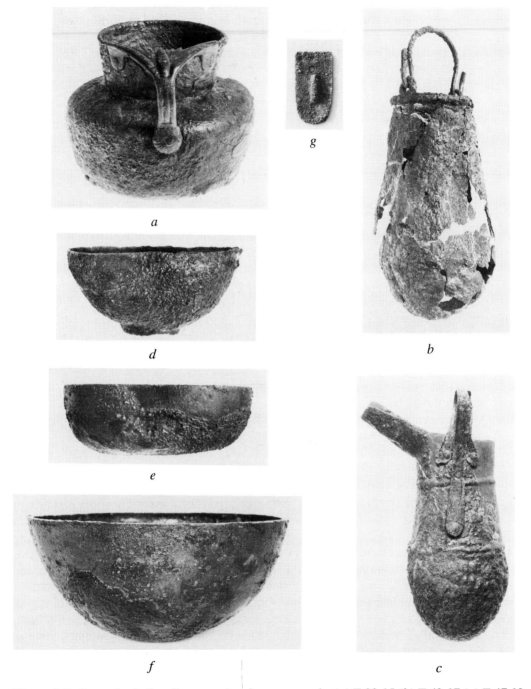

*Figure 2.5  From the Lefkandi cemeteries: bronze vessels, (a) T.33,15 (b) T.42,17 (c) T.47,18
(d) T.22,18 (e) T.31,20 (g) T.33,16, and a scale of bronze armour, (f) S.59,31*

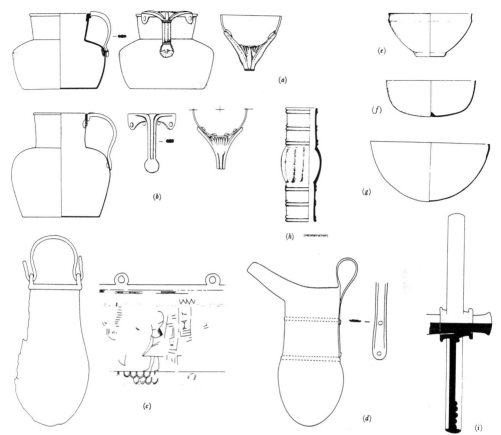

*Figure 2.6 From the Lefkandi cemetries: bronze vessels, (a) T.33,15 (b) T.39,31 (c) T.42,17 (d) T.47,18 (e) T.22,18 (f) T.31,20 (g) T.33,16, a bronze macehead (h) S.5,3 and bronze wheels (i) T.39,30.*

move up from behind. The whole scene is better preserved on two comparable bowls, one in Teheran Museum with no known provenance; the other was found in old excavations at Idalion in Cyprus. Apart from its other interest, our bowl provides what was missing, a firm chronology since it was found in a certain Late Protogeometric context. Some fifty years later another engraved Near Eastern bowl reached Athens and was deposited in a tomb of Middle Geometric date.

Less spectacular but intriguing are three other bronzes; a macehead (Fig. 2.6.h) of a type at home in the Near East with its closest parallels in Cyprus, a single scale from a suit of scale armour (Fig. 2.5.f) – surely a memento of some kind – and a pair of large enigmatic bronze wheels (Fig. 2.6.i), perhaps from a wheeled stand but, if so, it must have been much bigger than any which have survived on Cyprus where they are best represented and probably originate.

The tomb with the wheels was also particularly rich in another class of Near Eastern

*Mervyn Popham*

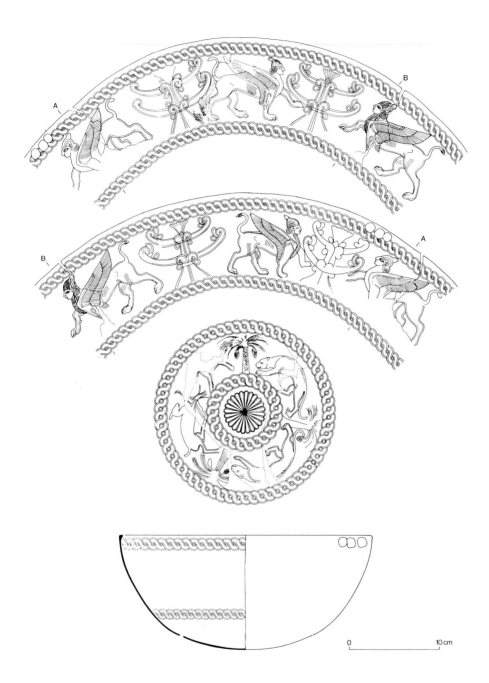

*Figure 2.7   Near Eastern engraved bronze bowl T.55,28.*

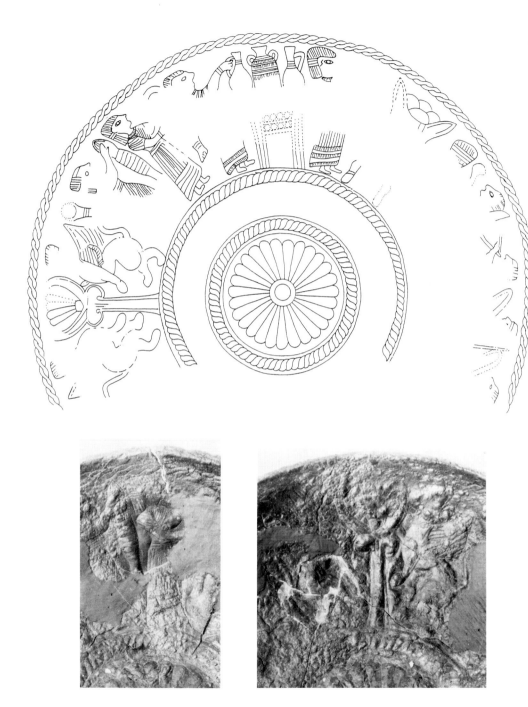

*Figure 2.8  Near Eastern engraved bronze bowl T.70,18, D. 15 cm.*

imports, those of faience and glass paste, which in various forms were deposited in many of the tombs at Toumba: two vases in the shape of a bunch of grapes, a flask, ring vase and plaque depicting a lion (Fig. 2.9); from other burials, two pomegranates, a bowl, and a necklace of pendents representing the Egyptian goddess Isis and a lion-headed goddess with an Egyptian crown, the latter thought to be a Phoenician conflation of two different Egyptian deities (Fig. 2.10.g). There are, in addition now, three rings with moulded bezel, the best preserved of which again points up the same Egyptian background, if no more, of several of the finds; in this case depicting the-ram-headed god of Egypt with solar disc and pectoral (Fig. 2.10.e).

On the most mundane level, we have recovered from the tombs well over 18,000 discs of faience segmented beads, which on the basis of one clearly distinct example, might represent some 60 necklaces. When I complain about the tedium of collecting them scattered among the tomb offerings and of later stringing them together in the museum, I try to keep in mind that even such simple imports are practically unknown elsewhere in Greece at the earliest stage.

For several of these objects we have already passed beyond the Protogeometric phase into Euboean Sub-Protogeometric as it is called, equivalent to Early Geometric and the beginning of Middle Geometric in Athens, say another 75 years or so, during which the flow of Near Eastern imports continued to reach Lefkandi, up to the point when our evidence fails us with the abandonment of the known cemeteries, around 825 BC.

To continue to discuss these individually would be tedious, so I illustrate only a few of the most outstanding, some of the scarabs, one in a gold mount, a rectangular prism with its sides carrying engraved signs, two other engraved seals, one with human head, another a recumbent lion (Fig. 2.10).

I end this review with a brief glance at the jewellery, much of which, like the discs and throat band worn by the lady buried in the Heroon, are of local manufacture or at least their decoration and shape are found elsewhere only on Skyros, which I shall later maintain was a Euboean outpost. Others, however, at the very least reflect a knowledge of Near Eastern ideas and techniques, like a small lunate-shaped pendent of gold with triangles of minute granulation, another similar but less finely made example, earrings with, in one instance, pendent clusters of granulation and in another hanging bars, and a necklace of spiral beads with a central disc (Fig. 2.11). We lack very close Near Eastern parallels at present; so if locally made, can it be that an immigrant Near Eastern craftsman had been induced to migrate to Lefkandi and settle there? The same suggestion has already been made to account for an elaborate pair of earrings found later at Athens, and, with much firmer evidence on Crete, to account for the oriental nature of the jewellery from Tekke, near Knossos, and for the earliest engraved metalwork, again at a somewhat later stage.

Here the Late Protogeometric settlement at Lefkandi made its contribution by having produced evidence in the form of clay moulds for the casting of decorated bronze tripods, and that at a far earlier date, around 900 BC, than had been anticipated for their manufacture in Greece. A resident or, at least itinerant, Cypriot metalsmith is suggested for the technology and character of the product.

I have attempted to bring Athens into the picture at various stages, but may have done less than justice to that city and the evidence there. It too receives Near Eastern imports but they

*Figure 2.9   Faience vases and plaque from the Toumba cemetery: (a) T.39,40 (b) T.39,39 (c) T.42,20 (d) T.59,38 (e) T.39,42 (f) T.59,37 (g) T.39,38.*

*Figure 2.10  Steatite, faience and glass seals, scarab, ring and beads from the Toumba cememtery: (a) T.36,21 (b) T.46,26 (c) T.47,24–6 (d) T.36,20 (e) T.39,37 (f) T.38,55 (g) T.22,28*

*Figure 2.11 Gold jewellery from the Toumba cemetery: (a) T.38,39 (b) T.59,26 (c) T.13,15 (d) T.5,10 (e) T.38,31 (f) T.13,16 (g) T.74,31 (h) T.80,59 (i) T.63,24.*

start later and are for this early stage far less in numbers. The same, as we shall see, is true of its exports.

This brings us to the other end of what it is fashionable to call the exchange network. What is the evidence in the Near East? Here we must resign ourselves to being restricted to pottery alone since whatever else the Euboeans traded it must have been perishable and has not survived.

A brief simplistic answer to the question would be merely to point to the distribution map at Fig. 2.12 of two of the vases most characteristic of Euboea and its area of influence – and I may add alien to Attica – the pendent semicircle skyphos and the larger shallow plate similarly decorated and which has only recently come into prominence (Fig. 2.15.a–c).

This answer is simplistic partly in that it combines nearly 200 years of exports. For, the skyphos changes only in details throughout most of this period and these are not readily perceivable in sherds which constitute the bulk of the evidence. Any modifications to the plate of chronological value have yet to be convincingly established, though none need be later than 800 BC.

Moreover, the map takes no account of quantities, deliberately, since to make use of large and small dots to indicate this would be to pretend that our present, often accidental, finds have more numerical significance than I believe can be ascribed to them in most cases.

For the Protogeometric stage, we can rely on a feature limited to that period which is found on different shapes of vase – the tall, markedly conical, foot which allows us to place a very small number of pots from Amathus on Cyprus to this early stage of intercommunication which include a circles skyphos and a cup with a somewhat carelessly painted zigzag on the rim, careless that is by Attic standards but usual on Euboean versions. Probably we should add to these a couple of imports at Tyre, if its earliest level with Greek pottery, Stratum XI, with its somewhat circular chronology, falls within this period.

Until we have more stratified evidence, it would be safer to allot most of the Greek imports in the Near East to the Euboean Sub-Protogeometric stage and to note that exports from that island continue well into Late Geometric by which time, of course, Eretria and Chalcis have become its main centres.

In passing, however, I may add that I reject the view of Kiersley in her study *The-Pendent-Semicircle Skyphos*, mentioned by Professor Snodgrass (Chapter 1), that the examples at Al Mina are all late and that they could belong to the Late Geometric stage. I myself doubt whether any were being made so late, and, among other reasons for holding this view, would point to their complete absence at Pithekoussai, whereas a few earlier ones did reach the West. Nor, as set out in the review of her work by Dr. Lemos and myself (in *Gnomon* 1992), were they being made in Cyprus, as she holds, except as obvious imitations. To hold this view is to ignore the clay analyses of such vases found at Al Mina and on Cyprus which have concluded that, with one exception, possibly Cycladic, the rest conform in their clay composition to that of Central Euboea. I remain content with the view that Al Mina was an important trading centre and that it involved Euboeans at least as traders, by 800 BC if not earlier. A fuller assessment of this issue will be possible when the hundreds of Greek sherds reported to have been found in the 'Amuq region, including 90 pendent semicircle sherds from three sites alone, have been published. Though it was with his study of the pottery from Al

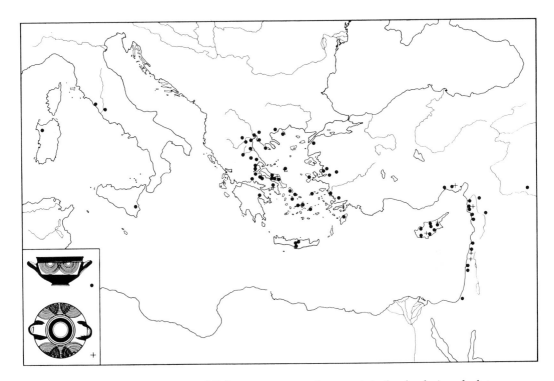

*Figure 2.12  Distribution map of Euboean type pendent-semicircle skyphoi and plates*

Mina that Professor Boardman first hoisted, courageously at the time, the Euboean flag, it may be that in the meanwhile we should put greater emphasis on the more recent, and better stratified material from Tyre, where in a fairly small area sherds of some 24 skyphoi, mostly with pendent semicircle decoration, were recovered together with fragments of seven plates. This emphasizes, too, how much we have yet to learn of that region in the Early Iron Age, where there are already indications that the range of vases imported was by no means restricted to the two shapes on which I have concentrated because of their more obvious and largely exclusively Euboean characteristics.

The predominance of Euboean-type pottery in the Near East, including Cyprus, is now firmly established and generally accepted. And we may add that the admittedly restricted number of clay analyses which have been made of it indicate Central Euboea as being by far the main centre of its manufacture.

What, then, was the role of Attica, since vases from there also reached the Near East? It is clear that its exports were far fewer, and as appears from Professor Coldstream's map (in *Geometric Greece*, fig. 29), now perhaps a little out-of-date, they had a more limited distribution. More than this, Coldstream wisely uses the term 'Atticising' since the Attic skyphoi with a panel of meanders or zigzags were imitated elsewhere, including as we know

Euboea. It is time, I suggest, that a detailed study was made of them, their fabric, manner of drawing and, especially of the composition of their clay, to allow greater precision in determining their provenance.

Of the earliest of the Attic vases at Tyre, Coldstream has said, with the enthusiasm of the convert, that the 'shapes fall within the considerable repertoire of Attic Middle Geometric exports to Lefkandi and so might well have been brought east in Euboean ships'. This, indeed, could be the case (the number, too, of Attic vases at Lefkandi is considerable) and it would find some support in the apparent emphasis in the East on pedestalled craters, such as the one accompanied by pendent semicircle skyphoi and plates in a royal burial at Salamis, which were rightly valued also by the Euboeans (Fig. 2.13.b).

However, joint ventures can, by no means, be excluded. Attica receives, too, its Near Eastern goodies, if mainly after 800 BC and Lefkandi obtained some outstanding Attic vases (Fig. 2.13.a). There are indications, too, at our site, in the form of some burials there which are locally uncharacteristic but typically Attic, that some Athenians might have intermarried with prominent Euboeans.

Another question needs addressing. Were the exchanges between Euboea and the Syro-Palestinian coast the result of direct communication – or trade – between the two regions, or was there an intermediary – a redistribution centre as it is now fashionable to call it? If the latter, Cyprus is the only obvious candidate for this role. It could be claimed that the island was re-establishing its probably similar function in the Late Bronze Age in the case of Mycenaean wares. It is a possibility, for the Cypriots were at least active in some of the same centres as have produced much of the Euboean pottery, but on the whole the evidence is at present against it. In the Late Bronze Age, the quantity of Mycenaean pottery in Cyprus is immense, quite different from the position with Euboean wares in the Early Iron Age. And, if this were the role of Cyprus, why is it that on present evidence little of the return exchange, at least in the shape of the luxury items which reached Lefkandi, was retained by the islanders? That picture could be changed with, for instance, the recent rescue excavations at Amathus, but the island has been already far more thoroughly explored than most regions and has a praiseworthy record of publication.

This is not, of course, to maintain that the Cypriots were not involved at all in Euboean trading activities; we have already seen ample evidence for this at Lefkandi. They may even have initially guided the Euboeans further east and operated in part with them and so claim to have been intermediaries in that more limited sense.

I come now to my final point, the direction of trade, eastward or westward, that is to say, Euboean enterprise or Phoenician expansion.

I have so far assumed that the goods exchanged between the Near East and Euboea were carried on Euboean ships. That assumption has been challenged by an alternative opinion which holds that these trading activities were part of the initial and continuing expansion of the Phoenicians who, having set up a colony at Kition on Cyprus, then went on to penetrate into the west Mediterranean and eventually settled there.

As I see it, the objections to Phoenician enterprise in the Aegean are great, and have yet to be answered by their protagonists.

We may start with a chronological problem. It would appear that the Phoenician settlement

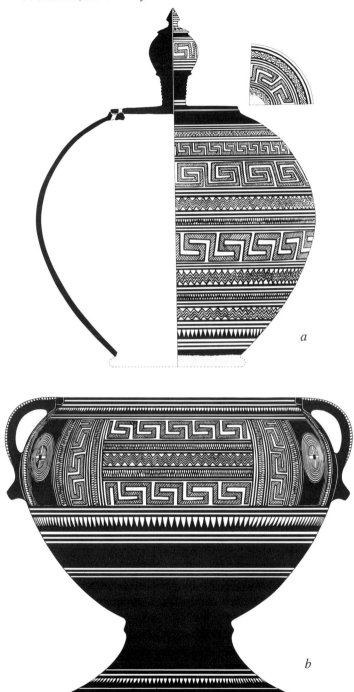

*Figure 2.13 Reconstructions of large Attic MG I vases from the Toumba cemetery: (a) pyxis Sq.XVI,14. Ht. 58 cm; (b) crater from Pyre 23, Ht. 47.5 cm.*

at Kition was not established until around 850 BC, at least 50 years after the flow of Near Eastern objects at Lefkandi was well underway, and those finds are the earliest in the Aegean. To this we may add that in the quite extensive excavations in the settlement of Kition, recently published, there are but two Greek sherds from the earliest levels – one Euboean, one Attic – later, two more of Euboean Sub-Protogeometric type up to the Late Geometric stage, when the site produced a further two Euboean sherds. Contrast that situation with the finds at the non-Phoenician city of Amathus, and it becomes negligible, even making allowance, as we should, for the comparison between settlement and cemetery evidence.

This aspect of distribution leads to the second main objection to this Phoenician bias. Why the overwhelming concentration of the Near Eastern objects at *Lefkandi* where they begin earlier than elsewhere and are not remotely rivalled in quantity in any part of Greece up to when the evidence from its cemeteries ceases around 825 BC?

Lefkandi is situated in a side water of the Aegean, not at all an obvious place to make your first main landing in Greek waters, and it is difficult to imagine any important commodity which Euboea had to offer which was not available closer to hand – certainly not just pottery. I say 'first main landing' since *en route* no such extensive exchanges can be documented, at least on present evidence, while on their return these presumed Phoenician traders would have had to distribute the pottery in their cargo pretty much equally between north Syria and their homeland proper.

Two scholars, Andrew and Susan Sherratt, in their wide-ranging article (*World Archaeology* 24 (1993), 361–78) on early Mediterranean economy are more explicit than others. They suggest that Lefkandi may have been a natural stopping place on a Phoenician route northwards through the straits of the Euripus. But, if this were so, they must have left nearly all their cargo there, since very little evidence exists for their presence further north, if we exclude the unsubstantiated and undatable reference in Herodotus (VI.47) to the Phoenicians mining silver on Thasos. There are a few Near Eastern trinkets, glass beads, at Marmariani in north Thessaly, rather more on Skyros for which there is another more cogent explanation. That island is almost wholly Central Euboean in character, indicating that its settlers came from this region and so may be expected to have profited somewhat in the fortunes of their homeland.

Early activities in the north Aegean *have*, however, their part to play in the argument. Again I could just point to the same distribution map of pendent semicircle skyphoi with the same chronological uncertainties, showing the presence of this type at Vergina and now at Dion in south Macedonia, with a concentration around Thessaloniki and extending eastward to Thasos and even to Troy. An added complication in this case is Thessaly, which shared many characteristics with Euboea, especially pottery, and with which it clearly had very close links. Far too little is at present known of this region to attempt to know the reasons and any part Thessalians may have played in these activities further north. It might, also, be wiser to have patience and await the publication of the results of the many Greek excavations taking place in west Macedonia, from where we hear talk of the finding of Euboean pottery extending to Late Geometric.

Even so, the evidence is much more than that produced by Professor Snodgrass in Chapter 1 in the case of Mende, though I share his belief in Euboean activity and settlement in the

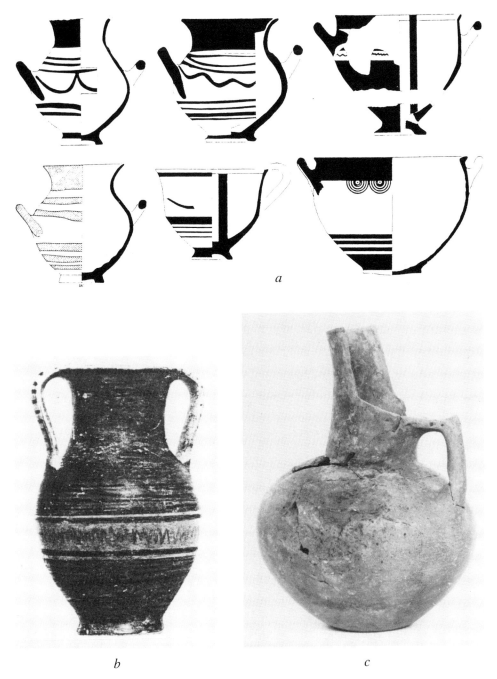

*Figure 2.14  N. Aegean connections; (a–b) vases from the cemetery at Torone, (c) jug from Toumba T.41,12, Ht. 22 cm.*

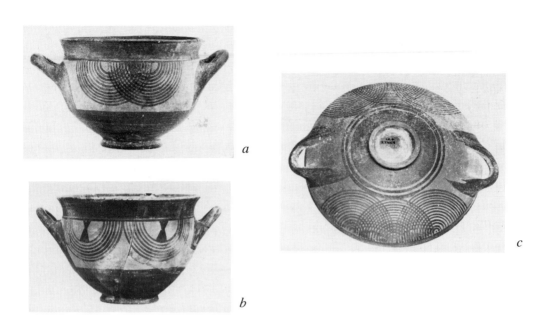

*Figure 2.15  Pendent-semicircle skyphoi and plate from Lefkandi: (a) T.59,2 (b) PP 3,14
(c) T.42,8; (d) pyxis with painting of a ship, T.61(fill), Ht. 29 cm*

area at a much earlier date than it is customary on very poor evidence to ascribe to it.

Today I shall merely point to the intriguing finds from Torone in Chalcidice a few of which have been illustrated so far (Fig. 2.14.a–b). Among these, the amphoriskoi with wavy line across the body are totally unexpected and must be very early, Early Protogeometric at the latest and their closest parallels are with Attica and Euboea, as too a cup, similarly decorated. Additionally a small amphora basically monochrome apart from its belly zone of a roughly painted zigzag is so close to Sub-Protogeometic II types at Lefkandi, no later than 850 BC, that I would not have been at all surprised to have found it at Lefkandi. A locally made skyphos, too, is of a shape which ought to be decorated with full circles but the local potter has conflated it with the pendent semicircle version, at least showing his acquaintance with the latter. Euboean links are to me certain and they are unexpectedly early, anticipating the more abundant evidence for Late Protogeometric which continues up to and including Late Geometric. Nor is evidence lacking at Lefkandi for early Macedonian contacts as we can see a few imports there which include a handmade and burnished jug found in a Late Protogeometric burial (Fig. 2.14.c). I feel confident that the next few years will establish firmly that Euboean enterprise had a northern prong as well. Pivotal to such a move was the island of Skyros set midway in the north Aegean seaways, possession of which has concerned all naval powers in the Aegean including the Athenians and the Venetians.

But I have strayed some way from our area of concern today – the East – and it is time to sum up. I have attempted to show that Greek communications with the East may well never have been entirely broken off and that the continuing link especially with Cyprus may have had its foundation in racial-linguistic bonds going back to the final stages of the Late Bronze Age. Those connections strengthen and become more obvious around 950 to 900 BC, the evidence for which is concentrated at Lefkandi. That this is not merely an accident of excavation but reflects a reality is confirmed by the predominance in the Near East of imports from Euboea which continue to hold their place until near the end of the eighth century.

This enterprise by the Euboeans in the east has its counterpart in the north Aegean, where signs of Phoenician activity are near non-existent. The culmination of this venturous spirit, the foundation by Euboeans of the first Greek settlement in the West, is discussed by other scholars in this volume.

We may end by wondering why this momentous Euboean enterprise had such a bad Greek press, or rather hardly any at all; even that the settlement at Pithekoussai was Euboean we learn from Livy. Political prejudice of some kind? Or was much of it too early for later Greek memory?

One author at least showed better knowledge and appreciation, the poet of the Delian Hymn to Apollo, who characterizes Euboea as being 'famous for its ships', *Euboia nausikleite*, a reputation perhaps celebrated too by a Lefkandian potter who included on his vase one of our earlier Greek pictorial representations, a painting of a ship (Fig. 2.15.d).

## ACKNOWLEDGEMENTS

My indebtedness to many people in the preparation of the lecture and text is wide. Here I single out Dr Irene Lemos for help and discussion on several topics, and especially on the 'Ionian Migration' and in the preparation of the distribution map at Fig. 2.12, Professor J. N.

Coldstream for constant advice on our Attic Geometric, Mrs Alison Wilkins for the drawing
of the distribution map in particular, and Mrs Lynda Smithson for typing several drafts and
the final version. Not least I must thank our editors for having invited me to participate in the
lecture series, which was such a success.

## SOURCES

I have left my text very much as the lecture which was delivered, and unencumbered by extensive references.
I was greatly indebted to the information and opinions given in three excellent surveys of the Early Iron Age,
which contain most of the references and more illustrations, those of V. R. D'A. Desborough, *The Greek Dark
Age* (London 1972), A. M. Snodgrass, *The Dark Age of Greece* (Edinburgh 1971) and J. N. Coldstream,
*Geometric Greece* (London 1977).

The excavation, finds, and the historical conclusions to be drawn from them, at Lefkandi have been
published in *Lefkandi I: The Iron Age Settlement and Cemeteries*, edited by M. R. Popham, L. H. Sackett and
P. G. Themelis (London 1979–80), and subsequently, joined by E. Touloupa, in 'Further Excavation of the
Toumba Cemetery at Lefkandi, 1981' in *BSA* 77 (1982), 213–48, as well as a later preliminary report in
'Further excavation of the Toumba Cemetery, at Lefkandi, 1984 and 1986' in *AR for 1988–9*, 117–29. A short
notice on the 1992 campaign is given in *AR for 1992–3*, 40. In the excavation of 1994, after the lecture was
given, further links with the Near East were found in the form of several fragmentary imports of 'Phoenician'
and Cypriot flasks.

The final report on the 'Heroon' is published as *Lefkandi II, Part 1: The Pottery* by R. W. Catling and I.
S. Lemos (London 1990) and in *Part 2: The Excavation, Architecture and Finds*, edited by M. R. Popham,
P. G. Calligas and L. H. Sackett (London 1993).

The evidence from Cyprus and the Near East, up to the date of their publication, is considered, with
references, in the surveys mentioned above. To these may be added, on Tyre, P. M. Bikai, *The Pottery of Tyre*
(1978) and J. N. Coldstream, 'Early pottery in Tyre and Cyprus: some preliminary comparisons' in *RDAC*
1988 (part 2), 35–44. The Greek pottery from the 'Amuq Plain is referred to, and the relative roles of north
Syrians and Phoenicians considered by J. Boardman in 'Al Mina and history', *OJA* 9 (1990), 169–90 and
especially note 4.

To earlier references to material from Cyprus, should be added V. Karageorghis, *Palaepaphos-Skales: An
Iron Age Cemetery in Cyprus* (Constanz 1983) and V. Karageorghis et al., *Excavations at Kition IV: The Non-
Cypriot Pottery* (Nicosia 1981).

Clay analyses of suspected Euboean vases in Cyprus and Al Mina are considered in M. Popham *et al.*,
'Euboean exports to Al Mina, Cyprus and Crete: a reassessment' in *BSA* 73 (1983), 281–90, with subsequent
analyses published by I. S. Lemos and H. Hatcher in 'Early Greek vases in Cyprus; Euboean and Attic', *OJA*
10 (1991), 197–207, where the early Euboean vases from Amathus are considered and illustrated.

For comparative material for the two engraved bowls from Lefkandi, see G. Markoe, *Phoenician Bronze
and Silver Bowls from Cyprus and the Mediterranean* (California 1985), especially his Cy3 (from Idalium)
and U6 (in Teheran).

Pottery from the cemetery at Torone is illustrated in *AR for 1985–6*, figs. 76–7, the source of Fig. 14.a–b,
and, together with vases from Dion, in *Ancient Macedonia* (Athens 1988), 18, no. 113.

## Chapter 3

# Phoenicians and Greeks in the West: a view from Pithekoussai

## David Ridgway

The first six words of my title conceal a major problem of archaeological explanation. Its nature is effectively demonstrated by the diametrically opposed readings of the same evidence that are proffered in two thoughtful and authoritative books first published less than ten years before I was invited to read the paper on which this chapter is based. I transcribe the key passages here in their recent and welcome English versions:

> "The expansion of the Greeks and the Phoenicians in the Mediterranean appears from early on to develop in mutual competition." (Burkert 1992, 21)

> "... the evidence seems to contradict [the] hypothesis of competitive spheres during the period of Phoenician expansion." (Aubet 1993, 314)

> "Phoenician expansion towards the West seems to be connected in some way with Euboean activity and there may well have been common interests and enterprises, at least in the years 760–700 BC." (Aubet 1993, 315)

Of these, the first appears in a work by Walter Burkert originally published in 1984 as *Die orientalisierende Epoche in der griechischen Religion und Literatur*; it is not without interest in the present context to note that its new English title, *The orientalizing revolution*, is inspired, with acknowledgement (Burkert 1992, 156 note 17), by John Boardman's (1990) timely and wide-ranging review of Al Mina and history. The statement by Burkert that I have quoted above is followed by a sensitive distinction between the trading connections set in motion "*first* by the Phoenicians and *then* by the Euboeans" (Burkert 1992, 21; emphasis added) on the one hand, and on the other the "more intimate cultural contacts and exchanges [that] took place on the level of skilled craftsmanship", occasioned by Eastern craftsmen fleeing from the Assyrian conquests at the end of the ninth century and passing on their skills to the Greeks in whose communities they took refuge. For Maria Eugenia Aubet, meanwhile, the "interests and enterprises" common to Phoenicians and Euboeans in the West c.760–700 (corresponding to the heyday of Pithekoussai on the Bay of Naples) are a natural extension of the earlier "symbiosis" in the East – and indeed of the "joint trading activities" they had developed towards the end of the ninth century at Al Mina and Tell Sukas on the Syro-Phoenician coast (Aubet 1993, 315).

I have learnt a great deal from both these authorities and their books, and I would certainly intend no disparagement of one if in this matter I had some overwhelming reason to prefer the other. In fact, I do not believe that the choice is anything like as simple as that between competition and collaboration *tout court*. Like Burkert, I find that two different relationships between the Greeks and their Eastern neighbours (a form of words I use deliberately) seem to have been in full working order well before 800 BC, and for at least a century after it. Mine, however, are not quite the same as his; and I wonder, too, if such differences as there are between them might in fact reside in nothing more arcane than their archaeological status as different material expressions, appropriate to different social and political circumstances, of the same underlying intention. At all events, my first relationship is documented in the archaeological record by the deposition of readily identifiable Eastern jewellery and other luxury items in certain privileged tenth- and ninth-century graves in Athens, Knossos and Lefkandi (references in Coldstream 1982 and Boardman 1990, 177–78). Similar (though rather less elaborate) items eventually reached the West, too, where some of them surface as trinkets "perhaps ... hawked by casual Phoenician traders" but more probably "conveyed to Italy ... by Euboean merchants who also had Levantine contacts" (Coldstream 1977, 224), along with the painted Geometric skyphoi with which the trinkets are associated in the indigenous *corredi* at Villanovan Veii, prehellenic Cumae and other native Tyrrhenian centres (Ridgway 1988; 1992, 129–38).

My second Phoenician-Greek relationship is less easy to define in archaeological terms, although it surely has something in common with Burkert's exchanges "on the level of skilled craftsmanship". That is something that we can certainly see happening in Euboea: we need look no further than the moulds for bronze tripods of Cypriot type from a foundry-refuse context dated *c.*900 at Lefkandi, and the cautious but surely convincing proposal that they may signify "the presence there of a bronzesmith trained in the East working as an itinerant craftsman ... [who] may well have brought with him the materials he needed for his work, as well as his expertise" (H. W. Catling in Popham *et al.* 1980, 96; and see Negbi 1992, 606) – with all that this implies for the continuous local development of metallurgy during the Greek Dark Age rather than its re-introduction to Greece when the Dark Age was over. For my own part, I am beginning to find it difficult to draw any meaningful distinction between the various activities in which itinerant craftsmen would be entirely plausible (and perhaps even indispensable) participants: technological evolution in Euboea; the kind of common interests and joint trading ventures abroad (in the East as well as in the West) postulated by Aubet; and the various roles that Giorgio Buchner (1978; 1982) and I have attributed in our time to certain "Oriental residents at Pithekoussai" (Buchner and Ridgway 1983; Ridgway 1992, 111–18).

It has long been, and still is, a commonplace that precolonial Euboeans in the West were attracted there to a significant extent by its mineral resources. The rulers of Tyre were perhaps even more single-minded in their quest for Western silver, gold, copper and tin, as has been well shown by Aubet (1993, 59–64, 74–6; see too Markoe 1992). Given that Phoenician trinkets and Euboean skyphoi are alike conspicuous by their absence from the archaeological record of the Tuscan Colline Metallifere, I once suggested that there might have been not so much "competition" as some kind of demarcation, tacit or otherwise, between the Phoenician and the Euboean exploitation of Western metals: Phoenicians in Sardinia, Euboeans along the Tyrrhenian coast of the peninsula (Ridgway 1986, 178). But that hypothesis, it seems to me now, has been demolished by the discovery of new evidence, especially in Sardinia (Ridgway and Serra Ridgway 1992). Before I discuss these matters further, however, I feel the need to attend to – I do not say answer – some of the questions that I have already begged.

*

The first question concerns the round date of 800 BC. For Boardman, this is the *terminus post quem* for "securely datable" Phoenician Iron Age finds in the West Mediterranean (well reviewed by Niemeyer 1984; see too 1990; and now 1994). "Securely datable" status requires association with a reliable chronological "yardstick" (Boardman 1990, 177), which in turn means diagnostic Greek pottery: it occurs to me that this procedure inhibits the detection of the kind of Phoenician chronological priority that Burkert postulates (above). Then comes the question of which Greek chronological yardstick should be used: whose dates for – to choose an example not quite at random – the crucial Euboean skyphoi with pendent concentric semicircles? When I compare the discussion of their absolute chronology in Kearsley (1989, 126–32) with the comments of Popham and Lemos (1992), I feel rather like a traveller trying to plan a journey by consulting two different timetables: and, based as I am in the Far West, I am only too well aware that neither of them has been compiled with my specific needs in mind.

Less metaphorically, I also wonder what "Phoenician" means. For the purposes of this paper, and in line with Aubet's (1993, 4) firm definition of the Phoenician "colonial period proper" as the eighth to sixth centuries, I suggest that this much-abused word can most suitably be used to signify the consequences in and for the West of the foundation, in the late ninth century, of Kition in Cyprus and of Carthage in North Africa (Burkert 1992, 11; Aubet 1993, 42–45, 187–99). Of these, it is reasonable to suppose that Kition inherited a good deal of earlier knowledge of the West, not least knowledge concerning the extensive mineral and human resources of Sardinia – knowledge which, never having been exclusively in Mycenaean hands, survived the Dark Age. Of course, if the Dark Age is a figment of our collective archaeological imagination, it is not necessary to argue the case for uninterrupted East-West contact down to 800. I freely confess that, unlike the possessors of younger and perhaps more supple minds (James *et al* 1991), I cannot bring myself to ignore the advice of the Egyptologists and lower the Mycenaean dates until the gap is closed. There is, in a word, no point in pretending that the Dark Age never happened: because it did. It was the Greeks' Dark Age and no-one else's; and the case for at least some degree of continuous exchange during its course between the non-Greek peoples of the East and of the West seems to me to be well founded (Ridgway and Serra Ridgway 1992).

There is another question, too, that is raised by the works of Burkert and Aubet that I have discussed above. I mean the potential for a Western extension of what Oswyn Murray (1993,

326) has recently described as the "orientalizing fantasies" generated by Martin Bernal (1987–91) in his search for the "Afroasiatic roots of classical civilization" (see also Dickinson 1994, 295). "Orientalizing fantasies" is an excellent definition, and like Murray I dissociate myself from them. I have found nothing in Bernal's work so far that assists me, in the area and period covered by this book, to achieve the only reputable goal of any archaeologist or historian: to get "closer to a more balanced indication of what happened, and even to some degree of why it happened" (Boardman 1990, 186). That, I hope, will not be read as a defence or minimization of the horrors of institutionalized racism in the nineteenth and twentieth centuries (Bernal's real target): scholarship was, and continues to be, by no means the least of its victims. But I am seriously perturbed by Bernal's apparent belief that this is the only reason why our predecessors drew what seem to us to be eccentric conclusions from the evidence that was available to them. As I dutifully read the first two volumes of his *oeuvre*, I began to feel that for him no-one can misinterpret evidence without being accused of bad faith or time-serving. This, I submit, is an extremely worrying concept for a working archaeologist. True, archaeology in general and text-free archaeology in particular has always been peculiarly and sometimes willingly vulnerable to manipulation for political ends. But over the past two centuries a number of archaeologists, and not a few historians, have also been guilty of the traditional academic vice of sloth and of a certain concomitant unwillingness to think things through; others again have drawn inferences that we are pleased to regard as "wrong" for the entirely innocent reason that they did not know what we believe we know now. *All* of these factors surely contributed to the "mistake" of nineteenth-century scholars in our field: which was to absorb fifth-century notions of Athenian superiority, formed in the contemporary circumstances admirably delineated by Edith Hall (1989), and to project them backwards in time as pre-Classical periods of Greek history and archaeology became available for inspection and study – and to do this without reflecting on what some Greek authors, notably historians, had written about the Eastern (especially the Phoenician) sources of Greek superiority. This is why "I do not consider that Bernal 1987[-91] supersedes Albright 1941" (Ridgway 1992, 153): and why I am more concerned here to point out that in our own time some scholars had made good progress along the path to truth before the *Black Athena* bandwagon began to roll in 1987. Ten years earlier, for example, in his first (and sadly his only) *Archaeological Report* on South Italy and Sicily, the late Martin Frederiksen (1977, 43) actually used the phrase "the Phoenicians are on the way back".

*

To my certain personal knowledge, Frederiksen came to this conclusion after a number of memorable visits to Ischia in the early 1970s, when it sometimes seemed to the latterday Pithekoussans there that the *Journal of Roman Studies* was being edited in Neapolis. Although he was the best, Frederiksen was by no means the first historian of Campania to visit Pithekoussai. Over a century ago, Julius Beloch concluded that while there was probably enough evidence to identify Monte di Vico (Lacco Ameno) as the acropolis of Pithekoussai from the fifth century, it did not necessarily follow that this was also the site that had attracted the Eretrian and Chalcidian pioneers mentioned by Strabo (V.4.9.) and Livy (VIII.22.5–6).

This – to us – oddly cautious hypothesis was formulated on the basis of what sounds more like a casual stroll than anything resembling a modern *ricognizione topografica*: "The surface of the hill is strewn with fragments of tiles and vases, and intact layers of them are revealed when the ground is scratched with a walking stick" (Beloch 1890, 208–209). And there the matter rested, and would no doubt have continued to rest in the state described well over a generation later by Alan Blakeway (1933, 200 note 3), if Buchner (1977, 142–43 note 28) had not happened to purchase the publisher's last copy of Beloch 1890 as a schoolboy. Time and chance enabled him to investigate Beloch's findings on the ground, and thereby to initiate an authentic revolution in the study and appreciation of the early Greeks overseas (of which Buchner and Ridgway 1993 at last provides a long overdue measure of definitive expression).

Although Beloch's "overt anti-Semitism" is a matter of public record (Burkert 1992, 3; *cf.* Bernal 1987, 373–77), we need not attach any sinister significance to the fact that his walking stick apparently failed to detect any fragments of Phoenician pottery on Monte di Vico. Quite what it did find is not wholly clear, but the reference in the passage quoted above to tile fragments (*Ziegeltrümmer*) suggests that it may have been a relatively late (Hellenistic?) domestic deposit, which might also account for his unwillingness to assume earlier settlement in the same place. At all events, it is enough to recall now that the Acropolis Dump on the east slope of Monte di Vico (Ridgway 1992, 83–91) has since yielded a substantial quantity of exceptionally fine Phoenician Red Slip (Buchner 1982). More Phoenician material has also been found in the Late Geometric graves in the adjacent Valle di San Montano, where a small and much-discussed fragment of a locally-made version of an Early Protocorinthian kantharos preserves two incised letters, tantalizingly incomprehensible but definitely Phoenician (Buchner and Ridgway 1993, 289–90 with pls. 95 and cxl: 232*–1); they need not be much earlier than the last decade of the eighth century. By then, in view of this evidence and a number of other considerations (Ridgway 1992, 111–18), I do not think it is excessive to infer that a few Phoenicians and a lot of Euboeans had been living together at Pithekoussai for at least a generation. Their circumstances provided an ideal context for the continuation in the West of exactly the kind of "intimate cultural contacts" that for Burkert (above) had been taking place in Greece since the end of the ninth century. It would be rash to expect all such "contacts" to be reflected – even indirectly – in writing. At the very least, in sum, we are surely justified in concluding that the relationship between Phoenicians and Euboeans at Pithekoussai went deeper than mere bargaining between resident Euboeans and itinerant Phoenician trinket-vendors, like those who kidnapped the infant Eumaeus (*Odyssey* XV.415–484) – and who may conceivably have hawked their *athyrmata* directly to the native Iron Age communities on the Campanian mainland and in Southern Etruria (above).

It is self-evidently true that the geographical situation of Pithekoussai, on a promontory on an island, recalls the "headlands and small offshore islands" mentioned by Thucydides in his description (VI.2) of the sites used by Phoenician traders in their dealings with the native communities in Sicily. This may well be a coincidence, or an indication that Phoenicians were not the only eighth-century merchant venturers capable of assessing and exploiting the topography of foreign lands. But at one kilometre from end to end by *c*.750 (Buchner and Ridgway 1993, *carta topografica*), Pithekoussai is presumably much bigger than the Phoenician trading posts in Sicily, as well as more permanent than they turned out to be: to this extent, perhaps, the Pithekoussans might be credited with eventually eroding the success of Phoenician operations in the West. To begin with, however, there are all the signs of Phoenician-Greek collaboration; and they are by no means confined to Pithekoussai.

\*

Excavations at Phoenician Sulcis in the mineral-rich south-west of Sardinia have produced not only early Phoenician material but also a handful of eighth-century Euboean and Euboeanizing painted sherds that would be entirely at home at Pithekoussai (Bartoloni *et al.* 1988; Bartoloni 1989). The same is clearly true of Carthage itself, where we have recently heard news of "12 coupes eubéennes, ou d'imitation eubéenne dans certains cas [that] puisent leurs meilleurs parallèles dans la poterie de Pithekoussai" (Vegas 1992, 188; see too Niemeyer and Docter 1993, 226–35 *ss.vv. importierte Feinkeramik, Transportamphoren*).

Sulcis, it will be remembered, has in addition given us the well-known painted urn, identified *de visu* by Buchner as "made in Ischia" (Ridgway 1986, 180). I wonder if the same might be true of the similar and undoubtedly related urn from Caere (Cerveteri) in Southern Etruria that was successfully concealed from prying eyes by the authorities for nearly four decades (Rizzo 1989, 29–33 with figs. 58–60)? There are good Euboean parallels for the main motif (facing birds) on both these pieces, and their shape and decoration are generally reminiscent of certain Corinthian Late Geometric globular pyxides that were exported to Syracuse and Naxos in Eastern Sicily and to Francavilla Marittima in Calabria (references in Ridgway 1986, 179–80; Rizzo 1989, 31–33 notes 72–76). These two urns are "well-connected" in Greek terms, then, which is hardly cause for comment in the case of the specimen now known to have been recovered in 1952 from the Etruscan Orientalizing Tumulo della Speranza at Caere; that from Sulcis, however, was used for the very different purposes of the Phoenician *tophet* in which it was found.

How could such things be? We have seen that both Phoenicians and Euboeans were hungry for metal, and that the Phoenicians of Kition in Cyprus will almost certainly have known about the human and metallurgical potential of the West – which in the late ninth century was more likely to mean Sardinia than anywhere else. The first Euboeans in the East, we may be sure, will not have been backward in drawing on the rich fund of traditional wisdom generated (especially in Cyprus) at the time when the Levant, Cyprus, Euboea and Sardinia were all involved in the outstanding feats of human ingenuity that achieved the remarkable degree of international physical standardization implicit in the Late Bronze Age distribution of ox-hide ingots of copper; when smithing tools in Sardinia (and in the West *only* Sardinia) found their closest parallels in the twelfth-century Enkomi hoards; and when Cypriot bronze tripods of the mid-eleventh century could be exported to Sardinia, to inspire an accomplished local school of bronzeworking that continued to flourish in the centuries corresponding to the Greek Dark Age (full references for these topics, and for more besides, will be found in Lo Schiavo *et al.* 1985; Vagnetti and Lo Schiavo 1989; Ridgway and Serra Ridgway 1992, and in press).

I accept that direct contact between Cyprus and Sardinia is unlikely to have been prolonged indefinitely after *c.*1050 (Boardman 1990, 177). This round date is a reasonable *terminus ante quem* for exports from Cyprus to Sardinia, but we should not infer from this that Sardinia was henceforth out of touch with the outside world, and least of all with those parts of it that were frequented by Phoenicians. Thus a hitherto enigmatic bronze in the Monte Sa Idda hoard (Decimoputzu, Cagliari province) has been identified at last as an obelos with close parallels in a family of types that has only one further exception to its otherwise exclusively Atlantic distribution: a funerary context of *c.*1000 at Amathus in Cyprus (Karageorghis and Lo Schiavo 1989). The typological family to which the Monte Sa Idda and Amathus obeloi belong is firmly based in the part of the Iberian peninsula that is now Portugal, where a strikingly early Phoenician presence is attested at Santarém (Roman Scallabis) on the Tagus, 50 km inland from its estuary (Lisbon). The indigenous Iron Age site concerned is on the direct route to the tin deposits of the interior; and, in the words of the excavator, Ana Margarida Arruda, it was "très fréquenté par des navigateurs orientaux, depuis le début du huitième siècle av. J-C."[1] Elsewhere, Lucia Vagnetti (1989) has identified a supposedly enigmatic impasto vase in tomb 2 at Khaniale Tekke in Crete as a common type of Late Bronze - Early Iron Age Sardinian askos; the tomb in which it was found is best known for its two "crocks of gold" (the stock in trade of a travelling Phoenician goldsmith?), and contained a number of depositions in the chronological range *c.* 850–680. Similar askoi, and a number of other Sardinian items, had reached the Colline Metallifere in Tuscany as early as the tenth century (Lo Schiavo and Ridgway 1987): which as we have seen is precisely the area that is traditionally supposed to have exerted an almost literally magnetic attraction on the precolonial Euboeans.

We have thus returned, perhaps not unexpectedly, to the familiar story of the imported and locally-imitated Euboean skyphoi in the native cemeteries of Tyrrhenian Italy. I would like to think that the new route we have taken will have helped to prepare us for the new situation that now compels us to reassess a good deal of well-known and seemingly well-understood evidence. I refer to certain discoveries made in 1990 at the nuragic village of Sant'Imbenia, near Alghero in northwest Sardinia. We must naturally wait for further details, and more especially for a full account of the appropriate and indispensable stratigraphical and contextual information. But in the meantime, our appetite has been well and truly whetted by the reference in a brief preliminary announcement by the excavator, Susanna Bafico (1991), to (*inter alia*): 44 kg of bun ingots; Phoenician plates and other forms; and fragments of painted skyphoi of the Euboean types with pendent concentric semicircles, chevrons and birds. On this showing, we have to come to terms with the fact that the Euboean precolonial story in the West *starts in Sardinia*: and starts moreover in a context that has intimate Phoenician and metallurgical connections, and may precede the establishment of Pithekoussai by perhaps as much as a century – an estimate that will naturally vary according to our choice of chronological yardstick.

*

I would like to end by returning to another subject that has already been mentioned above: literacy, which in the form of the alphabet itself is a sector in which Phoenicians and Greeks are traditionally linked. While it seems to be generally agreed that the Phoenicians taught the Greeks to write, there is no such consensus as to where or precisely when this momentous cultural act might have taken place. Under the first heading, it is now some time since Alan

Johnston (1983) made a strong case for Cyprus. More recently, Barry Powell (1991) has vigorously promoted the idea that the actual adaptation was in the hands of a single Euboean Palamedes – an idea for which I believe there is a good deal more to be said than there is for his attempt to revive the theory that the Greek alphabet was invented for the sole purpose of writing down the text of the Homeric epics. My own answer to the "where" question would be "somewhere where Euboeans and Phoenicians were seeing a lot of each other", whether at home in Greece (where it would surely qualify for inclusion in Burkert's category of "intimate cultural contacts"), or abroad (where, as we have seen at Pithekoussai, such contacts were entirely possible).

As to "when", one statement now has to be made with rather more emphasis than it has received hitherto. It is that the verses on the "Nestor" kotyle from Pithekoussai (Buchner and Ridgway 1993, 219 with pls. 72–73 and cxxvi-viii: 168–9) are not the first Greek writing in the West – although I hope I may be excused for my opinion that they are the first Greek writing anywhere that is actually worth reading. Even when allowance is made for the degree of *campanilismo* implicit in this judgement, one would expect something like a generation of less sophisticated writing before "Europe's first literary allusion" (Powell 1991, 167) went into the ground at a time corresponding to an early stage in the evolution of the Early Protocorinthian globular aryballos (Buchner and Ridgway 1993, 215 note 4). A few examples exist already, and now there is another one. It comes from a wholly unforeseen part of the indigenous West, and is extraordinarily (some would say embarassingly, or even impossibly) early.

The inscription that we must now define as the first Greek writing in the West, and among the very first anywhere, comes from the native Iron Age cemetery in the Osteria dell'Osa locality at Gabii: five letters scratched after firing on the side of a unique (but nevertheless surely local) impasto flask[2]. The *editio princeps* proposes the reading *eulin*; this might be the noun *eulinos* – or perhaps a name, Eulinos, on the analogy of the Demaratean craftsmen Eucheir and Eugrammos (Pliny *NH* XXXV.43.152). As luck and the *TLG* data-base would have it, the noun is not otherwise attested until the second century AD, when Pausanias VIII.21.31) tells us that the semi-mythical Olen the Lycian used it to qualify Eileithyia as "a clever spinner"; the name is not attested at all. The alternative reading *euoin* has also been proposed, and is said to represent the characteristic shriek of the Bacchanals (Peruzzi 1992). But what concerns me here, and more urgently than possible meanings, is the evidence for chronology and cultural context.

The excavator of Osteria dell'Osa, Anna Maria Bietti Sestieri, defines the inscribed flask as a grave offering, inserted with a cremation into a pre-existing inhumation grave. This is a most unusual procedure: but I have every confidence both in her skill as an excavator and in her ability to interpret the data she has retrieved in the field. If it had been stratigraphically possible for the inscribed vase to have been inserted after the two depositions, I have no doubt that the fact would have been noted. It is not, and I conclude that there can accordingly be no question of later interference. This needs to be said, because the two depositions involved were effected in a range that, in terms of the tried and tested local scheme of relative and absolute chronology, begins *c.*830 and ends *c.*770; I hasten to add that there are good reasons for attributing the cremation grave, and hence the inscribed vase, to the later part of this range.

Culturally, three comments are possible on the occurrence of these exceptionally early Greek letters in a native Italian Iron Age context. The first is that of the excavator herself, for whom it is "a striking example of the ability of the Latial society to acknowledge and absorb innovation of external origin even at an extremely early stage" (Bietti Sestieri 1992b, 217). I am not convinced that this is so: I see no evidence of literacy being "absorbed" during the eighth century by the native communities either at Osteria dell'Osa itself or elsewhere in Latium. Secondly, we may wish (with Peruzzi 1992) to recall that it was to Gabii that Romulus and Remus were sent when young – and so presumably *c.*770 – to be instructed in Greek learning (*paideia*), which naturally included letters (*grammata*: Dion. Hal. I.84.5). This is tempting: but it has to be said that, apart from the new inscription, no Greek writing of any period has ever been found at Gabii or anywhere in its territory. We are left, I believe, with a third possibility: that this Greek word was inscribed *for an exclusively Greek reason* on a local pot by an early precolonial Greek visitor to the area. He will have been roughly contemporary with the skyphos bearers who (with or without the assistance of Phoenician trinket-vendors) took their wares to Campania and Southern Etruria; his inscription may mean no more than "the owner of this pot spins well" – just the kind of logistic information that pioneer travellers (and prospectors) in strange lands might have agreed to share. What should strike us forcibly is that such an individual was already literate, at least to a point that enabled him to leave a message for anyone else like himself who came after him. Chronologically, we are closer than we have ever been to the date of the Phoenician-Greek transmission of the alphabet. There is food for thought in the fact that the result was put to use so soon and so far away from home, and the sea.

If my interpretation of this remarkable new find is anywhere near the truth, it is ironic indeed that our oldest evidence for the greatest gift that the Phoenicians and Greeks between them brought to the West comes from the homely sphere of spinning and weaving. And it is if anything even more ironic that the evidence was found in Latium vetus, an area that was at the time little more than a provincial backwater. The imminent change in Latial fortunes combines with the complex social and political structures that have emerged from the patient study of the eighth-century community at Osteria dell'Osa (Bietti Sestieri 1992a, 43–549; 1992b) to remind me irresistibly of *Middlemarch*, and of its setting in rural Warwickshire on the eve of an industrial revolution that was no less far-reaching in its effects than what we must now learn to call the Orientalizing revolution.

\*

*Middlemarch* provides an appropriate note on which to end. George Eliot's masterpiece has almost as many subplots as Sarah Morris' *Daidalos* (1992)[3], and the justly famous last paragraph of its finale refers movingly to "unhistoric acts", "hidden lives" and "unvisited tombs". The period and area that I have attempted to treat in these pages abound in all three.

## ACKNOWLEDGEMENT

I am most grateful to the organizers of the lecture series on which this book is based for their invitation to read an earlier version of the above paper in Oxford in February 1994: and for thus giving me the opportunity to say "look it up in *Pithekoussai* I" for the first time in public as a tribute to the author of *The Greeks overseas*.

## NOTES

1. These words are taken from the printed abstract of the memorable and well received paper ("Santarém: un site orientalisant dans la Vallée du Tage") that A. M. Arruda read to the international colloquium (*Interactions in the Iron Age: Phoenicians, Greeks and the indigenous peoples of the Western Mediterranean*) held at the Allard Pierson Museum, Amsterdam in March 1992. The proceedings of the colloquium are forthcoming in imminent volumes of *Hamburger Beiträge zur Archäologie*.

2. Bietti Sestieri *et al.* 1990, 83–88 (*editio princeps*); Bietti Sestieri 1992a, 209–12 with figs. 2f.1.14a-b (deposition and ritual), 273 with pl. 20 (typology), 686–87 with fig. 3a.270 (*corredo*); Bietti Sestieri 1992b, 121–25 with fig. 6.2, 185 with fig. 8.9. At just over 600 graves in the chronological range *c*. 900-580, Osteria dell'Osa is now the largest single Iron Age assemblage in Latium. See Holloway 1994, 103–13 for a brief account of the cemetery and this inscription (112, fig. 8.5). In my view, the present state of the evidence does not justify the affirmation (190, note 4) that the latter "raises the possibility that the Greeks adopted the alphabet in the West, very possibly at Ischia..." (see further Ridgway, in press).

3. Rightly in my view, Morris 1992 has been deemed "marvellous, thought-provoking" in the only review of it that I have seen (Sherratt 1993, 918). Many of Morris' subplots are highly relevant to the subject of this paper, and I am currently preparing a discussion of one of them under the provisional title "Daidalos and Pithekoussai".

## BIBLIOGRAPHY

ALBRIGHT, W. F. 1941: New light on the early history of Phoenician colonization. *BASOR* 83, 14–22.

AUBET, M. E. 1993: *The Phoenicians and the West* (Cambridge, U.P.).

BAFICO, S. 1991: Greci e Fenici ad Alghero. *Archeo* 74 (aprile), 18.

BARTOLONI, P. 1989: Nuove testimonianze arcaiche da Sulcis. *Nuovo Bullettino Archeologico Sardo*-2 [1985], 167–92.

BARTOLONI, P., BERNARDINI, P., TRONCHETTI, C. 1988: S. Antioco: area del Cronicario (campagne di scavo 1983–86). *Rivista di Studi Fenici* 16, 73–119.

BELOCH, J. 1890: *Campanien*, 3rd edn. (Breslau, Morgenstern).

BERNAL, M. 1987–91: *Black Athena*. I: *The fabrication of Ancient Greece 1785–1985*. II: *The archaeological and documentary evidence* (London, Free Association Books).

BIETTI SESTIERI, A. M. (ed.) 1992a: *La necropoli laziale di Osteria dell'Osa* (Rome, Quasar).

BIETTI SESTIERI, A. M. 1992b: *The Iron Age community of Osteria dell'Osa* (Cambridge, U.P.).

BIETTI SESTIERI, A. M., DE SANTIS, A., LA REGINA, A. 1990: Elementi di tipo cultuale e doni personali nella necropoli laziale di Osteria dell'Osa. *Scienze dell'Antichità* 3–4, 65–88.

BLAKEWAY, A. 1933: Prolegomena to the study of Greek commerce with Italy, Sicily and France in the eighth and seventh centuries BC. *BSA* 33, 170–208.

BOARDMAN, J. 1990: Al Mina and history. *OJA* 9, 169–90.

BUCHNER, G. 1977: Cuma nell'VIII secolo a.C., osservata dalla prospettiva di Pithecusa. In *I Campi Flegrei nell'archeologia e nella storia* (Rome, Atti dei Convegni Lincei 33), 131–148.

BUCHNER, G. 1978: Testimonianze epigrafiche semitiche dell'VIII secolo a.C. a Pithekoussai. *Parola del Passato* 33, 135–47.

BUCHNER, G. 1982: Die Beziehungen zwischen der euböischen Kolonie Pithekoussai auf der Insel Ischia und dem nordwestsemitischen Mittelmeerraum in der zweiten Hälfte des 8. Jhs. v. Chr. In *Niemeyer 1982*, 277–306.

BUCHNER, G. and RIDGWAY, D. 1983: Pithekoussai 944. *AION* 5, 1–9.

BUCHNER, G. and RIDGWAY, D. 1993: *Pithekoussai I. La necropoli: tombe 1–723*. Monumenti Antichi, serie monografica 4 (Rome, G. Bretschneider).

BURKERT, W. 1992: *The orientalizing revolution* (Harvard, U.P.).

COLDSTREAM, J. N. 1977: *Geometric Greece* (London, Benn).

COLDSTREAM, J. N. 1982: Greeks and Phoenicians in the Aegean. In *Niemeyer 1982*, 261–75.

DICKINSON, O. 1994: *The Aegean Bronze Age* (Cambridge, U.P.).

FREDERIKSEN, M. W. 1977: Archaeology in South Italy and Sicily, 1973–76. *AR for 1976–77*, 43–76.

HALL, E. 1989: *Inventing the barbarian: Greek self-definition through tragedy* (Oxford, Clarendon Press).

HOLLOWAY, R. R. 1994: *The archaeology of early Rome and Latium* (London, Routledge).

JAMES, P. *et al.* 1991: *Centuries of darkness* (London, Cape).

JOHNSTON, A. W. 1983: The extent and use of literacy: the archaeological evidence. In Hägg, R. (ed.), *The Greek Renaissance of the eighth century BC* (Stockholm, Svenska Istitutet i Athen), 63–68.

KARAGEORGHIS, V. and LO SCHIAVO, F. 1989: A West Mediterranean obelos from Amathus. *Rivista di Studi Fenici* 17, 15–29.

KEARSLEY, R. 1989: *The pendent semi-circle skyphos*. Bulletin Supplement 44 (London, Institute of Classical Studies).

LO SCHIAVO, F., MACNAMARA, E., VAGNETTI, L. 1985: Late Cypriot imports to Italy and their influence on local bronzework. *PBSR* 53, 1–71.

LO SCHIAVO, F. and RIDGWAY, D. 1987: La Sardegna e il Mediterraneo allo scorcio del II millennio. In *La Sardegna nel Mediterraneo tra il secondo e il primo millennio a.C.* (Cagliari, Atti del 2° Convegno ... di Selargius), 391–418.

MARKOE, G. E. 1992: In pursuit of metal: Phoenicians and Greeks in Italy. In Kopcke, G. and Tukumaru, I. (eds.), *Greece between East and West: 10th-8th centuries BC* (Mainz, von Zabern), 61–84.

MORRIS, S. P. 1992: *Daidalos and the origins of Greek art* (Princeton, U.P.).

MURRAY, O. 1993: *Early Greece*, 2nd edn. (London, Fontana).

NEGBI, O. 1992: Early Phoenician presence in the Mediterranean islands: a reappraisal. *AJA* 96, 599–615.

NIEMEYER, H. G. (ed.) 1982: *Phönizier im Westen*. Madrider Beiträge 8 (Mainz, von Zabern).

NIEMEYER, H. G. 1984: Die Phönizier und die Mittelmeerwelt im Zeitalter Homers. *JRGZ* 31, 3–94.

NIEMEYER, H. G. 1990: The Phoenicians in the Mediterranean: a non-Greek model for expansion and settlement in antiquity. In Descoeudres, J.-P. (ed.), *Greek colonists and native populations* (Oxford, Clarendon Press), 469–89.

NIEMEYER, H. G. 1994: Die Phönizier im Mittelmeerraum: Expansion oder Kolonisation? *Hamburger Beiträge zur Wissenschaftsgeschichte* 15, 321–47.

NIEMEYER, H. G. and DOCTER, R. F. 1993: Die Grabung unter dem Decumanus maximus von Karthago. *MDAI(R)* 100, 201–44.

PERUZZI, E. 1992: Cultura greca a Gabii nel secolo VIII. *Parola del Passato* 47, 459–68.

POPHAM, M. R. and LEMOS, I. S. 1992: review of Kearsley 1989. *Gnomon* 64, 152–55.

POPHAM, M. R., SACKETT, L. H., THEMELIS, P. G. (eds.) 1980: *Lefkandi I: text* (London, British School at Athens).

POWELL, B. B. 1991: *Homer and the origin of the Greek alphabet* (Cambridge, U.P.).

RIDGWAY, D. 1986: Sardinia and the first Western Greeks. In Balmuth, M. S. (ed.), *Studies in Sardinian Archaeology II: Sardinia in the Mediterranean* (University of Michigan Press), 173–85.

RIDGWAY, D. 1988: Western Geometric pottery: new light on interactions in Italy. In *Proceedings of the 3rd Symposium on ancient Greek and related pottery 1987* (Copenhagen), 489–505.

RIDGWAY, D. 1992: *The first Western Greeks* (Cambridge, U.P.).

RIDGWAY, D. In press: Greek letters at Osteria dell'Osa. *Opuscula Romana*.

RIDGWAY, D. and SERRA RIDGWAY, F. R. 1992: Sardinia and history. In Tykot, R. H. and Andrews, T. K. (eds.), *Sardinia in the Mediterranean: a footprint in the sea* (Studies Balmuth; Sheffield Academic Press), 355–63.

RIDGWAY, D. and SERRA RIDGWAY, F. R. In press: Su Tempiesu and the Ceri effect. *Acta Hyperborea*.

RIZZO, M. A. 1989: Ceramica etrusco-geometrica da Caere. In *Miscellanea Ceretana I* (Rome, Quaderni del Centro di Studio per l'archeologia etrusco-italica 17), 9–39.

SHERRATT, S. 1993: review of Morris 1992. *Antiquity* 67, 915–18.

VAGNETTI, L. 1989: A Sardinian askos from Crete. *BSA* 84, 355–60.

VAGNETTI, L. and LO SCHIAVO, F. 1989: Late Bronze Age long distance trade in the Mediterranean: the role of the Cypriots. In Peltenburg, E. (ed.), *Early Society in Cyprus* (Edinburgh, U.P.), 217–43.

VEGAS, M. 1992: Carthage: la ville archaïque. Céramique d'importation de la période du Géométrique Récent. In *Lixus. Actes du colloque ... Larache 1989* (Collection de l'Ecole Française de Rome 166), 181–89.

## Chapter 4

# Prospectors and Pioneers:
# Pithekoussai, Kyme and Central Italy

### J. N. Coldstream

In David Ridgway's paper, published in this volume, "Phoenicians and Greeks in the West", the order is significant. There he has put forward a soundly argued view that the first Euboean precolonial prospectors in the West were far from being the first in the field; on the contrary, they had to fit into a pre-existing network of East-West trade, beginning with exchanges of Cypriot copper for the iron of Sardinia as early as the twelfth and eleventh centuries BC. Meanwhile, a remarkably sophisticated Sardinian aristocracy, supporting a versatile bronze industry, was already exploiting the metal sources of northern Etruria, long before they were tapped by Phoenicians and, more indirectly, by Greeks (Ridgway 1992b). In Western waters the Phoenicians could even have been mentors to the Greeks, guiding them eventually towards suitable sites for settlement.

All this will help to fuel a healthy reaction against any Hellenocentric bias in previous generations of scholarship; but I think there is a danger of that reaction being carried too far. In its most extreme form, attributed to his "imaginary archaeologist" by Anthony Snodgrass in the opening paper in this volume, it not only excludes Greek settlers from Al Mina, but even argues against there being any positive evidence that Euboean merchants ventured outside the Aegean before 800; before then, the carrying of all imports to and exports from the Aegean is attributed to the heads of the ubiquitous Phoenicians; and, in the West, the earliest Euboean prospectors are downgraded from precolonial to paracolonial, no earlier than their first settlement at Pithekoussai.

For the East, Mervyn Popham's paper in this volume has put some powerful counter-arguments in favour of an active Euboean enterprise in that direction well before 800 BC. On that issue, well worth considering is the Eastern spread of the less well publicised Euboean shape with pendent semicircles – the plate; scarce at home in Euboea, where people seem to have preferred the skyphos for eating as well as drinking, but far more frequent as exports to Cyprus and the Levant, where the plate was an indispensable domestic chattel (Coldstream 1989, 92). As an example of this enthusiasm for the plate, there is a set of seven from the rich tomb 194 at Amathus, shortly to be published in *BCH*, and there are plenty more found at Tyre.[1] Do we, then, have a hint of Euboean market research, of an active response to a known overseas demand, of a willingness to manufacture especially for export? In the East, no doubt, the Euboean plates were appreciated for the excellence of their fabric, as luxurious alternatives to the local, more porous, versions. Here is but one reason why I believe that, long before 800 BC, the Euboeans had been no strangers to the waters outside the Aegean.

When Greek – and chiefly Euboean – fine pottery began to reach central Italy – and here no one doubted that the pots travelled in Euboean ships – the Italic recipients were perfectly happy with the favourite Greek shape, the skyphos, now in its Middle Geometric II stage, decorated with vertical chevrons, and in that form made in many parts of the Greek world. Can we be sure that these skyphoi are truly precolonial? Since Alan Blakeway's notion of "trade before the flag", the "flag" has, of course, been moved backwards in time with the discovery of Pithekoussai, to well before the middle of the eighth century; and "pre-" and "para-colonial" can have different meanings in different western contexts. Nevertheless, in spite of attempts (Vallet 1958, 34; Descoeudres 1983, 11–34)[2] to shunt these much-discussed vessels into a paracolonial siding, I still firmly believe that, apart from some of their looser local imitations, they are precolonial in an absolute sense, earlier than the foundation of the first colony. Typologically, they stand at the head of a sequence of two-handled drinking vessels, mainly Corinthian, which give us an archaeological measuring rod for the dating of all western colonial foundations throughout the eighth century. The chevron skyphos with its pronounced lip, a panhellenic shape, is absent from Pithekoussai, apart from the three sporadic finds among a vast body of material (Ridgway, 1981, fig. 1, frs. 1–2); otherwise, the earliest pieces there are from its successor, the proto-kotyle with only a minimal lip. This, in turn, gives place to the earliest, hemispherical, form of the lipless Corinthian kotyle, Sylvia Benton's Aëtos 666 type, still decorated with chevrons, and well represented among the earliest graves of Pithekoussai in the third quarter of the eighth century. Then follows the kotyle with herons facing over waves, a type still current during the settlement of the first colonies in Sicily. Finally, in the last two decades of the century, we have the deep or tall kotyle, a regular companion of the Early Protocorinthian globular aryballos; these two shapes occur in most graves of the second generation at Pithekoussai, but are among the very earliest finds in the colonies in the extreme south of Italy.[3]

This excursion into chronology has run into two facts of historical interest. First, the precolonial chevron skyphoi in Italy at once gave rise to local imitations, close enough to the work of resident Greek potters. Secondly, the imported fine pottery in the Euboean colonial graves of Pithekoussai is overwhelmingly Corinthian, rather than Euboean. To both these phenomena we shall return in due course; but this is a good moment to mention that the Euboeans may well have been forestalled by the Corinthians as the first post-Mycenaean Greek prospectors in Italy. For them, Italy was much more easily accessible, without having to brave the perils of Cape Malea; and on leaving the calm waters of the Corinthian Gulf, they had convenient forward stations in Ithaca and, eventually, their colony, Kerkyra. Their visits to the Italian mainland, however, were initially confined to the heel of Italy, especially to the Messapian site under modern Otranto where the entire sequence of eighth-century Corinthian fine pottery has been found, starting at least as early as, and possibly earlier than, the Euboean precolonial skyphoi further west (D'Andria 1990, 36–45). But for the time being, the Corinthians were content to limit their exploration to both sides of the Adriatic in activities which were pre- and para- but not actually colonial, until their seventh-century foundations on the Illyrian coast. As for Adriatic Italy, whatever commerce they were pursuing, they felt no need to have a colonial base there.

To return to the precolonial Euboeans. Their progress along the Tyrrhenian coastlands is charted by a scatter of Greek drinking vessels, mainly chevron skyphoi, as luxury ware in Italic burials. In Campania they were first noted at Kyme, in the prehellenic Osta cemetery (Gabrici 1913). Several of them occur in the cemeteries of Capua, preceding a series of paracolonial drinking vessels, mainly Euboean (Johannowsky 1969). The enormous cemetery of Pontecagnano, the ancient Picentia, offers a similar sequence but with more variety, including some Cycladic pieces (D'Agostino 1988, 44–7, pl. 16). Latium, so far, has produced no imported chevron skyphoi; but in Rome, under the church of San Omobono, a deposit of Euboean pottery includes some pieces with full concentric circles, quite likely to be precolonial (La Rocca 1975, fig. A). Fifteen miles east of Rome, at Gabii, where, according to Dionysius of Halicarnassus, the shepherd Faustulus taught Greek letters to Romulus and Remus, there is a puzzling graffito of five Greek letters in a local impasto flask, datable in the local sequence to not later than the early eighth century (Bietti-Sestieri *et al.* 1989–90). Passing into southern Etruria, it is at Veii that we find the greatest concentration of imported chevron skyphoi, together with the earliest imitations of them by Greek potters who took up residence there (Ridgway 1979). Precolonial pottery has not been found anywhere further north; but the visiting traders, and the expatriate artisans, would have noticed an extraordinary wealth and variety of metal objects, especially the copious bronze fibulae of types unfamiliar to them; they would also have had the impression of a well-organised and regimented society which, in the well-explored Quattro Fontanili cemetery, buried its dead in ever-increasing spirals around the top of the hill, to the delight of excavators seeking relative dates (Close-Brooks 1979).

With hindsight, because we know that iron from Elba was processed at Pithekoussai (Marinelli, *apud* Buchner 1969, 97–8), we are accustomed to infer that the chief motive of the precolonial Greek visitors was to prospect for ores from the north Etruscan metalliferous region. Veii would have been a place for negotiation, for exchange of gifts, for getting to know the middlemen through whose hands the ores might have been channelled.[4] But, unlike the Corinthians who could have operated up the Adriatic from their stations in the Ionian islands, the Euboean merchants felt very far from home; they needed also to prospect for a forward base. For this purpose, as we know, it was their earlier Campanian contacts which bore fruit; they chose Pithekoussai. Why? Possible answers will depend on our views on two debatable issues. First, was the pursuit of Etruscan metal ores their only motive in going west,[5] or did they also have their eye on other advantages – for example, enough good arable land for easy subsistence? And secondly, were they entirely free and strong enough to choose the best possible site for their needs, or were they obliged to fit into a previously existing network, in which Etruscans, Campanians, Sardinians and Phoenicians all had some say? As a first venture in colonial settlement, the choice of an offshore island was, no doubt, wise; the first settlers might well feel uneasy about their reception by possibly hostile and well-armed Italic mainlanders, whereas the indigenous occupation of Pithekoussai seems to have been slight (Ridgway 1992a, 86). But if their choice were entirely free, and if mineral wealth were their only motive, why choose an island three hundred kms. from metal sources? Why not somewhere like Pianosa, or Giglio, or even Monte Cristo? In that case, the choice was not entirely theirs – a conclusion in line with the absence of any *direct* contact with metalliferous Etruria in the form of Greek exports, or other Greek cultural contacts, until well after 600 BC. By way of contrast, consider the Phoenician and Phoenicianizing luxuries – silver vessels, faience objects and decorated ostrich eggs – found in the princely burials of Vetulonia and other north Etruscan cemeteries from the late eighth century onwards (Markoe 1992). On the other hand it is hard to think of Pithekoussai as a *pis aller*, allotted to the Euboean settlers by Phoenicians and other members of the "network" as a sort of consolation prize. Although their interest in metals cannot be denied, it was surely not their only motive in founding their first colony. The Euboeans must also have had a positive reason for choosing Pithekoussai – to be within easy reach of mainland Campania, rich not in metals but in arable land for future exploitation. Here let me hasten to declare a reluctance to be sidetracked into the general debate motives for founding colonies – a debate which can become sterile when extreme, polarised positions are taken up; "entirely for trade", or "entirely because of land hunger caused by overpopulation at home". Whatever the situation may have been in the late eighth century, it is hard to credit that Chalcis and Eretria, the founding cities, were suffering an explosion of population fifty years earlier, when Pithekoussai was founded. And yet, however strong the lure of the metals, the merchants would have also needed land for food and clothing. Let us explore the possibility that the first Pithekoussans wanted, and achieved, the best of both worlds.

Monte di Vico, a sheer headland forming the north-west corner of the volcanic island of Ischia, was the acropolis of Pithekoussai, a promontory with a harbour on each side. The attraction of the place persists into modern times, when much of the ancient site is now covered by the bathing resort of Lacco Ameno. Giorgio Buchner's largest excavation has been in the cemetery, in the quiet valley of San Montano. Through rescue digging[6] he has defined its full extent, of which he has excavated two portions, together containing some 1300 graves; the first of these is now fully published in *Pithekoussai* I. The acropolis of Monte di Vico is much eroded; but a large rubbish dump on its eastern flank, the Scarico Gosetti, has produced settlement pottery and other important finds going back to the colony's earliest years (Ridgway 1966a; Ridgway 1981). Near its point are traces of a temple, but not earlier than the sixth century. The third main excavation site is some way inland, on the Mezzavia ridge: this is the metalworkers' quarter on the Mazzola plot (Buchner 1971; Klein 1972), within easy reach of timber for the furnaces, and on a spot where the prevailing wind will have blown the noxious fumes away from the main settlement.

So much for the town of Pithekoussai, or as much of it as modern Lacco Ameno will allow us to glimpse; but the first colonists were not slow to exploit the rest of the island for their own subsistence. Finds of eighth-century Greek pottery, without any trace of indigenous presence, have turned up at three places (Fig. 4.1), all quite distant from the main settlement, under later volcanic deposits. One is near Buchner's house at Porto d'Ischia, near the island's north-eastern corner. Another is Punta Chiarito, a promontory on the south-western coast, found in 1992; Buchner interprets this site as an outlying farm, and excavations there are continuing (Fratta 1994). Further east, more eighth-century Greek sherds have turned up in canyons between Panza and San Angelo.[7]

This brief glimpse of the topography should satisfy us that we are not witnessing a small,

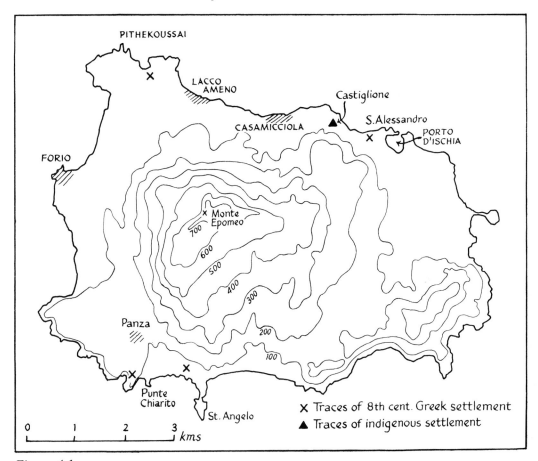

*Figure 4.1*

tentative experiment in overseas settlement. On the contrary, the newcomers arrived in force, and acted with premeditation. At once they occupied a defensible rock for their acropolis, and earmarked the western valley below for all their burials. The blacksmiths quickly settled down to process the ores from Etruria on an environmentally acceptable site; and others were not slow to farm the coastal land outside the settlement. From the first, the Pithekoussans acted like a true *polis*; and whatever ambitions they had as traders, they also aimed at being self-sufficient, the whole island being their *chora*. Their industrial energies, probably in league with some Phoenician colleagues, have been covered in Ridgway's paper in this volume; as he observed, "not all the first Western Greeks were Greek" (1990, 72). Here, then, is the place to underline the Greek aspects of Pithekoussai.

In the valley of San Montano we have that rare phenomenon, a complete and unrifled cemetery. It had been protected from looters by a deep overlay of alluvial material, and the hot steam in this highly thermal zone often caused the excavators to work at a temperature of sixty degrees Celsius, reducing much of the pottery to the consistency of soft cheese. Although over thirteen hundred graves have been cleared, these form only five per cent of the whole cemetery. Wisely, the excavators warn us against jumping to premature conclusions about the Pithekoussan social order, not least because the graves of the aristocratic élite have not yet come to light. Some general statements, however, are permissible. Two-thirds of the published graves belong to the mid- and late eighth century, the *floruit* of the colony before its decline from the seventh century onwards; and about twenty per cent fall into its first generation.[8] The forms of burial are wholly Greek, and consistent with what little we know of contemporary Euboean burials at home, mainly in Eretria. Well-to-do adults were cremated on pyres, and their ashes then placed under stone cairns; and family ties could encourage a single cairn to grow into a family of cairns. Pit inhumations were usual for children, and also for poorer adults, possibly slaves; infants were housed in large pots (Buchner 1982b; Ridgway 1992, 45–82).

Among such a vast assemblage of grave goods, the eastern *exotica* (Buchner 1982a) have naturally attracted much attention, as evidence of trade in that direction. There are the Phoenician transport amphorae, emptied of their imported contents, and then used for infant burials; the KW or "spaghetti" aryballoi of Cypriot type from a Dodecanesian unguent factory staffed by Phoenician entrepreneurs (Coldstream 1969); a few larger flasks, both Phoenician and North Syrian; faience and steatite scarabs, both Levantine imitations and Egyptian originals – including the well-known one bearing the cartouche of the ill-fated Pharaoh Bocchoris (Bosticco 1957, 218; Da Salvia 1978; Hölbl 1983); and the Lyre player class of stone seals, the scaraboids from Cilicia, found mainly in graves of small children, and especially in those of the first generation (Buchner and Boardman 1966b). This wide variety of *orientalia* may indicate a small minority of Levantine residents (Ridgway 1992a, 111–18). The fact remains, however, that the great majority of the pottery is Greek, whether imported or made locally. As grave offerings, very striking is the preference for Corinthian fine ware and its local imitations, a taste apparently not shared by the Euboeans at home; but in Pithekoussai the Euboean style predominates only in the settlement deposits. During the colony's second generation, we have clear evidence of Corinthian master-potters actually residing at Pithekoussai or Kyme, to become bold pioneers of Orientalizing decoration in the vanguard of the Early Protocorinthian style (Williams 1986; Neeft 1987, 59).

This Corinthian strain was an essential ingredient in a hybrid colonial style, of which we find no trace in the Euboean homeland; Euboean birds with raised wings, for example, on larger unguent vessels such as the Corinthian conical lekythos, and other shapes with fine Corinthian banding (Buchner 1964, 268–9, fig.3). Again, in Euboean graves at home we have no large figured vases alluding to death, as in Athens; but this eclectic school of Pithekoussai produced some obviously funerary vases, including a krater showing a mourning woman between two horse panels (Buchner and Ridgway 1993, pl. 235). This is a sporadic find within the cemetery, and the horses could supply a hint of the as yet missing aristocracy. Horses are much better represented in the local settlement pottery, whether feeding indoors at the manger, or grazing out in the field (Buchner 1969, fig. 27). Both images were inherited from the creator of the large Cesnola krater (Coldstream 1971); he would have included among his patrons the landed aristocrats of Chalcis and Euboea, for whom the well-fed horse was a symbol of power and wealth, prestige and the possession of good pasture land (Coldstream

1981, 244–5). Unlike later Greek aristocrats, those of the eighth and seventh centuries did not disdain the role of trader; on the model of the Corinthian Bacchiads, with their mercantile enthusiasms (Strabo VIII.6.22), the Euboean commercial ventures in the West would also have been directed by an élite (Buchner 1982b, 279). But, for aristocratic families accustomed to the bounteous Lelantine plain at home, opportunities for grazing horses on this volcanic island might not have been great. Here, perhaps, we have one reason, among several others, for the eventual move to Kyme, where the élite would have had a better chance of enjoying both worlds.

We cannot leave Pithekoussai without some thought for its Italic population. If the burial customs and pottery are overwhelmingly Greek, the bronze fibulae, the commonest category of dress ornament, tell quite a different story. Far from including any Greek types, they conform instead to the Villanovan sequence, diffused in the eighth century throughout Etruria, Latium and Campania (Buchner 1979, 133; Toms 1986). Furthermore, a miscast fibula of Villanovan type has been found in the blacksmiths' quarter on the Mezzavia ridge, showing that such fibulae were locally produced (Buchner 1971, 66).[9] To explain the prevalence of these Italic dress ornaments in the early colonial graves, Buchner has reasonably argued for widespread intermarriage between the first Euboean colonists and women from Italy (1979, 135). In a previous paper I have pursued the wider implications of this hypothesis (let us not call it a model!), envisaging how such liaisons could have begun with precolonial contacts, and especially considering the role of bilingual children from such marriages in the subsequent sharing of ideas between Greek settlers and Italic peoples, not least in the spreading of alphabetic literacy, in the first instance to the Etruscans (Coldstream 1993). I should, however, acknowledge that, as Buchner (pers. comm. 31.4.93) has pointed out to me, I put too much emphasis on southern Etruria as a potential source of Pithekoussan brides, having underestimated the amazing homogeneity of Villanovan fibulae in all the Tyrrehenian coastlands of central Italy. Indeed, some wives could have come from no farther afield than the island's small indigenous settlement of the Early Iron Age at Castiglione, on its north coast between Lacco Ameno and Porto d'Ischia; others from precolonial encounters in Campania, notably Pontecagnano and prehellenic Kyme.

Among ancient authors, Livy (VIII.22) deserves our special respect, in that he alone, perhaps from his command of Etruscan sources, knew that Pithekoussai had been the earliest of all Greek settlements in Italy. In his account, the Chalcidians first settled in the island of Aenaria, or Ischia, before they dared (*ausi*) to establish themselves on the mainland at Kyme. At first, he implies, they contemplated a mainland settlement but, uncertain of their reception, they did not dare. Thinking of the illustrious future of Kyme, it is easy to accuse Livy of hindsight – of imputing to the Euboeans a grand design, first settling cautiously on an offshore island, with an eye towards a more spacious colony in mainland Campania when the time became ripe; but this reconstruction would be quite consistent with the precolonial visits to Campania, as along as we can accept that such visits had a local purpose, rather than merely providing staging posts on the way to Etruria. As for the date when the Euboeans settled at Kyme, it still lies in an archaeological lacuna; no prehellenic graves of the Osta cemetery are later than the early eighth century (Close-Brooks 1979), whereas the pottery from the first Greek graves is Early Protocorinthian, no earlier than in those of the first Sicilian colonies.

Strabo, however (V.4.8), would have us believe that Kyme was founded before any of the Sicilian colonies; hence, on present evidence, I follow Martin Frederiksen's (1984, 59) approximate date of *c.* 740 – about a generation, that is, after the beginning of Pithekoussai.

Here, in parenthesis, let us note that, in spite of Livy's statement, there is no archaeological sign that Pithekoussai was at once depleted by the foundation of Kyme. On the contrary, the published graves of the second generation, contemporary with the earliest of Kyme, are three times as numerous as those of the preceding first generation (Ridgway 1992, 69).[10] In the numbers of burials, the decline of Pithekoussai begins only after 700; and one telling symptom of commercial decline, to which Buchner has drawn my attention, is the very sharp drop after *c.* 700 BC in the import to Pithekoussai of Egyptian and Egyptianizing trinkets (De Salvia 1993, 770). Although too little of the settlement has been excavated to reveal any general volcanic damage,[11] the earthquake and eruptions mentioned by Strabo (V.4.9) might well have caused an exodus.

Kyme could, of course, provide a refuge from such disturbances; but, as we shall see, some Pithekoussans of the second generation, especially those of mixed parentage, might also have had positive reasons for seeking their fortunes in the mainland colony.

For the earliest Greek period at Kyme, the quality of our evidence falls far short of what we now have for Pithekoussai, the cemeteries having been dug mainly in the nineteenth century and without much care. Until recently, even the ancient topography could be misunderstood; thus, the straight modern shoreline gave rise to the idea that Kyme had no harbour, and therefore was a purely agrarian settlement (Vallet 1958, 57, n.3). It is now clear that the sea has receded since ancient times, and the reconstruction by Werner Johannowsky (1975) allows for a substantial harbour south of the rocky acropolis, so that Kyme would have been just as well placed for trade as was Pithekoussai. The acropolis, though very little explored at the deeper levels, has nevertheless produced an intriguing Late Geometric sherd showing a galloping horseman (Buchner 1954, 52, fig. 3) – an unusual theme in Geometric vase painting, but less rare in Euboean contexts than elsewhere (Coldstream 1981, 245–6). Rearing horses should not have been difficult in the spacious plains around Kyme; but it is the aristocratic element in the cemeteries that needs our special attention, because there we find what is at present missing at Pithekoussai. For the rest of this paper I shall concentrate on the richest among an élite group of burials, tomb 104 on the Fondo Artiaco plot, 600 yards inland from the acropolis, found intact, dug with care, and promptly published by Pellegrini in 1903. Precise dating is not easy, since the élite did not favour the humble pot; the only clay vessel is a plain Attic amphora of the SOS type, datable in broad terms to *c.* 700. The high status of the tomb is expressed in the 51 metal finds, of which we shall consider a selection.

In a cist tomb of well-cut tufa blocks, the cremation of a warrior was protected by an Etruscan bronze shield with concentric zones of decoration. It rested on the mouth of a huge bronze cauldron, half a metre across. Inside that was a smaller cauldron, sealed with cork and leaves, and covered by a linen cloth preserving traces of purple. This, in turn, enclosed a silver bowl with its lid, 26 cms. across, containing the warrior's ashes and some choice granulated jewellery, badly damaged in the pyre. Elsewhere in the tomb were two more bronze cauldrons, one inside the other, sharing the same lid, and resting on a bulbous conical stand of eastern type like the well-known Orientalizing vessel from the Barberini tomb at Praeneste, on a smaller scale; the outer vessel has lotus handles resembling a type current in Cyprus two centuries earlier, in the rich tombs of Old Paphos. In a heap of fused iron lay the warrior's horse bits and his weaponry, including at least eight spearheads, and a sword in a silver-plated scabbard of Italic "carp's tongue" type, found also in the earlier prehellenic burials of the Osta cemetery. There were two more fragmentary silver vessels, a Phoenician piriform jug with palmette handle, and a deep kotyle of Corinthian shape; and a set of massive electrum fibulae, up to 13 cms. long, extreme elaborations of current Villanovan types; and an Etruscan Orientalizing bolt fibula in silver with miniature sculpture tricked out in granulation: two Hathor heads, and rows of bearded sphinxes perched upon the plates.

The Italic character of the ornaments and weapons has persuaded Ingrid Ström (1971, 147) that our splendid warrior is no Greek colonist, but rather an Etruscan grandee living among Greeks at a time when Etruscan cultural influence had spread far and wide into Campania. One might add that the abundance of silver is unusual in a purely Greek context, even though the Greeks at home had the ores at their disposal. In the West, Glenn Markoe (1992) has made a persuasive case that the acquisition and working of silver was initially a concern of the Phoenicians rather that the Greeks; and, indeed, no other Phoenician palmette jug has occurred in a Greek orbit. More generally, ostentatious display of wealth in Greece at this time is found not in graves but in sanctuaries.

There is, however, a good metropolitan parallel for the burial rites, in the warrior graves by the West Gate at Eretria. There, too, we have cremation ashes in bronze cauldrons which also contain some personal jewellery, and are associated with large numbers of weapons (Bérard 1970). Hence Buchner, among others, prefers to see this élite cremation as that of a wealthy and aristocratic Euboean colonist (1979). The metal urns and the cloth wrapping will inevitably recall Homeric practices, as do the cairns of Pithekoussai in which the intact and unburnt oinochoai suggest the quenching of the pyre with wine (Buchner 1966a, 5–6). At the other limit of the Greek world, in the Royal Tombs of Salamis in Cyprus, we have a similar confrontation between the Homeric horse burials and the Near Eastern finery in ivory inlays for the furniture, and bronze accoutrements for the chariots (Karageorghis 1974); but no one, so far, has doubted that those are the burials of a Greek Cypriot élite.

Both interpretations of the Artiaco tomb must be respected, and they need not be in conflict if we pursue the consequences of mixed marriage in the previous generation. I would attribute this burial to the son of mixed Euboean and Italic parentage, a son of the aristocracy at present missing from the Pithekoussan cemetery who, lured by the prospect of a more spacious estate in the mainland, had moved to Kyme and there consolidated his power and prosperity. For his bereaved family, the need to make such a show at his burial was dictated not so much by Greek tradition, but rather by the example of the "tombe principesche" in Etruria, Latium and Campania, in which all his luxurious offerings can be matched; and some of those tombs, like the Warrior Tombs of Tarquinii and Veii, can be shown to be earlier that the Artiaco burial (Ström 1971, 148). This remarkable *koine* of precious artefacts suggests to me a good deal of gift exchange and guest friendship, perhaps cemented by matrimonial links, between the Greek colonial aristocracy and their Italic peers with whom they had trading relations.

My aim has been to argue that Kyme was a continuation of Pithekoussai on a larger scale and, incidentally, to lay to rest the suspicion that Pithekoussai was "different" from any subsequent western Greek settlement. This myth may have started with Strabo (V.4.4), who knew about Pithekoussai, and yet called Kyme the earliest Greek western colony; Pithekoussai, by implication, was not a true colony. Now, in the light of the excavated finds, it is often categorised as a mere *emporion*, a toe-hold for traders, an Al Mina in reverse with a few Levantine entrepreneurs living among a Greek majority. Trade was indeed a major concern. and probably supplied the original motive for emigration. But the recent discoveries in the ancient Ischian countryside show that the colonists quickly aimed at becoming self-sufficient from whatever land there was to farm; in other words, they were true pioneers in establishing a real Greek *apoikia*. The decline of the island colony in the seventh century can be seen in various lights: perhaps the colonists became victims of their own commercial success, and found themselves with too little arable land to support a rapidly rising population at the end of the eighth century (Frederiksen 1984, 67); perhaps the volcano and its works caused many colonists to move to Kyme. For the earlier years, too, there are still many serious gaps in the archaeological record, especially the missing élite burials of Pithekoussai, and the lacuna of the mid-eighth century at Kyme which denies us any clue as to how the Euboeans were able to acquire their mainland colony. If the Etruscans were then as influential in Campania as the material evidence suggests, their connivance must have been obtained, especially of those living only 25 kms. away at Capua. At all events, by the end of the eighth century, we have the impression of a healthy equilibrium between the Euboean colonists and their wealthy and prosperous Italic neighbours; exchanges were peaceful, and immensely profitable for all concerned.

## ACKNOWLEDGEMENTS

I am grateful to Dr Giorgio Buchner and to Mr David Ridgway for reading this paper and offering valuable advice. Dr Buchner has most generously permitted me to mention the recent discoveries of early Greek settlement on Ischia outside Pithekoussai, of which he has kindly supplied me with details.

## NOTES

1. Coldstream and Bikai 1988, 38–9, pl. 10.9–18.
2. Vallet's objections to a precolonial date for the chevron skyphoi have been met by subsequent finds from Veii, and study of the abundant sequence there of Villanovan fibulae which help to correlate the prehellenic Osta graves of Kyme with the precolonial Facies IIa and perhaps early IIb (Close-Brooks, 1979). Descoeudres' lower dates for the skyphoi from Veii rest largely on fragmentary chevron skyphoi found with some LG pottery in sanctuary and settlement deposits in Greece, context for which he surely expects too narrow a chronological bracket. Against his arguments must be weighed the total absence of the chevron skyphos, whether in its Corinthian or Euboean form, from the many hundreds of LG single burials at Pithekoussai.
3. This eighth-century sequence is illustrated in: Coldstream 1968, pls. 4e, 17h, 18d (chevron skyphoi); 17e (proto-kotyle); 19j (Aëtos 666 kotyle); 19k,l (heron kotyle); 21e–f (deep kotyle); 21h–j (globular aryballos). *Cf.* Coldstream 1982, esp. pl. 3.
4. Very recently (Zifferero, forthcoming) metal ores have been reported from southern Etruria, including silver and gold.
5. At home, suitable iron ores were freely available in Euboea and Boeotia (Bakhuizen 1976, 45–57).
6. Buchner and Ridgway 1993, *carta topographica*.

7. Buchner pers. comm. 31.4.93, 8.2.94, 5.4.94 for these discoveries at various points on the island. Dr C. Gialanella and Dr M. Lauro carried out the excavations on the Punta Chiarito site, of which a preliminary report will be published in 1994 in *AION* by Dr S. De Caro (Soprintendente, Napoli) and Dr Gialanella. Dr Buchner kindly informs me that the eighth-century structures there were covered by a deposit about a metre thick of lapilli and ash, probably from a local volcanic eruption. The same spot was then resettled in the second half of the seventh century; a house of that date was remarkably well preserved under a deep flow of tufa detritus from Monte Epomeo, representing a more general catastrophe which affected much of the southern part of the island.

8. In the portion of the cemetery excavated in 1965–1980 (plan, n. 6, n. 2) which will be published as *Pithekoussai* II, Dr Buchner tells me that the graves of the first generation actually form the majority.

9. The miscast piece belongs to the *fibula ad arco a sanguisuga* (*i.e.* leech-shaped bow) class: Toms 1986, 77–80. A second Villanovan type, the *fibula ad arco rivestito*, *i.e.* with segments of bone threaded on to the bow (Toms 1986, 81) was also evidently manufactured on the Mazzola site, to judge from the discovery there of small regular bone plaques from which the segments had been cut out (Buchner, pers. comm. 5.4.94), leaving rows of elliptical holes. Dr Buchner refers to these plaques in his entry, Ischia, in *Enciclopedia dell'Arte Antica*, 2nd Suppl. 219–24 (forthcoming).

10. See, however, n. 8 above.

11. The four excavated buildings in the metalworkers' quarter on the Mazzola site have produced no pottery later than *c.* 675 BC (Buchner 1971, 64; Klein 1972, 36); later Archaic finds, however, have been made elsewhere in the Mezzavia area, as Dr Buchner informs me. For volcanic disturbances elsewhere on the island, see n. 7 above.

## BIBLIOGRAPHY

BAKHUIZEN, S. C. 1976: *Chalcis-in-Euboea, iron and Chalcidians abroad. Chalcidian Studies* 3 (*Studies of the Dutch Archaeological and Historical Society* 5) (Leiden).

BÉRARD, C. 1970: *Érétria* III. *L'Héröon à la porte de l'Ouest* (Bern).

BIETTI-SESTIERI, A. M., DE SANTIS, A. and LA REGINA, A. 1989–90: Elementi di tipo cultuale e doni personali nella necropoli laziale di Osteria dell'Osa. In *Atti del Congresso Internazionale, Anathema: regime delle offerte e vita dei santuari nel Mediterraneo antico, Roma 1989* (*Scienze dell'Antichita: storia archeologia antropologica*) 3/4, 65–88.

BOSTICCO, P. 1957: Scarabei egiziani della necropoli di Pithecusa. *Parola del Passato* 12, 215–29.

BUCHNER, G. 1954: Figürlich bemalte spätgeometrische Vasen aus Pithekusai und Kyme. *MDAI(R)* 60/61, 37–55.

BUCHNER, G. 1964: Intervento. In *Metropoli e Colonie di Magna Grecia, Atti del Terzo Convegno di Studi sulla Magna Grecia, Taranto 1963* (Napoli) 263–74.

BUCHNER, G. 1966a: Pithekoussai, oldest Greek colony in the West. *Expedition* 8, 4–12.

BUCHNER, G. and BOARDMAN, J. 1966b: Seals from Ischia and the Lyre Player Group. *JdI* 81, 1–62.

BUCHNER, G. 1969: Mostra di scavi di Pithecusa. *DdA* 3, 85–101.

BUCHNER, G. 1971: Recent work at Pithekoussai (Ischia), 1965–71. *AR* for 1971–72, 63–7.

BUCHNER, G. 1979: Early Orientalizing aspects of the Euboean connection. In D. and F. Ridgway (edd.), *Italy before the Romans* (London, New York, San Francisco), 129–44.

BUCHNER, G. 1982a: Die Beziehungen zwischen der euböischen Kolonie Pithekoussai auf der Insel Ischia und dem nordwestsemitischen Mittelmeerraum in der zweiten Hälfte des 8 Jhs v. Chr., in H.G. Niemeyer (ed.), *Phönizier im Westen* (*Madrider Beiträge* 8), 277–97.

BUCHNER, G. 1982b: Articolazione sociale, differenze di rituale a composizione dei corredi nella necropoli di Pithecusa. In G. Gnoli and J. P. Vernant (edd.) *La mort, les morts dans les sociétés anciennes* (Cambridge), 275–87.

BUCHNER, G. and RIDGWAY, D. 1993: *Pithekoussai I. La Necropoli: tombe 1–723 scavate dal 1952 al 1961. Monumenti Antichi, Serie Monografica* IV (Roma).

CLOSE-BROOKS, J. 1979: Proposal for a division into phases: the archaic *facies* of Etruria, chronological considerations. In D. and F. Ridgway (edd.), *Italy before the Romans* (London, New York, San Francisco), 95–113.

COLDSTREAM, J. N. 1968: *Greek Geometric Pottery, a survey of ten local styles and their chronology* (London).

COLDSTREAM, J. N. 1969: The Phoenicians of Ialysos. *BICS* 16, 1–8.

COLDSTREAM, J. N. 1971: The Cesnola painter: a change of address. *BICS* 18 1–15.

COLDSTREAM, J. N. 1981: Some Peculiarities of the Euboean Geometric figured style. *ASAA* 59, N.S. 43, 241–9.

COLDSTREAM, J. N. Some problems of eighth-century pottery in the West, seen from the Greek angle. In *La céramique grecque ou de tradition grecque au VIIIᵉ in Italie centrale et méridionale* (Centre J. Bérard, Naples), 21–37.

COLDSTREAM, J. N. and BIKAI, P. M. 1988: Early Greek pottery in Tyre and Cyprus: some preliminary comparisons. *RDAC* (part 2), 35–44.

COLDSTREAM, J. N. 1989: Early Greek visitors to Cyprus and the eastern Mediterranean. In V. Tatton-Brown (ed.), *Cyprus and the east Mediterranean in the Iron Age. Proceedings of the seventh British Museum Classical Colloquium, 1988* (London), 90–96.

COLDSTREAM, J. N. 1993: Mixed marriages at the frontiers of the Greek world. *OJA* 12, 89–107.

D'AGOSTINO, B. 1988: *Pontecagnano II: la necropoli del Picentino* I. Le tombe della Prima Età del Ferro (Napoli).

D'ANDRIA, F. 1978: *Archeologia dei Messapi. Catalogo della Mostra, Lecce, Museo Provinciale* (Bari).

DE SALVIA, F. 1978: Un ruolo apotropaico dello scarabeo egizio nel contexto culturale greco-arcaico di Pithekoussai (Ischia), in *Hommages à M. J. Vermaseren* III (Leiden), 1003–61.

DE SALVIA, F. 1993: Appendice II. I reperti di tipo egiziano. In *Buchner and Ridgway* 1993, 761–811.

DESCOEUDRES, J. P. and KEARLSEY, R. 1983: Greek pottery at Veii, another look. *BSA* 78, 9–53.

FRATTA, A. 1994: Nuovi scavi a Ischia. *Il Mattino* (Napoli) 31.1.1994, 10 (newspaper report).

FREDERIKSEN, M. 1984: *Campania*, ed. N. Purcell. (British School at Rome).

GABRICI, E. 1913: La civiltà preellenica di Cuma. *Monumenti Antichi* 22, 61–212.

HÖLBL, G. 1983: Die Aegyptiaca des griechischen, italischen, und westphönikischen Raumes aus der Zeit des Pharao Bocchoris (718/17–712 v. Chr.). *Grazer Beiträge* 10, 1–20.

JOHANNOWSKY, W. 1969: Scambi tra ambiente greco e ambiente italico nel periodo precoloniale e protocoloniale. *DdA* 3, 31–43.

JOHANNOWSKY, W. 1975: Problemi relativi a Cuma arcaica, in *Contributions à l'étude de la société et de la colonisation eubéennes* (Centre J. Bérard, Naples), 98–105.

KARAGEORGHIS, V. 1974: *Excavations in the necropolis of Salamis* III (Department of Antiquities, Cyprus).

KLEIN, J. 1972: A Greek metalworking quarter of the eighth century BC: excavations in Ischia. *Expedition* 14, 34–9.

LA ROCCA, E. 1975: Due tombe dell'Esquilino. Alcune novità sul commercio euboico in Italia centrale nell'VIII sec. A.C. *DdA* 1, 86–103.

MARKOE, G. 1992: The pursuit of Italian metal: Greeks and Phoenicians. In G. Kopcke and I. Tokamaru (edd.), *Greece between East and West, 10th - 8th centuries BC* (Institute of Fine Arts, New York University), 61–84.

NEEFT, C. 1987: *Protocorinthian Subgeometric Aryballoi* (Amsterdam, Allard Pierson Museum).

PELLEGRINI, G. 1903: Tombe greche archaiche di Cuma. *Monumenti Antichi* 13, 201–294.

RIDGWAY, D. 1973: The first Western Greeks: Campanian coasts and Southern Etruria. In C. F. C. Hawkes (ed.), *Greeks, Celts and Romans* (London), 5–38.

RIDGWAY, D. 1979: "Cycladic" cups at Veii. In D. and F. Ridgway (edd.), *Italy before the Romans* (London, New York and San Francisco), 113–27.

RIDGWAY, D. 1981: The foundation of Pithekoussai. In *Nouvelle contribution à l'étude de la société et de la colonisation eubéennes* (Centre J. Bérard, Naples), 45–56.

RIDGWAY, D. 1982: The eighth century pottery at Pithekoussai: an interim report. In *La céramique grecque ou de tradition grecque au VIIIᵉ siècle et Italie centrale et méridionale* (Centre J. Bérard, Naples), 69–102.

RIDGWAY, D. 1990: The first Western Greeks amd their neighbours. In J. P. Descoeudres (ed.), *Greek colonists and native populations* (Canberra and Oxford), 61–72.

RIDGWAY, D. 1992a: *The first Western Greeks* (Cambridge, U.P.).

RIDGWAY, D. 1992b: Demaratus and his predecessors. In G. Kopcke and I. Tokamaru (edd.), *Greece between East and West, 10th-8th centuries BC* (Institute of Fine Arts, New York University), 85–93.

STRÖM, I. 1971: *Problems concerning the origin and development of the Etruscan Orientalizing style* (Odense).

TOMS, J. 1986: The relative chronology of the Villanovan cemetery of Quattro Fontanili at Veii. *AION* 8, 41–97.

VALLET, G. 1958: *Rhégion et Zancle: histoire, commerce et civilisation des cités chalcidiennes du détroit de Messine* (Paris).

WILLIAMS, D. 1986: Greek potters and their descendants in Campania and Southern Etruria, *c.* 720–630 BC. In J. Swaddling (ed.), *Italian Iron Age Artefacts: Papers of the sixth British Museum Classical Colloquium* (London), 295–304.

ZIFFERERO, A. forthcoming: Miniere e metallurgia estrattiva in Etruria Meridionale. *Studi Etruschi*.

# *Chapter 5*

# Massalia and Colonization in the North-Western Mediterranean

## B. B. Shefton

A glance at the map shows very tellingly the foolhardiness of the Greek adventurers who made their way to the southern coast of France and the north-east of Spain. It was in many ways a much greater hazard than those undertaken by sailors, merchants and settlers in Sicily or the southern and western Italian coastlines. Here in the north-west they were truly cut off from their kindred through long and uncertain lines of communication, more problematical perhaps than those encountered elsewhere in the Mediterranean. Nor do we know their approach lines, nor for that matter the incentives which would have attracted them to these faraway shores.

We are told that the first settlers on their way made contact with the Rome of Tarquinius, the origin, according to some sources, of the long *amicitia* with Rome.[1] This may or may not be based upon a solid tradition. Contact *en route* with Etruscan centres is inherently probable, but there is no certainty about details of the route taken beyond central Italy. Corsica would be a plausible staging port, or the route could have followed along the Ligurian coast towards the mouth of the Rhone.[2]

What would they have found there? According to legend they were a group of well-born adventurers from Phocaea in Aegean Asia Minor who presented themselves to the local ruler, one of them married his daughter and they were given land to settle.[3] This is dated in our sources to near enough 600 BC.[4] Archaeological investigations have shown that the site was virgin.[5]

Though this is evidently the first Greek settlement in this part of the world, the area as a whole was by no means entirely *terra incognita*. It is clear that the coastline had been known, explored and according to some, even settled by Etruscan enterprise. In fact, of all areas of Etruscan maritime endeavour, the southern French coastal area had by this time already become the most intensively cultivated.[6] The evidence for this Etruscan exploitation goes back into the early third quarter of the seventh century at any rate and the evidence is largely provided by the abundance of Etruscan wine amphorae and the Etruscan drinking vessel which seems to have accompanied their distribution, the bucchero kantharos above all.[7] The site which is almost emblematic of this phenomenon is one not far from present-day Marseilles, but much nearer the mouth of the Rhone. It is the site of St Blaise.[8] The recovery of St Blaise is essentially a post-war discovery. It was excavated by Henri Rolland and after his death the

work of scholarly exploitation of the finds has above all been in the hands of Bernard
Bouloumié of the University of Provence in Aix.

This yield amplified our knowledge of the Etruscan impetus, and also gave us an idea of
the richness of the material which reached this settlement, this *emporion*. There is a
recognizable amount of elaborate East Greek still of the seventh century, also reportedly Attic
SOS oil amphorae of the second half of the seventh century. Of East Greek there are a number
of bird bowls of the late seventh century.[9]

Now the volume of early Etruscan import at St Blaise is considerably larger than that on
other coastal sites along the Gulf of Lions and Bouloumié claims for St Blaise a privileged
status vis-à-vis the rest. At one stage one even thought of Etruscan settlers there, though in
the more recent literature that claim is no longer pressed.

Can we think of any reason for the particular attractiveness of St Blaise for Etruscan trade?
The site itself goes back into the Bronze Age, even earlier. Level 8, which sees the earliest
Etruscan imports, is associated by Bouloumié with salt production. It is also the earliest level
which shows signs of urbanization – there are also traces of local artisanship, perhaps even
jewellery work in coral.[10]

It is questionable whether a salt trade alone would be sufficient to explain the Etruscan
concentration, particularly as it is likely that Etruria had indigenous resources in this mineral
so vital for the preservation of food even over a short time span.[11]

If we were to look for other reasons one could of course cite the closeness of the site to
the Rhone delta and presumably access routes inland and indeed over great distances. There
is, let it be said, no direct evidence so far that St Blaise was actually involved in such an
inland penetration – or shall I put it rather differently – there is no evidence so far that St
Blaise was the kind of *emporion* to which natural resources from the hinterland or even further
afield were brought to be exchanged for Etruscan, or Greek, or other exotic luxury goods.

The one thing though that we can say is that Mediterranean luxury goods did as a matter
of fact penetrate the hinterland reaching far into the heartland of Europe and there are
indications that some of them went up the Rhone entry route and this well before the
foundation of Marseilles. We shall come back to this phenomenon presently.

St Blaise is the most important *emporion* in that region, but there are others such as Cap
Couronne and Tamaris[12] all in this same part of the coast, and all of them with imported
material earlier than the foundation of Marseilles. It is presumably in the tow of such an
Etruscan trade movement that the Greek, Phocaean adventurer colonists made their way to that
same coast, though to a site rather further away from and east of the Rhone mouth.

Now this crescent along the Gulf of Lions had traces of early central Mediterranean goods
on other sites, rather more remote from the Rhone mouth. For these we have to turn quite a
bit further west to the area where the Hérault, Orb and Aude rivers discharged into the Gulf
of Lions at close intervals between the present-day Agde[13] and Narbonne. Let me straightway
point out that this is again near a potential entry route to the inland, the Garonne valley which
going past Toulouse leads eventually to the Atlantic coast with all that is implied by it,
including possibly tin resources of north-western France and beyond. However we must be
cautious here. There is infinitely more compelling evidence that the Rhone entry route into
the heart of Europe was in use at this time than there is for an Aude-Garonne route for the

penetration of luxury goods. Perhaps when the Agen conference of the *Association française pour l'étude de l'Age du Fer* which dealt with this very region a few years ago is published, we may hear more of any evidence there may be for the penetration of Mediterranen goods at an early period. Meanwhile we may quote Jean-Jacques Jully, writing about his home region of Agde "par sa proximité de lagunes aux eaux calmes, par son arrière-pays riche en cuivre et plomb argentifère, par l'amer du Mont d'Agde – l'actuel Mont Saint-Loup – qui signalait aux navigateurs, cette région parait avoir eu un mouvement commercial qui lui était, en grande partie, propre. Les embouchures deltaiques de Hérault favorisaient la pénétration dans l'intérieur des terres."[14]

The work of André Nickels at the necropolis of Agde brought to light some rare Greek type skyphoi and cups which seem to be third quarter of the seventh century, if not somewhat earlier. Similar material came further inland from Mailhac just north of the Aude valley; all of Greek type, nothing early Etruscan.[15] The extremely small number of pieces involved make it impracticable to draw too many conclusions. They were incidentally found in relatively well equipped élite graves. The date of this earliest relevant material is near enough to that of the early Etruscan import further east, and the absence of Etruscan material of the same very early period in this more westerly area is interesting and does perhaps support the view that the Etruscan preoccupation at St Blaise may be connected with the Rhone valley route. There is however another factor which may well be relevant in any assessment. The western part of this crescent, Roussillon and Catalunya in modern terms, had very strong Western Phoenician influence manifested in extensive imports of transport amphorae and also perfume containers.[16] This may have inhibited the demand for Etruscan imports in these parts at the very early period at any rate.

It was at the eastern end then of this crescent that the Phocaean settlement was established about 600 BC at the eastern edge of the area visited and cultivated by the Etruscans.[17] It is no wonder therefore that much of the early imported material so far recovered at the newly established colony is Etruscan too, and this to such an extent that did we not know better, we might easily have been inclined on the strength of these finds to consider Marseilles to have been an Etruscan foundation. I ought to say that this newly excavated material, much of it from rescue excavations in the historical centre between 1985 and 1990,[18] is not yet available in a publication, but François Villard and Lucien-François Gantès, the latter being one of the two then appointed city archaeologists, have in the Proceedings of the 1990 Marseilles conference on *Marseille Grecque* described and analyzed these new finds and come out with some interesting conclusions.[19] In the earliest quarter-century 600–575, the imported fine pottery is Greek, largely East Greek and Corinthian, rather than Etruscan, but this changed radically in the second quarter when both fine pottery and imported wine amphorae are predominantly Etruscan. This quarter-century distinction may turn out to be rather artificial and forced and it may be preferable at this stage to follow Villard who presses the numerical preponderance of Etruscan imports both kantharoi of bucchero, a few bucchero cups and aryballoi and a fair amount of Etrusco-Corinthian[20] and wine amphorae during the first half ot the sixth century, though he stresses that the spread of shapes and the total volume are inferior to that found at St Blaise. It should be said that this recognition of the Etruscan numerical preponderance is in fact perhaps the most significant contribution of the recent excavations and this includes the identification of impasto kitchen ware from Etruria! As for the Greek material, East Greek (latish Wild Goat style, also Chiot chalices) of the first quarter of the sixth century and a certain amount of Corinthian including some fine column kraters[21] the position has not changed materially from what had been known previously, mainly through the work of Villard in 1960 and the original publication by Vasseur (and Pottier) in 1914.[22]

The dramatic decline of Etruscan imports after the middle of the sixth century is remarkable.[23] Attic imports become relatively copious after the middle of the century and abundant after about 530 BC. Yet already before the middle of the century Attic, even if relatively rare, had been represented by significant pieces. In fact virtually with the foundation of the colony works by the Gorgon Painter and his neighbourhood were arriving.[24] This observation is of intriguing importance, as the presence of this very early sixth-century material seems, comparatively speaking, more concentrated here in Marseilles than on Etruscan sites, where such pieces rank amongst the earliest imports of Attic decorated pottery to the West.[25] Now it has rightly been stressed repeatedly by François Villard that the early sixth-century presence in Marseilles of fine Corinthian kraters and Attic pieces closely matches the kind of material found in Etruria, and may therefore be due to secondary importation from there.[26] Yet this concentration in Marseilles might even suggest that this early Attic material came direct from the Aegean and that the presence of the Gorgon Painter's products and that of his school in Etruria could be regarded as *en route* depositions in *emporia* such as Graviscat[27]. In this respect it is perhaps significant that the presence of his work has also been reported from Phocaean Aleria.[28] Perhaps Herodotus' often-quoted assertion (I, 163) of the role of Phocaea in opening up the path to Etruria (amongst other destinations) may find a context in such a scenario, though even so it can hardly be taken literally.[29]

During much of the Archaic period and predominantly in the third quarter of the sixth century the most frequent type of cup is the Ionian cup, but Attic cups were imported in large quantities too.

The rescue excavations at Marseilles during the last ten years or so have thus gone a good way towards confirming the dating of the beginning of the Greek colony; they have also given more of an idea of its original extent and growth during the first century or so of its existence.[30] It is clear now more than ever before that in the first two generations the place was quite small covering little more than the triangle formed by the heights behind Fort Saint Jean, the site of the productive excavations by Vasseur early in the century, which produced some of the most representative finds of Archaic and Classical pottery imports up to the most recent activities reviewed just now. Amongst the finds in the first generation we may mention the building near the Church of St Laurent as the oldest example of domestic architecture so far discovered in Marseilles, going back to the beginning of the settlement. Here, in one of the three rooms explored, the intriguing find was made of a native modelled (not wheel-thrown) pot covered with a lid made of local light clay and wheel-thrown, a very early example of colonial Massaliote pottery. This has been taken by the excavators as "an archaeologically documented witness of peaceful relations between Greek arrivals and natives in the first phases of Marseilles's existence".[31]

From 540 onwards to the end of the Archaic period the inhabited area grew considerably both northwards and along the Lacydon basin. The extent eastwards reached the site of the

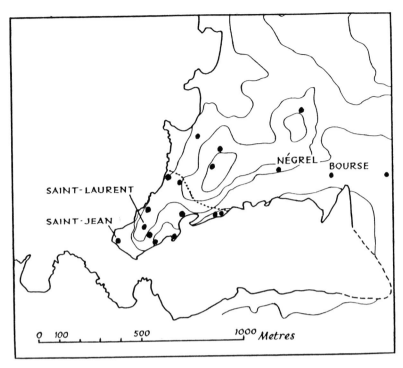

*Figure 5.1   Marseilles. Growth and development to c. 480 BC with location of structural and other remains of the period. The dotted line indicates the probable extent by c. 540 BC. (After Gantès, in Marseille Grecque, 73, fig. 2)*

Bourse, prefiguring in fact almost its full extent in later centuries.[32] The northward extension was more limited to the promontory at the height of the old Seminary. (Fig. 5.1)

The third quarter of the sixth century, near 540 perhaps, was evidently a crucial period for Marseilles, marked not only by a considerable topographic extension of the city[33] but also by other developments. Of these one of obvious importance is the appearance of a strong and increasingly significant pottery industry, producing a very characteristic shape of transport amphora for wine.[34]

There is every reason to suppose that it was local, Massaliote wine which must have been nurtured by the Greek city to the extent that a good surplus had by now become available for both local consumption and for export.[35] Such an industry is not traceable before about 540 BC. There is another aspect of this development, namely that it is only now that the first evidence appears for an active interest of Marseilles in relationships and trade into the heart of Europe, which can be traced for about two generations at least.

Let us for a moment stay here and reflect. We had already brought up, though only fleetingly, the point that Marseilles by virtue of its position could be presumed to have been placed where it was because of its nearness to the mouth of the Rhone. Yet there is no evidence available at all that she had been involved at this early stage in any activity targeted at the heartland of Europe.

If then there was no traceable early activity of Marseilles vis-à-vis its distant hinterland, what were the activities of Marseilles then during the first two generations of its existence, apart from just surviving in potentially hostile surroundings and exploiting the harvest of the sea?[36] This is not easy to answer. Marseilles's territory ('*chora*') was apparently never very extensive in the hinterland, but there must have been contacts and a compelling superiority.[37] There are some very early settlements, *oppida* to be, where there is a respectable stream of quite early and fine Greek imports, undoubtably channelled through Marseilles. Notable amongst them is Baou de St Marcel[38] some 7 km inland to the east of Marseilles. Here a new site was settled before 575, almost a generation after the foundation of Marseilles. It became a fortified native post at the head of a valley, which as the imported material shows was in close contact with the Greek colony. Here as we have said, there is Greek, Attic, material dating back even into the first quarter of the century.[39] So much for the immediate vicinity. The early activity of Marseilles is however likely to have extended along the crescent of the Gulf of Lions, though the precise details are by no means evident. There is at the far end of the crescent the Greek colonial site of Ampurias, to which we shall turn in due course.[40]

What of the numerous native sites (Fig. 5.2) between these two extremities? Here, though the evidence for the late sixth and for the fifth centuries is rich, for the earliest period, which we want to address just now, it provides little to help us. What we are looking for is Massaliote influence in the first two generations of the colony's existence and some evidence that early Greek imports there were due to the intermediacy of Marseilles, rather than other factors such as the activity of Ampurias. What we find is meagre indeed, but not entirely unhelpful.

From Béziers we have a fragment of a large closed pot by the Gorgon Painter or his close circle and we have already noted the strong presence of his work in Marseilles and its immediate neighbourhood. Again from Agde we have a fragment of a Chiot chalice, certainly of the first half of the century, probably from its first quarter. Here again the links are entirely with Marseilles rather than with any other site in the north west. The same can be said of the fragment of the Laconian cup by the Hunt Painter from Ensérune, which should date broadly speaking to the middle of the sixth century, or somewhat earlier. Here too the links are entirely with Marseilles.[42] These are all rather telling pointers, seeing that the sites involved are by no means close to Marseilles, on the contrary rather in the western sector of the Gulf of Lions.

At the middle of the century and beyond, in the third quarter, the situation appears for the present at any rate to be more ambivalent. Thus works by Exekias seem at present to be in the western sector, including Ampurias, only; in fact this concentration of works by Exekias may be considered specially noteworthy.[43] However with more exploration this westward tilt of the evidence may well be redressed by finds in Marseilles.[44]

Though there are still big gaps in our knowledge we are thus perhaps no longer entirely at a loss to account for Marseilles's activities during the first two generations of its existence. There was indeed activity westwards in the Gulf of Lions. That the situation is clearer to a great extent after that, that is to say in the last third of the sixth century and the beginning of the fifth, is due largely to the evidence provided by finds in the interior of western Europe.[45]

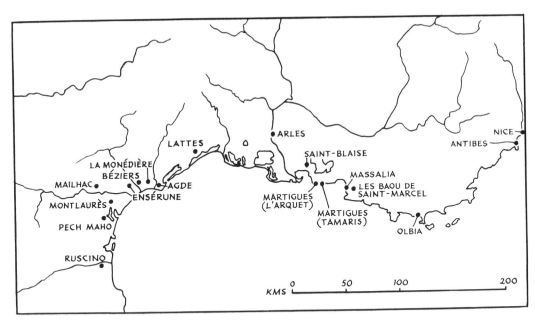

*Figure 5.2   Sites along the Gulf of Lions. (After Bats, in Marseille Grecque, 276, fig. 4)*

We do not know how the earliest systematic imports of Mediterranean luxury goods reached the continental hinterland in Europe. What is clear however is that they include luxury objects which antedate the foundation of Marseilles. Of these some by their distribution pattern suggest strongly that they reached their destination through the Rhone valley and then further up the Saône and Doubs to the upper Rhine areas. These are above all the "Rhodian" bronze oinochoai which have an almost linear distribution along that way. Their date is in the last third of the seventh century.[46] There are some other Mediterranean imports of about the same period which might have crossed the Alps rather than gone via the sSouthern coast of France. Numerically speaking though the "Rhodian" bronze jugs are the biggest and therefore most telling group of imports which must antedate the foundation of Marseilles. Even more significant for the status of Mediterranean import in the precolonial period are the series of bronze cauldrons, some of them with griffin attachments which appear to have made their first appearance in the late seventh century but go on being fashionable and desirable prestige objects into the middle of the sixth century and beyond.[47] Here again we cannot say for certain how these objects reached their destination – the earliest of them surely not via Marseilles, which had not then been established. The sixth-century successors could theoretically speaking indeed have come via Marseilles, but there is no positive reason which would make this particularly likely.

In view of this situation I do not want to spend any time on this group of early prestige objects of bronze, which evidently played an important role in the status determination and treasurization of the Hallstatt élite in an area which extended from the lower Loire across France to the area of Stuttgart in Germany.

Why then have I mentioned, if only briefly, these early imports reaching from the later seventh century down to perhaps the forties of the sixth century? Really to make two points. For one that there was quite independently of Marseilles, indeed existing already at the time of its foundation, some traffic in specific prestige objects to the aristocracy of the interior of western Europe; secondly that this traffic did not include any Greek pottery, for which there was evidently no interest at all amongst this aristocracy.

It is about 540 that there becomes apparent a change and the beginning of a stream of imports up the Rhone valley and the Saône and Doubs which are now well documented through the finds at Mont Lassois/Vix, just north of Châtillon-sur-Seine, the finds at Châtillon-sur-Glâne, near Fribourg in Switzerland and then again at the Heuneburg overlooking the upper Danube, to mention only those sites which have up to now provided the richest yield.[48]

It is, I think, important to underline the relative suddenness of the irruption of this Attic material into the heart of Europe. The episode included Little Master cups, at least one with Greek inscription which must have been the earliest examples of alphabetic writing seen in the heart of Europe north of the Alps.[49] Somewhat later came an assortment of volute kraters, amphorae, hydriai and also dinoi of a splendour which was seen in this part of Europe during a period of a generation or a little more and never again after that. The appeal was evidently to a very select number of great hillforts which have been identified as the key Hallstatt centres, amongst them Mont Lassois, the Münsterberg near Breisach, the Marienberg overlooking the present-day Würzburg, the Asperg, north of Stuttgart and the Heuneburg. These seats of power concentration were customers for this quite new-fangled prestige drinking ware and the wine which came with it (or the other way round). This wine came mostly in Massaliote amphorae, but not exclusively so.[50]

Now the role of Marseilles in this sudden irruption of Greek imports would hardly be noticeable from the finds in Marseilles itself, except insofar as much of the black figure material found in the heart of Europe is just the kind of material which has turned up in Marseilles too in some quantity. Moreover a recently found wreck at Pointe Lequin has produced some more of similar character, at least as far as cups are concerned.[51]

Now there is some reason to believe that some at least of the initiative for this trade with the Hallstatt interior of Western Europe was deliberately fostered by the oligarchic regime which governed Marseilles. In my published view the Vix krater which must have gone north at near enough the beginning of this period of irruption of Greek imports into Hallstatt Europe, and for that matter the slightly earlier Hochdorf cauldron as well, are likely to have gone north as "introductory gifts" to the local rulers at particularly critical points perhaps at the beginning of the establishment of these trade links.[52] This view of the Vix krater is not only buttressed by the existence of parallel phenomena, but also by the observation that certain repairs to the cast ornamental rim enhancement, which fractured during the journey, were carried out at its destination by a process of soft soldering, which was not then known amongst native metalsmiths. The presumption is that on this occasion at any rate a trained metalsmith will have accompanied the gift from the south.[53] That the gift emanated from Marseilles and indeed had an official character seems a very enticing hypothesis. The obvious parallel is of course the Spartan gift to King Kroisos reported by Herodotus (I.70), a gift which never arrived, as it was taken over *en route* by the Samians.

The precise modalities of the injection of Greek goods into the heart of Europe are not yet entirely clear. Was there a kind of symbiosis between wine imports in Massaliote, but not exclusively Massaliote transport amphorae, and Greek drinking ware, or did Greek drinking vessels take on an autonomous surge on their own?[54] We cannot say. It does seem however that after the first decade or so of the fifth century this import stops. Not so however within some regions of the western sector, that is to say the present-day France. Here the situation is even now shifting by reason of recent excavations in Bourges, where fine amphorae, stamnoi and cups and other Attic material go on, albeit in small quantities so far, well beyond the middle of the fifth century.[55]

As yet we have no means of telling how these imports reached the area of Bourges. Was it a continuation of the stream from Marseilles or is it part of what was a new line of approach via the Alps and the Jura of which other evidence is available, and which was predominantly nourished by Etruscan activity? Here De Marini's excavations at Mantua may give us further clues in the future.[56]

As to the function of Marseilles in the fifth century, it is often claimed that there must have been a recession. There is said to have been less import of Attic pottery. Yet we must be cautious. A single new deposit in Marseilles could change this situation radically, and I have been told recently by L.-F. Gantès that this is in fact so and that a new deposit of fifth-century Attic red figure and black glaze has turned up, which will alter our preconceptions considerably.

Yet even without these new finds we could have presumed that the situation at Marseilles was by no means as bleak as has been held to be the case. For it is during the fifth century that the sites along the crescent of the Gulf of Lions reach high points of imported Attic pottery, some of it of considerable quality.[57] It is an interesting lot of sites, the best known ones are some distance away from Marseilles.[58] The nearest is at Arles, where recent excavations in the Winter Garden (Jardin d'Hiver) by Arcelin are being worked on by Pierre Rouillard. Further west is the site of La Monédière near Bessan upstream from Agde; there are also important new finds at Béziers. Other rich sites as Ensérune, Mailhac, Montlaurès, Pech-Maho, both near Narbonne, and Ruscino near Perpignan are of course well known.[59] In all these sites the mass of Attic red figure cups, and the rarer kraters of various sorts as well as other containers such as lekanides of the fifth century is extremely impressive and it is difficult not to think of Marseilles as the direct provider of these vases, even if the most westerly sites amongst them may well have been provisioned from Ampurias.[60] Nor is it easy to think of another fringe area of the Mediterranean which has so intensive a concentration of Attic ceramic imports on a closely contiguous string of native hill settlements. (Fig. 5.3)

The intensity of the use of Attic pottery must also betoken an increasing hellenization of this part of Mediterranean France, probably more profound than had been the case in the sixth century.[61]

There is one rather unexpected, but all the more telling for that, testimony for this hellenization dating to the "second third" of the fifth century BC. It is the recently discovered document written on lead from Pech-Maho, near Narbonne. This now famous piece had lain some thirty years in a box amongst lead debris before it was realized that the shapeless lump was in fact a rolled up document. It was fully published in 1988 by Lejeune, Poullioux and Solier.[62] On one side was an Etruscan letter which we cannot interpret (apart from a reference to Marseilles), but which,on palaeographic grounds, has been associated with Corsica, more particularly with Aleria. The other side is in Greek, in Ionian alphabet and dialect and is nothing less than a statement of payment and surety arrangements for a boat bought (or hired) in Ampurias. Some provisions are also recorded concerning the deposit and instalments. The name of the *rapporteur* and the owner are not preserved in the main text, but those of the witnesses are and they are native names *Basigerros* and *Bleryas* and *Golo.biur* and *Sedegon*. Some more names at the end are mutilated but seem native as well. On the other side, written at right angles to the Etruscan text stands the name of *Heronoiios*, who may have been the *rapporteur*. We have here therefore a document linking a native coastal settlement of the mid-fifth century to both Marseilles, probably also to Aleria and certainly Ampurias, the Greek colony in Catalunya. Whether the *rapporteur* and writer was a Greek himself or only had a highly hellenized name cannot be certain; what is certain is that his witnesses, whether they lived at the Greek colony of Ampurias or at the indigenous settlement of Pech-Maho, were natives who can be presumed to have known Greek and who could cope with the legal and technical terminology of this document, in other words to have been highly hellenized. The witnesses' names have been identified as Iberian by Michel Lejeune.[63]

This valuable correspondence between archaeological evidence of imports and the document is a happy coincidence. My own knowledge of the sites is insufficient to say whether the architectural evidence of buidings and planning is available for the late sixth and the fifth centuries. At Pech-Maho, Solier has claimed that the planning of the rebuilt settlement and its fortification after about 480/460 has Hellenic influence behind it. A locally carved Ionic capital of small size has with some probabilty been claimed to date to this same fifth century.[64]

This brings us geographically to Ampurias, also a Phocaean colony. I do not want to say too much about its topography except to remark that here, unlike Marseilles, no later settlement obscured the ancient remains, as far as the Neapolis is concerned, and they were always identified as such from the reports of our Classical sources including the description in Strabo (III, 4, 8), though proper investigations did not start until 1908. The Palaiopolis to the north is built over even nowadays by the hamlet of Sant Marti d'Empúries and is therefore only little explored. Moreover, what is visible to-day at the Neapolis is largely of Late Hellenistic/Roman Republican date. Only within the last decade have the systematic and stratigraphic excavations conducted by Enrique Sanmartí given us further details of early structural remains, and have gone much further in elucidating the fortification sequence during the Classical and Archaic periods.[65] Particularly in the area of the later Asklepios sanctuary they have given us some idea of a fifth century BC extramural sanctuary and possibly also traces of the indigenous habitation we hear of in our literary sources.[66]

Sanmartí certainly regards the first implantation to have been the establishment of a trading settlement, an *emporion*, on a small island next to the mouth of the Fluvia river rather than the foundation of a colony with planned civic organization. This Palaiopolis, as it came to be

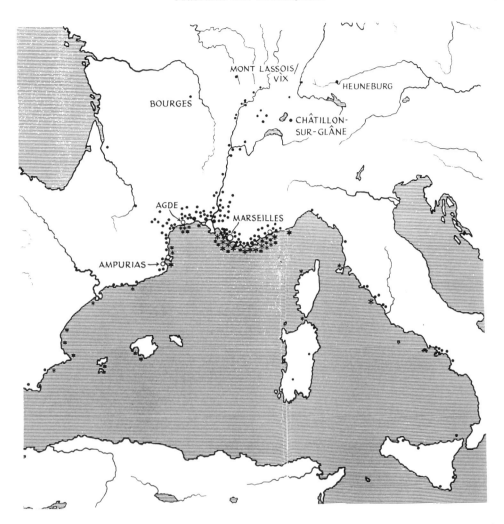

*Figure 5.3  Distribution of Massaliote wine amphorae between c. 540 and 350 BC. (After Bats, in Les Amphores, 276-7)*

known, dated to about 600 BC on a site that had been settled by natives as early perhaps as the 7th century or even before, though it is not clear whether the native settlement still existed when the Phocaeans arrived. It was only about a generation or a little more later that a bigger settlement was established as a proper *polis* on the mainland a short distance further south. This 'Neapolis' – a modern term – was to be the real Emporion.

We might well ask what the reason was for the original establishment. There is no obvious answer to this as far as I can see. Quite a few scholars, including Morel, Sanmartí and Dominguez Monedero tend to subscribe to a view which makes Emporion a staging post and depot on the route from southern Spain, particularly Tartessos to the north, or rather the other way round, from Marseilles along the Levant coast towards the Malaga coastal strip and beyond. In other words on this view the Phocaeans whom we know from Herodotus to have had close contacts with the Tartessians – remember their links with King Arganthonios (Herodotus I.163) – went there via Marseilles and along the north-west Mediterranean coastline then via Catalunya, Valencia down to the southern coastal strip of Malaga and through the Straits of Gibraltar to Tartessos.[67]

I myself have always found this view hard to follow. For one thing what may be considered the first symptoms of Phocaean links with southern Spain are apparent long before the foundation of Marseilles. They go back well into the third quarter of the seventh century[68] even if the more massive imports of Greek pottery found in Huelva[69] and also in Malaga[70] come later, in the very early sixth century. In my view the Phocaean traders on their way to the far west, (*i.e.* southern Spain) used the same approach route as that taken by the Phoenicians before, namely along the north coast of Africa, crossing over at a certain point to the southern coastal strip of Andalusia.[71] Phocaeans then arrived in the south in the wake of the Phoenicians, just as a little later they were to arrive in the north west in the wake of the Etruscans, as we saw when dicussing the foundation of Marseilles! Subsequently Phocaean activity came to extend northwards to Alicante and Valencia, the Levant coast.[72] I have set this down in detail in several papers and need not labour it here. It is clear then that we have to separate sharply what happened in the north, that is the Greek activity ranging from Marseilles to Ampurias, from what had been going on in the south, where there had been a long history of Phoenician activity and settlement, which left little if any room for Greek settlement. This Phoenician activity had included a role as purveyors of Greek goods, such as Attic SOS amphorae filled with oil and other pottery.[73] In due course direct Greek involvement began well before the end of the seventh century, to which I have alluded just now, and there is good reason to associate this activity with the Phocaeans. That in contrast with what happenend in the north, this southern prong of Phocaean trade never led to the formation of colonies is an interesting fact, which we have to take on board.

As to the reports in later Greek geographical writings that there was a Greek colony at Mainake on the southern coastal strip and similarly so at Hemeroskopeion further north on the Le·ant coast, H. G. Niemeyer's paper in *Historia* some years ago dealt very convincingly with that problem.[74] His identification of Mainake with present-day Toscanos, near Vélez Malaga, a Phoenician settlement going back to the early 8th century is entirely persuasive. As to Hemeroskopeion, which is usually placed in the Contestania area north-east of Alicante, there is so far no evidence at all of Greek settlement. Recently Rouillard has voiced the opinion that Alonis, another Greek (Massaliote) colony claimed in literary evidence, is to be sought south of Alicante at Santa Pola. However, though he himself is excavating there, nothing of any moment has yet turned up to give substance to that claim.[75]

If I were to be pressed to think of a place where there might have been Greek settlement, not a colony but perhaps some semi-permanent presence for a period of time at any rate, I would be inclined to settle for Los Nietos at the southern edge of the Mar Menor in the region of Cartagena, adjacent to a metalliferous zone.[76] The site seems to me to have yielded the kind of Attic material, albeit in minimal quantity, which might indicate some Greek presence. Yet even here what we find turns out on calmer reflection to be no more than what is encountered

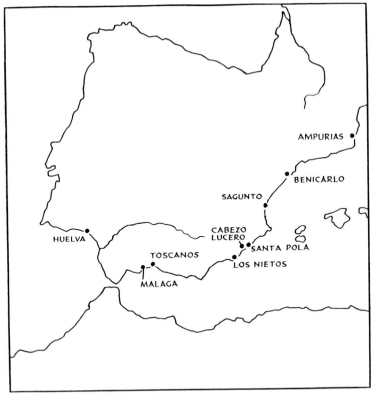

*Figure 5.4   Iberian peninsula. Sites mentioned in the text.*

on the native settlements along the Gulf of Lions rather than on attested Greek colonial establishments, and the site will probably have to be viewed in that light.

It is worth perhaps looking a little more closely at Los Nietos, as it has quite far south, indeed almost beyond the Levant coast, material which could really only have come from the concentration of Attic further north, in fact from Ampurias or the native settlements along the Gulf of Lions, if not actually from Marseilles. I refer here to the coral-red dish and the rather later Penthesilean circle cup by the Painter of Bologna 417. We encounter here perhaps the earliest symptoms of Ampuritan interest in the regions further south along the coastline and this perhaps as early as the first quarter of the 5th century. We have similar evidence roughly contemporary from Cabezo Lucero at the mouth of the Segura river – the Brygan circle cup[77] – and also from the Puig at Benicarló, just north of Castellon – the Penthesilea Painter's cup, so well published by Enrique Sanmartí.[78] Los Nietos, however, provides the clearest indication for these new links from the north as there in the shape of the coral-red dish some quite rare imports to Ampurias are replicated in a way unique for the Peninsula so far.[79] (Fig. 5.4)

Let me conclude with another recent documentary find which conceivably can shed some light on what I have just argued. At about the same time that the Pech-Maho lead document became known the intense investigations by Sanmartí in the northern quarter of Ampurias in search of the classical habitation levels discovered in a room in a fifth-century context a rolled up letter on lead. It is written in Ionian alphabet and also in an East Greek dialect, with some elements which are also known in Chiot. It ought to be said that much of the material in the said room belongs to the first half of the fifth century, but there are a few pieces which are from the second half and therefore break the closed context. The rolled-up lead document has however on palaeographic grounds been dated to the later sixth century BC. Intriguingly it provides the earliest mention of the name of the *polis* of the Emporitans, the citizens of Emporion-Ampurias. The letter – this time it is addressed to a person with instructions – speaks of a ship with merchandise and mentions Sagunto (north of Valencia) and speaks of the necessity to purchase wine. Here again a native name occurs several times of one *Baspedas*, who may have been the merchant in Sagunto with whom the writer was in trading contact. Where the letter originally emanated from is not clear. It is evidently addressed to the recipient in Ampurias. Possibly it originated from Marseilles, but this is a guess only.[81]

The document, if it is truly as early as the editors (Sanmartí and Santiago) claim, would provide evidence even earlier than that of archaeology for Ampuritan interest and activity along the coast to the south, as far as the neighbourhood of Valencia at any rate. There the correspondent was, to judge by the name, a local Iberian. That a process of hellenization may well have accompanied these new links, and led to the use of Attic fine ware is entirely possible, just as we were able to observe it further north on the native settlements along the Gulf of Lions. Are Los Nietos, and perhaps also Benicarló and even Cabezo Lucero then to be regarded in a similar light?

Even so such an approach could hardly account for a hellenization, which already in the later sixth century embraces much of the hinterland of the Levant coast. In the absence of any Greek colonial settlements in this part of the peninsula this deep influence, discernible not so much in the import of Greek pottery or other goods as in the style of much of the local sculpture of the later sixth and the fifth century, is bound to give rise to perplexity, particularly as the phenomenon there is unparalleled elsewhere within the Phocaean ambit in the West.[82] On the one hand it stimulates a desperate, and up to now unsuccessful search for Greek colonial settlements in this area, whence such influence could radiate through immediate close contact;[83] on the other hand there is speculation about immigrant or itinerant Greek sculptors under local patronage[84] or again we must operate with more intangible factors.[85] Nor are these alternatives mutually exclusive.

Such problems should remind us that we have in this paper touched upon only a small part of a phenomenon which has even wider implications, of the kind which were addressed many years ago by Ernst Langlotz on the role of Phocaea as the civilizing force in the West.[86] The linguistic evidence provided by the recently discovered written documents from Ampurias and Pech-Maho has indeed confirmed the Phocaean character and background of the personnel involved in Greek activity in these parts, even as late as the advanced fifth century BC. However there were by this time other factors at play too. Their importance has recently been thrown into relief by the newly recomposed Porcuna sculptures, now in the Museum at Jaén.[87] There is much work yet to be done here of the kind which has always engaged the penetrating apprehension of the honorand of this volume, from whom we may confidently expect further illumination in this field.

# ABBREVIATIONS

*ACorsa:* Archéologia Corsa (Aleria)
*AntClass:* L'Antiquité Classique (Brussels)
*ArchEspA:* Archivo Español de Arqueologia
*AthMit:* Mitteilungen des Deutschen Archäologischen Instituts, Athenische Abteilung
*AulaOrient:* Aula Orientalis (Barcelona)
*BulMusHongrBeauxArts:* Bulletin du Musée Hongrois des Beaux-Arts (Budapest)
*BulSocNatAntiquFr:* Bulletin de la Société Nationale des Antiquaires de France (Paris)
*CahLigurPréhArch:* Cahiers Ligures de Préhistoire et d'Archéologie (Bordighera)
*CuadernPrehA:* Cuadernos de Prehistoria y Arqueologia Castellonenses (Castellon de la Plana)
*CVA:* Corpus Vasorum Antiquorum
*DocumArchMérid:* Documents d'Archéologie Méridionale (Lattes)
*IstMit:* Istanbuler Mitteilungen
*MadMit:* Madrider Mitteilungen
*NotScav:* Atti della Accademia dei Lincei. Notizie degli Scavi di Antichità
*OpRom:* Opuscula Romana. Skrifter utgivena av Svenska Institutet i Rom
*ParPass:* La Parola del Passato (Naples)
*RANarbon:* Revue Archéologique de Narbonnaise (Paris)
*RBelgPhilHist:* Revue Belge de Philologie et d'Histoire
*RStLig:* Rivista di Studi Liguri (Bordighera)
*StEtr:* Studi Etruschi

# BIBLIOGRAPHY

*Addenda²*: *Beazley Addenda.* Additional references to *ABV, ARV²* and *Paralipomena.* Second edition compiled by T. H. Carpenter, Oxford 1989.

*Les amphores*: Bats, M. (ed.), *Les amphores de Marseille grecque. Chronologie et diffusion (VIᵉ–Iᵉʳ s. av. J.-C.).* Actes table-ronde de Lattes 1989, Lattes and Aix-en-Provence (Etudes Massaliètes 2, 1990).

Beazley, J. D., *ABV: Attic Black-Figure Vase-Painters* (Oxford 1956).

Beazley, J. D., *Paralipomena*: Additions to *Attic Black-Figure Vase-Painters* and to *Attic Red-Figure Vase-Painters* (Oxford 1971)

*Centre Bérard 1976*: *Les Céramiques de la Grèce de l'Est et leur diffusion en Occident. Colloque Centre Jean Bérard* (Institut Français de Naples) 1976. Paris and Naples 1978. (Colloques Internationaux du Centre National de la Recherche Scientifique No. 569, Sciences Humaines).

*Cortona*: *Forme di contatto e processo di transformazione nella società antica.* (Atti Convegno di Cortona 1981. Rome & Paris (Coll. de l'École Française de Rome 67, 1983). (For French title see here note 15).

Jully, J.-J., *Céramiques*: *Céramiques grecques ou de type grecque et autres céramiques en Languedoc méditerranéen, Roussillon et Catalogne aux VIIᵉ-IVᵉ s. av. n.è. et leur contexte socio-culturel* (Annales Litteraires Univ. de Besançon 275, 3 vols, Paris 1982–83).

*Marseille Grecque*: Bats, M., Berucchi, G., Congès, G. & Tréziny, H. (eds) *Marseille Grecque et la Gaule.* Actes, Colloque international d'histoire et d'archéologie et du Vᵉ congrès archéologique de Gaule méridionale, Marseille 1990. Lattes and Aix-en-Provence (Etudes Massaliètes 3, 1992).

*Marseille Itinéraire*: Gantès, L.-F. & Moliner, M., *Marseille, Itinéraire d'une Mémoire. Cinq années d'archéologie municipale.* (Exhibition catalogue, Marseilles, Musée d'Histoire 1990).

*Ravello*: Hackens, T. (ed.), *Navies and Commerce of the Greeks, the Carthaginians and the Etruscans in the Tyrrhenian Sea.* Proceedings European Symposium at Ravello 1987. Strasbourg and Ravello (Pact 20, 1988).

Shefton, B. B., *Bronzekannen*: *Die "rhodischen" Bronzekannen* (Marburger Studien zur Vor- und Frühgeschichte 2, Mainz 1979).

Shefton, B. B. 1982: Greeks and Greek imports in the South of the Iberian Peninsula. In Niemeyer, H. G. (ed.), *Phönizier im Westen. Beiträge des internationalen Symposiums über 'Die Phönizische Expansion im westlichen Mittelmeerraum', Köln 1979* (Madrider Beiträge 8, Mainz 1982) 337–70.

Shefton, B. B. 1989: Zum Import und Einfluss mediterraner Güter in Alteuropa, *Kölner Jahrbuch für Vor- und Frühgeschichte* 22, 207–220.

Shefton, B. B. 1994 forthcoming: Leaven in the Dough: Greek and Etruscan imports North of the Alps – The Classical period. In Swaddling, J. & Walker, S. (eds), *Italy in Europe: Economic Relations 700 BC to AD 50.* (16th British Museum Classical Colloquium 1992). British Museum Occasional Paper, No. 97.

*Territoire*: Bats, M. & Tréziny, H. (eds), *Le territoire de Marseille grecque*. Actes table ronde d'Aix-en Provence 1985. Aix-en-Provence (Etudes Massaliètes 1, 1986).

*Voyage en Massalie*: Aubert, M. & Lescure, B. (edd.), *Voyage en Massalie. 100 ans d'archéologie en Gaule du Sud*. Exhibition catalogue, Musées de Marseille (Vieille Charité) 1990–91. Marseilles 1990.

## NOTES

(*Editorial Note:* The text of this chapter was received too late for the Editors to rework these Notes into the style of the rest of the volume.)

1. On the very early links with Rome: G. Nenci, *RStudLigur* 24, 1958 (1–2) 24–97; M. Bats in *Marseille dans le monde antique* (note 18 *infra*) 80–87, esp. 82 and 84ff. (on the common bond through the cult of Ephesian Artemis).

2. Thus the Giglio wreck, Campese Bay, might have been *en route* to Marseilles via Corsican waters (presumably a Greek ship of the beginnning of the 6th century BC, see M. Bound in: M. Cristofani *et al.* (eds), *Il Commercio Etrusco arcaico*, Incontro di Studio Roma 1983, Rome 1985, 65–70; *id.*, Studi e Materiali. *Scienze dell'Antichità in Toscana* 6, 1991, 181–244 – First and Second Seasons report; *id.*, The Giglio wreck. A wreck of the Archaic period (c. 600 BC) off the Tuscan island of Giglio, *Enalia* Suppl. 1, Athens 1991; *cf.* P. Rendini in: *Ravello* 191–200 – for links with Corsica and beyond. M. Cristofani in: *Italy in Europe* (16th Brit. Mus. Classical Colloquium, December 1992), forthcoming. Bound suggests that the ship had just loaded granite anchor stocks at Giglio.) The Etruscan Antibes wreck of the mid-6th century is on the other hand typical of the traffic from Etruria to these parts along the Ligurian coastline (Cl. Albore Livadie, L'épave étrusque du Cap d'Antibes, *RStudLig* 33, 1967 (Omaggio F. Benoit I) 300–326; B. Bouloumié, *L'épave étrusque d'Antibes et le commerce en mediterranée occidentale au VI^e siècle av. J.-C.*, Marburg 1982; *cf.* id in *Voyage en Massalie*, 43–45; also *Les Etrusques et l'Europe* (note 6 *infra*), 170–71 (illustr.); 254–256 (illustr.)) We also note the heavy concentration of later wrecks along the Ligurian coast, certifying a well-used route, *cf.* e.g. M. Bats (ed.), *Les amphores* (as in note 34 *infra*) 65, fig. 38, *ibid.*, 276 (maps); *cf.* also *Marseille Grecque*, 230, fig. 50 – archaic period wrecks.

3. Justin 43, 3, 4–13; Strabo IV, 1, 4; Aristotle ap. Athen, 13, 576; D. Pralon in *Marseille Grecque*, 51–56.

4. For the date of about 600 B.C. in the literary tradition: Ps. Scymnus 211–214, quoting Timaeus "120 years before the battle of Salamis" (= Jacoby *FGH* III B 566 F 71). Solinus II, 52 (similar date with anachronistic motivation of the foundation). Aristotle's Constitution of Massalia is reported by Harpokration to have accepted an early date too. Note also Villard in *Marseille Grecque*, 164, n. 2. For the divergent version of a later foundation *cf.* Nenci (note 1 *supra*) 50. J. Brunel, Marseille et les fugitifs de Phocée, *REA* 50, 1948, 5–26.

5. Marseilles as virgin site: Gantès in *Marseille Grecque*, 72.

6. M. Cristofani, *Gli Etruschi del Mare*, Milan 1983, 47ff. B. Bouloumié in *Les Etrusques et l'Europe*, Exhib. Cat. Paris, Grand Palais 1992 = Berlin, Altes Museum 1993, 168–173 (on Etruscan sea-borne trade with the southern coast of France).

7. Above all Morel's fundamental survey article: Le commerce étrusque en France, en Espagne et en Afrique in *Etruria Mineraria*. Atti XII ConvegnoStudEtrItal (Firenze, Populonia, Piombino 1979) Florence 1981, 463–508; *cf.* also Shefton 1989, 213 ff. nn. 28–29, 38 with further literature, esp. M. Py, Les amphores étrusques de Gaule méridionale in *Commercio Etrusco arcaico* (note 2 *supra*) 73–94 (important study with

the requisite geographical and chronological discrimination). For an instructive map with the bucchero import to the south of France shown in relation to the general distribution of the fabric: F.-W. von Hase, Der etruskische Bucchero aus Karthago. Ein Beitrag zu den frühen Handelsbeziehungen im westlichen Mittelmeergebiet, *JbRGZM* Mainz 36, 1989, 329, fig.1 (representing a maximalist view in respect of some of the more exotic provenances).

8. B. Bouloumié, Un oppidum gaulois à St. Blaise en Provence (= *Histoire et Archéologie. Les Dossiers* 84, June 1984); *id.*, in *Voyage en Massalie*, 33–41 (good selection); *Les Etrusques et l'Europe* (note 6 *supra*) 256, nos. 286–90; *cf.* also Shefton 1989, 213, n. 28.

9. East Greek Bird bowls: *cf.* references in Shefton, *Bronzekannen* 52; *cf.* also *id.*, 1982, 353, n. 45 (Add: Cap Couronne, see note 12 *infra*, also de Wever, *AntClass* 35, 1966, 85) with 347, fig. 2 – map. For map of precolonial East Greek within the region, Bouloumié & Lagrand in, S. Boucher (ed.), *Actes IVe Colloque International sur les bronzes antiques, Lyon 1976*, Annales Université Jean-Moulin – Lettres 1977, 27ff., fig 6. Bird bowls were apparently no longer current at the time of Marseilles's foundation; at least none have so far been found there (Gantès in *Marseille Grecque*, 173). For their latest appearance on Etruscan sites *cf.* M. Martelli Cristofani, La ceramica Greco-Orientale in Etruria, in *Centre Bérard 1956*, 153–7, esp. 154f. with ref to *ead.*, *StudEtr* 41, 1973, 105, n. 27 (Populonia, Tomba dei Flabelli). On the question of who brought the Greek goods to these shores in precolonial days, Greeks or Etruscans, no decision seems possible, perhaps both; *cf.* Shefton, *Bronzekannen* 33.; *id.* 1989, 215f with references.

10. Bouloumié, St Blaise (note 8 *supra*) 46.

11. Bouloumié claims that home-produced salt was scarce in Etruria, *Les Etrusques et l'Europe* (note 6 *supra*) 173; also *id.*, St Blaise (note 8 *supra*) 69 with map of salt resources in Italy.

12. Cap Couronne (L'Arquet) and Tamaris: Ch. Lagrand, *Gallia* 17, 1959, 155ff; *id.*, *CahLiguresPréhA* 10, 1961, 207-209 (Cap Couronne); *id.*, in *Territoire,* 127 ff.

13. For Agde *cf. Voyage en Massalie*, 183–189 (O. Bérard, A. Nickels & M. Schwaller) – summary with bibl. *cf.* also O. Bérard, *Musée d'archéologie sous-marine*, Cap d'Agde 1987, 64–67 on goods for export and import from local wrecks, incl. the Roman-period imported metal ingots. M. Gras, Agde et le commerce préromain dans le Languedoc archaïque in: Actes du colloque Géographie commerciale de la Gaule, Tours 1976, *Caesarodunum* 12 (1), 1977, 152–159 (argues for a Phocaean establishment there since the foundation of Marseilles and Ampurias, with increase about 540 BC).

14. Quoted from J.-J. Jully, Les importations attiques dans la Néapolis d'Ampurias du VIᵉ au IVᵉ s., *RBelgPhilHist* 54, 1976, 47.

15. For the very early Greek imported pottery in Agde and also Mailhac *cf.* survey by A. Nickels in *Modes de contacts et processus de transformation dans les sociétés anciennes, Colloque de Cortone 1981*, Paris/Rome 1983, 412ff.; *cf.* also references in Shefton 1989, 213, n. 28.

16. Phoenician imports in Roussillon: O. Arteaga, J. Padró & E. Sanmartí, La expansión fenicia par las costas de Cataluñya y del Languedoc, *AulaOrient* 4, 1986 (= G. del Olmo Lete & M. E. Aubet Semmler (eds), *Los fenicios en la Peninsula Iberica* II), 303–314, esp. 309, map 3 (settlements and cemeteries with Phoenician imports); *cf.* also map in Bouloumié, *L'épave* (note 2 *supra*) 66, fig. 17 (for 6th cent., with more sites indicated for Roussillon); J. Miró, Anforas arcaicas en el litoral Catalán, *ArchEspA* 62, 1989, 21–70, esp. 23, fig.1 – map of Western Phoenician amphoras.

17. On Massalia: for the earlier literature, Shefton 1989, 212, n. 26. For our purposes we note particularly G. Vasseur, *L'origine de Marseille*, Marseilles 1914 (= Annales du Musée d'Histoire Naturelle de Marseille 13); Fr. Villard, *La céramique grecque du Marseille*, Paris 1960. For the results of the very recent (and still current) rescue excavations, see note 18 *infra*.

18. For the recent (since 1985) and ongoing rescue excavations: Marseille dans le monde antique, *Les Dossiers d'Archéologie* 154, Nov. 1990 (informative contributions by those involved). L.-F. Gantès & M. Moliner (eds) *Marseille, Itinéraire d'une Mémoire. Cinq années d'archéologie municipale*, Marseilles 1990 (selection of material, including Greek and Etruscan). M. Bats *et al.* (eds), *Marseille Grecque et la Gaule*. Actes du Colloque International d'Histoire et d'Archéologie et du Vᵉ Congrès archéologique de Gaule

méridionale 1990, Lattes 1992 (Etudes Massaliètes 3) – the basic source.

19. Villard, La céramique archaique de Marseille, in *Marseille Grecque,* 163–170; Gantès, L'apport des fouilles récentes à l'étude quantitative de l'économie massaliète, *ibid.,* 171–178 esp. 172–75 – imports by fabrics.

20. Villard in *Marseille Grecque,* 165; Gantès, *ibid.,* 173; *id., Marseille Itinéraire,* 66, right column, middle and below. For this recently found Etrusco-Corinthian now J. G. Szilágyi, Quelques remarques à propos de l'histoire de l'atelier "senza graffito" de Tarquinia, *BulMusHongrBeauxArts* (Budapest) 78, 1993, 21–37, esp. 34f.

21. East Greek and Corinthian: Villard in *Marseille Grecque,* 164; Gantès, *ibid.,* 173–74. For the previous finds of fine Corinthian, Vasseur (note 17 *supra*) pl. 5, 5 (probably by the Three Maidens Painter, so Villard, *Céramique* (note 17 *supra*) 14, n. 1) and two more Middle Corinthian kraters.

22. See note 17 *supra.*

23. This has been connected with the establishment of Phocaean Aleria *c.* 565 BC, *cf.* Morel in *Ravello,* 460; but Etruscan imports continue strongly in St. Blaise, so Bouloumié, *St. Blaise* (note 8 *supra*) 81. For the progressive but differing rates of decline in Southern France of imported Etruscan bucchero and transport amphorae respectively, see Py (note 7 *supra*) 86, fig. 12. There is strong evidence however for continuing Etruscan influence at the end of the sixth century and beyond, such as Etruscan script used by the indigenous owner of domestic vessels in Lattes (Hérault), *cf.* G. Colonna, Graffiti etruschi in Linguadoca, *StudEtr* 48, 1980, 181–5. Equally telling is the presence of Massaliote Auriol type coins in the Volterra hoard of the early fifth century, *cf.* Villard, *Céramique* (note 17 *supra*) 124, n. 1; M. Martelli in *L'Etruria Mineraria* (note 7 *supra*) 413; M. Cristofani & M. Martelli, *ACorsa,* 6–7, 1981–2, 8. (The Volterra hoard: M. Thompson, O. Mørkholm & C. M. Kraay, *Greek Coin Hoards,* New York 1973, no 1875 ("buried *c.* 500 BC"). Subsequently the partial recovery of the hoard and its publication by M. Martelli in 1975; *cf.* A. E. Furtwängler, *Monnaies grecques en Gaule. Le trésor d'Auriol,* Fribourg 1978, 40ff).

24. Gorgon Painter olpe fragment, recent find: Villard in *Marseille Grecque,* 164; Gantès, *ibid.,* 174; *id., Marseille Itinéraire,* 76, upper panel top left. Previous finds: Vasseur (note 17 *supra*) pl. 10, 12 (Beazley, *ABV* 11 no. 8), Villard, *Céramique* (note 17 *supra*) 18f.; *cf. ibid.,* 19 with pl. 5, 1 – early Horse Head amphora; also note 39 *infra* (Baou de Saint-Marcel). Note also Vasseur, pl. 11, 5 (Villard 19 "column-krater ca: 580 B.C."), now attributed to the workshop of Sophilos: G. Bakir, *Sophilos,* Mainz 1981, 75 (B.23) with pl. 84, 175.

25. There were more works by the Gorgon Painter and his circle in Etruria though than a perusal of Beazley, *ABV* and *Paralipomena,* where not a single Etruscan provenance is recorded, might make one think. For one thing the Louvre amphora *ABV* 9, no. 9; *Paralipomena* 7 is ex Campana (Villard, *CVA Louvre* fasc 11, text p. 105 preliminary note on III H e). In other cases the collections of which vases are part were formed in Italy, thus *Paralipomena* 7, mid-page no. 9 *bis,* Avallon, for which Cl. Rolley, *BCH* 85, 1961, 539, though this could of course include Southern Italy, where his work is also represented, *cf.* L. Forti in *Leuca, Archeologia e Storia Antica,* Università di Lecce 1, Galatina 1978, 117–120. Again other pieces in the Louvre which though not by the Gorgon Painter are yet close in date and style are also ex Campana. Thus *CVA* 11, pl 122, 5–6; pl. 123, 1–2; *cf.* in general I. Scheibler, *JDAI* 76, 1961, 31, n. 89. For post-Beazley determinations: Gravisca, note 27 *infra*; Tarquinia, C. Tronchetti, *Ceramica attica a figure nere,* Museo Archeologico di Tarquinia, Rome 1983, pl. 1, a-b.; Poggio Pelliccia, M. Cristofani, *Gli Etruschi in Maremma,* Milan 1981, 205, fig. 180; Cortona, *StudEtr* 40, 1972, pl. 65. I am indebted to the Beazley Archive, Oxford for help here.

26. For the correlation between Corinthian and Attic imports to Marseilles with those to Etruria *cf.* Villard, *Céramique* (note 17 *supra*) 18; 33f., also *id.,* in *Marseille Grecque,* 165. *A propos* rather later similar contacts within the second quarter of the 6th century we might note that the statement in Gantès, *Marseille Itinéraire,* 75 (illustration on 76 top panel, lower left) that Marseilles has produced a Tyrrhenian amphora (Attic products otherwise confined to Etruria) should be treated with caution. I noted that the inside was black, i.e. that the fragment came from an open shape, perhaps a dinos? My judgement was based upon

a glimpse through the case at a difficult angle. The piece is cited as "Tyrrhenian amphora" also by Villard in *Marseille Grecque,* 164 with 165, fig. 2 as part of the argument for specially close links with Etruria. Note also the identification in *id.*, Céramique (note 17 *supra*) 19 with pl. 5, 9.

27. M. Torelli, *Parola del Passato* 37, 1982, 308–323 argues that Gravisca may have been established as part of Phocaean enterprise at the time of Massalia's foundation; *cf.* id., in *Ravello,* 181; note in this respect also the musings by Morel in *Marseille Grecque,* 19. The Gorgon Painter's work is actually represented amongst the early imports to Gravisca, F. Boitani, *NotScav* 1971, 244, fig. 58.

28. Villard & Vallet, *Parola del Passato* 21, 1966, 181, n. 43 (fragment of dinos "like the Louvre eponymous dinos") citing Jehasse, *Etudes Corses* 22, 1955, 19, fig. 1 – which is not accessible to me. It must be said though that a piece by the Gorgon Painter would be a surprising find for a place only settled in *c.* 565BC.

29. I am aware that I am now at odds with my earlier suggestion in *Bronzekannen,* 23f. that the "Rhodian" bronze oinochoai found in Etruria amongst other places in the late 7th century are in fact diagnostic of early Phocaean activity. However all this is speculative.

30. For the successive stages of the colony's growth L.-F. Gantès, La topographie de Marseille grecque. Bilan de recherches (1829–1991) in *Marseille Grecque,* 71–88 with plans.

31. Gantès in *Marseille Grecque,* 75; *id.*, in *Les Dossiers d'Archéologie* (note 1 *supra*) 14 (illustr.), 16. On the effects of intermarriage *cf.* Morel in *Territoire,* 164.

32. See Gantès in *Marseille Grecque,* 73, map 2 (state before 540 BC and extensions up to 480), see here Fig. 5.1.

33. Could the extensions of the city after 540 BC have been occasioned by population influx at the time of Phocaea's abandonment through Harpagos' pressure? Aleria too was at this time given up by the Phocaeans in favour of Velia, but could nonetheless have provided new immigrants and strength; *cf.* J. Brunel, Marseille et les fugitifs de Phocée, *REA* 50, 1948, 5–26. It is the period too which saw the establishment of the Massaliote Treasury in Delphi *cf.* G. Daux, *BCH* 82, 1958, 360–64. F. Salviat, Le Trésor des Marseillais à Delphes et sa dédicace, *Archéologie du Midi méditerranéen* (Centre de Recherches Archéologiques, Valbonne) 3, 1981, 7–16 was unfortunately inaccessible to me. For the date and the connection of the dedication with the battle of Alalia, *cf.* M. Gras, Marseille, la bataille d'Alalia et Delphes, *DHA* 13, 1987, 161–181. Such a view would however lose much of its force if the Treasury turns out to have been appreciably later; thus E. Hansen reported in J.-F. Bommelaer & D. Laroche, *Guide de Delphes, Le site* (Ecole Française d'Athènes, Sites et Monuments 7) Paris 1991, 63 ("540–500 with preference for the later end").

Of finds from this and the succeeding period of the early fifth century we may note in particular the forty odd limestone naiskoi from rue Négrel with archaic East Greek representations of an enthroned goddess presumed to be Kybele. Discovered in the last century they represent the largest body of Greek sculpture ever found on metropolitan French soil. Gantès in *Marseille Grecque,* 78; F. Salviat, *ibid* 147 ff. (with illustr.); *cf.* also Fr. Naumann, *Die Ikonographie der Kybele in der phrygischen und der griechischen Kunst*, Tübingen 1983 (*IstMitt,* Beih. 28) 139ff, 303f, nos. 69–108, pl. 19, 1–2.

34. For these amphorae now M. Bats (ed.) *Les amphores de Marseille grecque. Chronologie et diffusion (VI<sup>e</sup>-*I<sup>er</sup> *S. av. J.-C.)*, Lattes 1990 (Etudes Massaliètes 2) – esp. for distribution . G. Bertucchi, *Les amphores et le vin de Marseille. VI<sup>e</sup> s. avant J.-C. – II<sup>e</sup> s. après J.-C.* (RANarbon Suppl. 25) Paris 1992 – detailed study of type evolution; problems of contents; useful testimonia for wine in Marseilles. See here the distribution map Fig. 5.3.

35. Marseilles had become rich in wine and oil, but was poor in corn (Strabo IV.1.5). This had to come from elsewhere. Note in this respect the many silos, though of later date, in Languedoc and Catalunia, M. Bats in *Marseille Grecque,* 266 (Languedoc); Morel, *ibid.*, 18 – with further bibl. (Ampurias); *id.*, in *Territoire,* 167. Villard's suggestion, *Céramique* (note 17 *supra*) 64, that Marseilles imported Aegean wine for its own consumption and exported its own production was developed by Yu. B. Tsirkin in the Second Tskaltubo conference 1979 (cf. Morel in *Territoire,* 169f.). For imports of foodstuff and wine during the initial period after the colony's establishment in *à la brosse* amphorae, M. Gras in *Ravello,* 294; *cf.* also

Morel, *ibid.*, 460.

36. The perplexities concerning the early role of Massalia are also implicit in Morel's formulation in *Ravello*, 459: "Marseille, lors de sa fondation, reste de toute façon le type même d'un avant-poste vers l'Occident, d'une intermédière vers quelque chose d'autre (plutôt que d'une colonie entretenant des trafics de type colonial)". He goes on to say that this could be Gaul alone, but he toys strongly with the Tartessian hypothesis, whilst admitting (*ibid.* 458) that there is for the time being little, if any, explicit archaeological evidence for it. For this Tartessian hypothesis, see below and note 67. The hypothesis seems also implicit in B. Cunliffe's formulation of the role of Massalia in his *Greeks, Romans and Barbarians. Spheres of interaction*, London 1988, 22.

37. On the precarious relations with the surrounding tribes and the expansion of the territory, Justin 43, 4 and comments by M. Bats in *Territoire,* 26ff. Note above all the detailed treatment of its development by P. Arcelin in *Territoire,* 43–104, esp. 52–58; also Bats *ibid.*, 21–23 on acculturation and transfer of skills between Greeks and the indigenous neighbours. P. Arcelin, Société indigène et propositions culturelles massaliotes en basse Provence occidentale in *Marseille Grecque*, 305–336.

38. Baou de St Marcel: G. Rayssiguier & C. Guichard in *Marseille dans le monde antique* (note 1 *supra*) 61–9; *eid.* in *Territoire* 105–7; *eid.*, in *Voyage en Massalie* 47–53 (summary with bibl. and selection of material).

39. L.-F. Gantès & G. Rayssiguier, *DocumArchMérid* 3, 1980, 79 ("last quarter 6th cent."); 74, fig. 9, 1 (sejant lion facing backwards) should be close to the Gorgon Painter (though the way the tail pases over the body, set off by incision is at odds with his normal practice) – from an amphora? The lion's mouth and teeth at the edge of the break seem peculiar in the published drawing! The piece was presumably found after the publication of the archaic pottery from the site in *RANarbon* 11, 1978, 1–18. *Voyage en Massalie*, 50, no. 2 mentions a fragment of an "olpe, School of the Gorgon Painter", which is a different piece, to judge by the description.

40. To the east Marseilles' thrust seems (with the exception of Antibes) much less evident in the early and the Archaic periods. Here the effort came during the Classical and later times and was to include such sites as the present-day Nice: *cf.* J. Ducat, Antipolis et Nikaia, Implantations et activités économiques, *Ktema* 7, 1982, 89–99; *cf.* also *Histoire et Archéologie. Les Dossiers* no. 57 (Oct. 1981) Côte d'Azur. Antibes however had early imports from Marseilles, including a Chiot chalice, Bats in *Voyage en Massalie,* 221.

41. For these sites in their physical setting note the map in M. Bats, Marseille, les colonies massaliètes et les relais indigènes dans le trafic le long du littoral méditerranéen gaulois in *Marseille Grecque*, 276, fig. 4; see here Fig. 5.2. For a diachronic survey account, taking account of their natural resources, Cunliffe (note 36 *supra*) 39–49. On Greek pottery imports in this region note particularly the work of J.-J. Jully, *Céramiques Grecques ou de type grec et autres céramiques en Languedoc méditerranéen, Roussillon et Catalogne aux VII^e-IV^e s. av. n. è. et leur contexte socio-culturel*, Paris 1982–83 (3 volumes. Annales Litteraires, Besançon 275). It is unfortunately user-unfriendly. More accessible and useful is his short version, Importations de céramiques, influences commerciales et ambiance culturelle en Languedoc méditerranéen et Roussillon de la fin de VII^e s. avant notre ère à la fin du IV^e s., *Caesarodunum* 12(1), 1977, 160–196. A number of his other studies on these problems are cited here, where apposite.

42. **Béziers**: Gorgon Painter or near, floral ornament. F. Mouret, *CVA Ensérune* (France 6, 1927) pl. 55,1; Jully, *Céramiques* II, 2, pl. B 87. The attribution of the fragment which formerly was considered Corinthian appears to be Jully's.
   **Agde** (La Monédière): Chiot chalice fragment. A. Nickels, Un calice de Chios dans l'arrière-pays d'Agde à Bessan, Hérault, *RA* 1975(1), 13–18, fig. 1a-b – with reference to the material in Marseilles. *Cf.* also A. A. Lemos, *Archaic Pottery of Chios*, Oxford 1991, 197, no. 26. Her reference there "to more finds in Provence" and her misplaced distribution map entry (p. 193, no. 26) need greater precision. These finds are Antibes (note 40 *supra*), L'Arquet-Cap Couronne (note 12 *supra*), St Blaise and Agde-La Monédière. They all come from maritime *emporia* or settlements in the immediate hinterland within the ambit of

Marseilles. In the 'Far West' too we have now, not unexpectedly, several Chiot chalices from Huelva, R Olmos Romera, *ParPass* 37, 1982, 398, D 1-4 (see below in this note). But these are part of the story of Tartessos; *cf.* note 69 *infra*.

**Ensérune**: Hunt Painter's cup fragment: Jully, *Céramique laconienne et céramique attique de l'habitat de hauteur languedocien d'Ensérune (Hérault), fouilles 1929–1967*, *DHA* 4, 1978, 347–373, fig. 1 (p. 365); *id.*, *Céramiques* (note 41 *supra*) II, 2 pl. B93, 248. There are no other Laconian decorated cups in this part of the Mediterranean apart from the relatively numerous examples in Marseilles. For Laconian black vessels in Ampurias, see Shefton in T. J. Dunbabin (ed.), *Perachora* II, 383, n. 1. (For Tartessian Huelva, beyond the Straits of Gibraltar *cf.* references in Shefton 1989, 211, n. 19 – Naucratis Painter (P. Cabrera & R. Olmos, Die Griechen in Huelva, *MadMit* 26, 1985, 70, fig. 8); now more pieces in *Tartessos y Huelva* (note 69 *infra*) 57, (Cabrera); *cf.* also the aryballos, Olmos Romera, as above in this note, 398, C 1).

In the face of this evidence Villard's (and Jully's) denial of an early interest of Marseilles in the western Languedoc (*Marseille Grecque,* 167, n. 8) should be reconsidered.

43. For Exekias we have here the biggest concentration of his vases outside Athens and Etruria. We note the 'Onetorides kalos' fragments of a neck amphora from Ampurias, the fragment of a stately type A panel amphora, also from Ampurias; the well-known neck amphora fragments from Montlaurès in Narbonne and the fragments of one or two more fine panel amphorae from La Monédière, once in the collection of the Abbé Giry. References: Onetorides kalos fragments from Ampurias (attrib. Shefton): G. Trias de Arribas, *Ceramicas Griegas de la Peninsula Iberica*, Valencia 1968, pl. 20, 1–2; Beazley, *ABV* 148 "near Exekias"; *id.*, *Paralipomena* 62; *Addenda²*, 41. Panel amphora, Ampurias (attrib. E. Sanmartí): R. Marcet & E. Sanmartí, *Ampurias*, Barcelona 1990, 21, fig. Narbonne fragments (attrib. P. Jacobsthal): *ABV* 144, no. 2; recent illustrations: Salviat & Barruol, *Provence et Languedoc, Livret Guide* (note 64 *infra*) 237, fig. 1; Narbonne et la Mer (note 64 *infra*) 47 top; Jully, *Céramiques* (note 41 *supra*) II, 2 (1983) pl. B45 with *ibid.*, II, 1, 362–63 (most complete coverage). La Monédière fragments (attrib. D. von Bothmer): Jully, *OpRom* 8, 1974, 59, n. 50, pl. 10; *id.*, *Céramiques* II, 2, pl. B 79; B 80; B 82; B 83, 1–3.

44. M. Py, *Civilisations indigènes et urbanisation durant la protohistoire en Languedoc-Roussillon*, *Ktema* 7, 1982, 101–119 points (*ibid.* 108) to the richer resources of the western Languedoc as against the pastoral economy of the eastern part with smaller surpluses. Hence, though further away from Marseilles, these settlements were able to acquire more opulent goods from the Greek city.

45. For what follows I may in general refer to Shefton 1989, 213–16; *cf.* also Cl. Rolley, Le rôle de la voie rhodanienne dans les relations de la Gaule et de la Méditerranée (VIIᵉ-Vᵉ s. av. J.-C.) in *Marseille Grecque,* 411–418, with different perspective and differing interpretation of the evidence.

46. For the Rhodian bronze oinochoai *cf.* Shefton, *Bronzekannen* with *id.*, 1989, 213, n. 31 (also on the chronology). Add now another in Freiburg/Br. from nearby Gündlingen, conveniently in C. F. E. Pare, *JbRGZM* 36, 1989, 445, fig. 15 top; 467 ("Liste 4").

47. Shefton 1989, 214f. with nn. 33–36.

48. Shefton 1989, 216f. Now also L. Pauli in H. Bender, L. Pauli & I. Stork, *Der Münsterberg in Breisach II (Hallstatt und Latènezeit)*, Munich 1993 (interesting topographical consideration of the "Fürstensitze"). The three sites mentioned: **Mont Lassois**: R. Joffroy, *L'oppidum de Vix et la civilisation Hallstattienne Final*, Paris 1960, 120ff, pl. 67–70; also in part W. Kimmig, Die griechische Kolonisation im westlichen Mittelmeergebiet und ihre Wirkung auf die Landschaften des westlichen Mitteleuropa, *JbRGZM* 30, 1983, pl. 7,3. Some of the more impressive shapes (with cups, which are common imports, excluded): volute-krater, column-krater, amphora, hydria. **Châtillon-sur-Glâne**: H. Schwab (and L. Kahil), *Germania* 53, 1975, 79ff, esp. 80–81; *ead.*, *Germania* 61(2), 1983, 405–458, esp. 438–44 – in both publications the identification of shapes is left disappointingly vague. For a general account of the site see D. Ramseyer, Châtillon-sur-Glâne (FR), un habitat de hauteur du Hallstatt final. Synthèse de huit années de fouilles (1974–1981), *Annuaire de la Société Suisse de Préhistoire et d'Archéologie (Bâle)* 66, 1983, 161–188. Ramseyer, Amphores massaliètes en territoire helvétique in: Bats (ed.), *Amphores* (note 34 *supra*) 259–61.

Many krater fragments: the fine dinos fragment is a more recent find: Ramseyer and Kahil, La céramique de Châtillon-sur-Glâne, *Histoire et Archéologie, Les Dossiers* 62 (April 1982) 54, fig. **Heuneburg**: *cf.* Shefton 1989, 216, n. 45. W. Kimmig, *Die Heuneburg an der oberen Donau*², 1983, 136ff. figs 82–85; more in P. S. Wells, *Culture contact and culture exchange*, Cambridge 1980, 25, fig 3.4 (= *Expedition* (Philadelphia) 21 (4), 1979, 21, fig 4) – volute-krater, column-krater, calyx-krater(?), oinochoe. These three sites are marked on the map, Fig. 5.3.

49. Little Master (Lip-cup) cup with inscriptions from the Heuneburg: Kimmig, *Heuneburg* (note 48 *supra*) 138f, fig. 83–84; also Kimmig, *Kolonisation* (note 48 *supra*) pl. 6, 1, a-b. Another fragment of the same cup gives the nonsense inscription in the handle zone. The restored drawing so far published is unfortunately somewhat misleading, insofar as the pair of wrestlers should engage dead centre in the frieze. It is remarkable that lip-cups, which are particularly delicate and liable to fracture, should have been sent north on the distant overland journey into Barbary. For another stemmed cup from the Heuneburg with a "kalos" (?) inscription in the tondo see Wells (note 48 *supra*) 25, fig 3.4 second down, left. These two are the only inscribed vases that I know of north of the Alps. By contrast the inscribed Attic vases reaching the literate Tartessos are hugely more assertive beginning with the splendid Kleitias fragment from Huelva, P Cabrera & R Olmos, *ArchEspA* 53, 1980, 5-14 & fig.; also *ParPass* 37, 1982, 397, fig 2 (Olmos Romera) and carried on by the Eucheiros cup from Medellin e.g. *MadMitt* 20, 1979, pl. 27a (*cf.* Shefton 1982, 357, n. 58 for refs to the publication by M. Almagro Gorbea and elsewhere). On writing in "barbarian" western Europe, G. Woolf, Power and the spread of writing in the West, in: A. R. Bowman & G. Woolf (eds), *Literacy and power in the ancient world*, Cambridge 1994, 84–98. Earlier bibl. in P.-Y. Lambert, Diffusion de l'écriture gallo-grecque en milieu indigène in *Marseille Grecque*, 289–294.

50. H. van den Boom, Amphoren der Heuneburg, in Bats (ed.), *Amphores* (note 34 *supra*) 263–266.

51. For the arguments that the Attic ware came via Marseilles and the Rhone valley rather than across the Alps, Shefton 1989, 217, n. 47. For Pointe Lequin 1 A, *Ravello* 411; L. Long *et al.* in *Voyage en Massalie*, 232–236 with earlier bibl.; *eid.* in *Marseille Grecque*, 199–234 (fullest publication); *cf.* also P. Pomey & L. Long, *ibid.*, 193.

52. Re introductory presents: Shefton 1989, 218, n. 50; *id.*, 1994 forthcoming, n. 37.

53. For the Vix krater see Shefton 1989, 218f. n. 50 (introductory gifts); n. 54 (use of soft solder in the repair).

54. The spread of Attic cups was wider than that of transport amphorae. Whilst the major centres of Hallstatt power just mentioned had both transport amphorae and drinking ware of the more sophisticated kind, including kraters, many of the minor sites had Attic cups alone without kraters and such like vessels; nor have they produced evidence that these transport amphoras ever reached them. It is thus not unlikely that wine was redistributed to them from the major centres in skins or other perishable containers.

55. J. Gran Aymerich & M. Almagro-Gorbea, Les fouilles récentes à Bourges et les recherches sur les importations étrusco-italiques, *BulSocNatAntiquFr* 1991, 312–39; Gran Aymerich in *Italy in Europe* (16th British Museum Classical Colloquium, December 1992) forthcoming 1994. It should be noted though that Bourges has so far not produced imports of Mediterranean pottery before the early fifth century. For the approach route *cf.* also Shefton 1989, 217, n. 47 *ad fin.*

56. *cf.* Shefton 1989, 217, n. 47 *ad fin.*; *id.*, 1994 forthcoming, n. 3.

57. H. Gallet de Santerre, above others, had always resisted the common belief in a decline of imports during the 5th century, and cautioned against arguments ex silentio; see now his article, La diffusion de la céramique attique aux Vᵉ et IVᵉ siècles av. J.-C. sur les rivages français de la Méditerranée, *RANarbon* 10, 1977, 33–57; and especially *id.*, Les exportations de céramique attique pendant la première moitié du Vᵉ siècle av. J.-C. dans la Midi de la France in *Stele. Memorial volume for N. Kondoleon*, Athens 1980, 187–93. Note also now Bertucchi, *Les amphores* (note 34 *supra*) 312ff. stressing the evidence for prosperity in 5th century Marseilles. Contra however arguing for a decline in much of the 5th century of the level of Attic import Villard in *Marseille Grecque*, 169 and others before him, e.g. J. Jannoray,

*Ensérune. Contribution à l'étude des civilisations préromaines de la Gaule méridionale*, Paris 1955, 314–15 ("hiatus between late 6th cent. and the Meidian period"). Note also now Rouillard, La place de Marseille dans le commerce des vases attiques à figures rouges on Méditerranée occidentale (V$^e$-IV$^e$ s. av. J.-C.) in *Marseille Grecque*, 179–87. In general *cf.* J.-J. Jully, *Les importations de céramique attique en Languedoc méditerranéen, Roussillon et Catalogne*, Besançon 1980 (Annales Litteraires no. 231).

58. See note 44 *supra*.

59. Some references to the material and its whereabouts. For all these and more consult the detailed discussion by Gallet de Santerre (note 57 *supra*, two articles).

**Arles**: P. Rouillard in *Marseille Grecque*, 183; new excavations – material in Arles.

**La Monédière**: J.-J. Jully, *La céramique attique de La Monédière, Bessan, Hérault*, Brussels 1973 – material ex Coulouma in Montpellier; more from other collections in Jully, *Céramiques* II, 2, pl. B79-B86.

**Béziers**: D. Ugolini & O. Olive, La céramique attique de Béziers (VI$^e$-V$^e$ s.). Approche de la diffusion et de l'utilisation de la vaiselle attique en Languedoc occidental, in *Sur les pas des Grecs en Occident. Hommages A. Nickels* (Etudes Massaliètes 4), Lattes 1994, forthcoming – material, much of it from recent excavations, in Ensérune, more in Béziers, Musée du Biterrois, Jully, *Céramiques* II, 2, pl. B87–B90.

**Ensérune**: CVA (note 42 *supra*); Jannoray (note 57 *supra*); Jully (note 42 *supra*, under Ensérune); Jully, *Céramiques* II, 2, pl. B 93–143 – material in site museum.

**Mailhac**: M. Louis, O. & J. Taffanel, *Le premier Age du Fer languedocien* I, Montpellier 1955, 115 ("at least 37 Attic cups incl. 10 red-figured cups, 20 Castulo cups"). Very little is published; *cf. ibid.*, fig. 88; fig. 100 for r.f.; fig. 89 for Castulo cups; Jully, *Céramiques* II, 2, pl. B 25–44 – material, from excavations, in site museum.

**Montlaurès**: Jully & Solier, Les céramiques attiques de Montlaurès, in *Narbonne. Archéologie et histoire*, Montpellier 1973, 113–126; Jully, *Céramiques* II, 2, pls B 43–56 – material in Narbonne.

**Pech-Maho** is unpublished. Note however Gallet de Santerre, *Diffusion* (note 57 *supra*) 48; also Solier in Salviat & Barruol (note 64 *infra*) 258, figs 4–5; Jully, *Céramiques* II, 2, pls B66 & B74; *cf.* his note on page preceding pl. B66 – material in Sigean.

**Ruscino**: Jully & Rouillard, La céramique attique de Ruscino, in G. Barruol (ed.), *Ruscino, Château-Roussillon, Perpignan I*, Actes Colloque Perpignan 1975, Paris 1980 (RANarbon suppl. 7); Jully, *Céramiques* II, 2, pls B 150-55 – material still in Perpignan?

60. For this *cf.* e.g. Jully, Importations attiques dans la Néapolis d'Ampurias (note 14 *supra*) 44–47 ("the links between Ampurias and Roussillon and western Languedoc are particularly significant in the 5th century"); also Rouillard (note 57 *supra*) 181. As we have seen however the situation for Marseilles is now in a flux and new finds may well change this perception. It is also worth noting that Ruscino, which has little early- and mid-fifth century red figure is, of the sites listed in note 59, actually the closest to Ampurias which is very well endowed with early and mid-5th century red figure. So why this gap in Ruscino, if the supply came from Ampurias?

61. For criteria of hellenization, see Aleksandra Wasowicz, Les facteurs de la civilisation et de l'urbanisation des côtes de la Mer Noire à l'époque de la colonisation grecque, in *La città antica comme fatto di cultura* (Atti del Convegno di Como e Bellagio 1979, Como 1983) 67–77, summarized by Morel in *Territoire*, 165 – interesting reflections of relevance also to Mediterranean France, as Morel points out; *cf.* also Shefton 1989, 217 with n. 48 referring to the situation north of the Alps. For a good, brief account of the impact of the new influences on local settlement patterns M. Bats & M. Py, Les premiès villes. Etablissements massaliètes et agglomérations proto-urbaines en Gaule méditerranéenne, in J.-P. Mohen *et al.*, *Archéologie de la France*, Paris 1990, 289–295; more extensively M. Py, Civilisations indigènes et urbanisation durant la protohistoire en Languedoc-Roussillon, *Ktema* 7, 1982, 101–119. In general still (even if superseded in some respects) H. Gallet de Santerre, Les civilisations classiques en Languedoc méditerranéen et Roussillon, in *Le rayonnement des civilisations grecque et romaine sur les cultures périphériques* (= 8th International Congress of Classical Archaeology Paris 1963) Paris 1965, 625–641. Important also the existence of presumably local ownership graffiti with Greek names on Attic red-figure

from native sites. Thus J.-J. Jully, Graffiti sur vases attiques en Languedoc méditerranéen, Roussillon et Catalogne, *DHA* 2, 1976, 53–70; also *id.*, Les importations (note 57 *supra*, ad fin.) 45 – examples from Montlaurès, Peyriac-de-Mer (Aude); Ruscino; La Monédière; *cf.* also M. Bats, L'écriture en Gaule méridionale protohistorique, *RANarbon* 21, 1988, 127.

62. M. Lejeune, J. Pouilloux & Y. Solier, Etrusque et Ionien archaiques sur un plomb de Pech Maho (Aude), *RANarbon* 21, 1988, 19–59; also Pouilloux in *La Magna Grecia e il Lontano Occidente* (note 65 *infra*) 205–12. On the Etruscan text: M. Cristofani, *StEtr* 57, 1991, 285–87 ("mataliai" = Massalia; also 'kappa' used in the Alerian manner); *id.*, in *Italy and Europe* (note 55 *supra*) forthcoming. Good reproduction in *Les Etrusques et l'Europe* (note 6 *supra*), 172–73; 256, no. 293 (with bibl.).
(Regrettably when writing the above I was unaware of some important further work on both the Greek and Etruscan texts. On the Greek text see now M. Lejeune, Ambiguités du texte de Peche Maho, *REG* 104, 1991, 311–29, reviewing also J. Chadwick, The Pech Maho lead, *ZPE* 82, 1990, 161–6. On the Etruscan text see M. Cristofani, Il testo di Pech Maho, Aleria e il traffico del V secolo A.C., *MEFRA* 105 (2), 1993, 833ff.).

63. For the role of Iberians as traders in the Hérault, *cf.* J. Untermann, *RANarbon* 25, 1992, 19–27 (use of Iberian language and script); also J. de Hoz in *La Magna Grecia e il Lontano Occidente* (note 65 *infra*) 212f.

64. Pech-Maho: F. Salviat & G. Barruol (eds), *Provence et Languedoc méditerranéon. Sites protohistoriques et gallo-romains*, Paris 1976, (Livret-Guide of excursion. 9th Internat. Congress U.I.S.P.P, Nice 1976), 253–262 (Y. Solier); The Ionic, non-architectural capital, *ibid.*, 260, fig. 6; also *Narbonne et la Mer de l'antiquité à nos jours*, exhib. cat. Narbonne 1990, 49 top (illustr.), 65, no. 42 (commentary). *cf.* also Solier (note 62 *supra*) 58.

65. On Ampurias: The most recent surveys are by Enric Sanmartí & Josep M. Nolla, *Empuries, Guide and Itinerary*, Barcelona 1988; and more fully, the well illustrated R. Marcet & E. Sanmartí, *Ampurias*, Barcelona 1990. These incorporate the recent excavation results. Both give interesting and judicious surveys of the history of the site's archaeological exploration. Good summary of history and early monumental development as revealed by recent excavations in E. Sanmartí, Emporion, Port grec à vocation Iberique, in *La Magna Grecia e il Lontano Occidente* (Atti 29⁰ Convegno di Studi sulla Magna Grecia, Taranto 1989 (1990), 389–410 (with bibl. of recent excavation reports). A series of earlier important publications on the site and its material were due to Martin Almagro Basch; *cf.* also J.-P. Morel, *BCH* 99, 1975, 865, n. 49; Rouillard, *Les Grecs* (note 75 *infra*) 244–81.

66. E. Sanmartí-Grego, Massalia et Emporion, in *Marseille Grecque,* 31f.

67. J.-P. Morel, in *Marseille Grecque*, 16ff. Sanmartí, *Emporion* (note 65 *supra*) 394; A. J. Dominguez Monedero, La función económica de la ciudad griega de Emporion, in *Protohistoria Catalana* (VI Colloqui Internacional d'Arqueologia de Puigcerdà) Puigcerdà 1984, 193–99. Note also that Paloma Cabrera in her full treatment of the early imports to Huelva (note 69 *infra*), operates with "Massaliote imports", thus *ibid.*, 63f. "from second quarter of 6th cent some Massaliote imitations of Ionian cups, also basins and ewers reach Huelva" (cf. *ibid.*, 91ff, fig. 5, 79–87; also fig. 12, 213–15; *cf.* also the basins fig. 6, 99–100). If these identifications are confirmed, they would raise some intriguing questions, but not necessarily prove that there was a direct contact between Marseilles and Tartessos along the Levant coast at an early period, that is to say the late 7th and the earlier 6th centuries BC. Against such contacts must count the absence of any germane material during the 7th and most of the 6th century along that coast; *cf.* the concise, but authoritative account by A. Fernandez, C. Gomez & A. Ribera, Las anforas griegas, etruscas y fenico-punicas en las costas del Pais Valenciano, in *Ravello* 317–33. This shows little, if anything, which cannot be accounted for as part of the Phocaean enterprise of the 6th century which by then had reached the Levant (see text here to note 72 *infra*). For Massaliote transport amphorae in the crucial areas *cf.* also Rouillard in *Amphores*, 179ff., where the finds along the Levant coast and on land are reported as not earlier than the 5th century. Huelva though has produced perhaps three amphorae of the later 6th century (ibid. 181). To what period then is the source of Avienus' *Ora Maritima* to be

assigned?

68. For the earliest material, which includes East Greek bird bowls, Shefton 1982, 346–53 with maps figs 2 and 3. For bird bowls see here note 9 *supra*. They are apparently no longer found in Marseilles! This also in answer to Morel's difficulties raised in *Marseille Grecque*, 16, nn. 1 & 3.

69. For the massive Greek pottery imports in Huelva, which begin not before the early 6th century *cf*. refs. in Shefton 1989, 211, n. 19 to which add now J. Fernandez Jurado, *Tartessos y Huelva* (Huelva Arqueologica X-XI (1)-(3) with 'cuadro resumen') Huelva 1988–89, (1990). These very important volumes give for the first time the full range of the imported material with specialist contributions (in vol. 3) by Paloma Cabrera (Greek imports) and Jurado (Etruscan imports). We note from the new material the lip fragment of an Ionian Little Master cup, the like of which had not hitherto been seen west of Aegina (East Greek Little Master cups are also known from Gravisca). Thus put Cabrera *cit*. 97 fig. 196 (with text 71) beside Kunze, *AthMit* 59, 1934, 97f, Beil. 7, 5 from Aegina (W. Felten however in *Alt-Agina II, 1* (1982) 19 with pl. 8, 112 considers the Aegina cup to be Laconian, but I prefer to follow Kunze and Stibbe in taking it to be an East Greek (Samian?) imitation of Laconian, for which now see *Greek Vases in the J. Paul Getty Museum* 4, Malibu 1989, 59 with nn. 54, 55; also *ibid.*, 69 with n. 80). Considerations of this sort suggest that much of the East Greek material in Huelva came direct from the Aegean; *cf*. Shefton 1982, 353; also the remarks on the Laconian imports by Cabrera, *loc. cit.* 57.

70. For Malaga *cf*. refs. in Shefton 1989, 211, n. 20 and now J. Gran-Aymerich, *Malaga phénicienne et punique*, Paris 1991 (with complete bibl.).

71. Shefton 1989, 208, n. 3 with ref. to *id.*, 1982, 353 ff.

72. Shefton 1982, 354–59 with map on 349, fig. 4.

73. Shefton 1982, 338–43; *id.*, 1989, 209–11.

74. H. G. Niemeyer, Auf der Suche nach Mainake, *Historia* 29, 1980, 165–189 (= *Habis* 10–11, 1979–80, 279ff. in Spanish). For the sites mentioned here and in subsequent notes see the map, Fig. 5.4.

75. J.-P. Morel, L'expansion Phocéenne en Occident, *BCH* 99, 1975, 887, n. 124, as modified in P. Rouillard, Les colonies Grecques du Sud-Est de la Péninsule Ibérique, *ParPass* 37, 1982, 417ff. Now Rouillard, *Les Grecs et la Péninsule Ibérique*, Paris 1991, 299ff. (Hemeroskopeion); *ibid.*, 303ff. (Alonis).

76. Los Nietos: E. Diehl & P. San Martin Moro & H. Schubart, Los Nietos – Ein Handelsplatz des 5. bis 3. Jhdt. an der spanischen Levanteküste, *MadMit* 3, 1962, 45–83, esp. 59f, no. 1 (coral-red dish, *ibid.*, pl 16a); no. 2 (cup by Painter of Bologna 417, *ibid.*, pl. 17a). Some of the material also in Gloria Trias de Arribas, *Ceramicas Griegas de la Peninsula Iberica*, Valencia 1968, pls. 177–78; J. M. Garcia Cano, *Ceramicas griegas de la region de Murcia*, Murcia 1982, 248–60, pls 16–18. For subsequent exploration of the cemetery and the remarkable find of a magazine with eight early 4th cent. Attic bell kraters, C. Garcia Cano & J. M. Garcia Cano, *ArchEspA* 65, 1992, 3ff.; see *ibid.*, 31 on the nearby mines of La Union "ricas en plata y plomo, come parece indicar la gran cantidad de minerales y escorias de fundición de estos metales, que se han atestiguado durante el curso de excavación". For summary of the site and its finds J. M. Garcia Cano in, J. Blanquez Perez & V. Antona del Val (eds), *Congreso de Arqueologia Iberica: Las Necropolis*, Madrid 1991, 328ff.

77. For Cabezo Lucero, see now C. Aranegui, A. Jodin, E. Llobregat, P. Rouillard & J. Uroz, *La nécropole iberique de Cabezo Lucero*, Madrid – Alicante 1993. For the Brygan cup, *ibid.*, pl. 69; also *CRAI* 1990 (April-June), 551, fig. 7; good detail as cover picture of Rouillard, *Les Grecs* (note 75 *supra*). Note also that black cups type C, which date to the beginning of the 5th century, are relatively frequent at the site, Aranegui *et al.*, *cit.* 89. Similarly so for instance at Pech-Maho (see note 59 *supra* with ref. to Gallet de Santerre), Montlaurès and Ruscino.

78. Puig de Benicarló: E. Sanmartí & F. Gusi Jener, *CuadernPrehACastellon* 3, 1976, 205–18, figs; Sanmartí Grego, *ibid.*, 219ff, (cup type C).

79. We refer to the coral-red small dish, which enjoys a puzzling popularity in certain parts of the Mediterranean, to which I hope to return elsewhere. Of relevance here is the remarkable concentration in the north west of the Mediterranean: Baou de St. Marcel (*RANarbon* 11, 1978, 6, fig. 2, 19); Arles?

(*Marseille Grecque* 183); Béziers; Ruscino (*Ruscino, Château-Roussillon, Perpignan* I, 1980, RANarbon Suppl. 7, 175 E below; cf also *ibid.*, fig. 5, 15); Ampurias (quite a few; *cf.* Sanmartí-Grego & Santiago (note 80 *infra*), 6, fig. 2, 23 with ref. to A. Arribas & G. Trias, *ArchEspA* 32, 1959, 93ff.; *cf.* also M. Almagro, *RStLig* 15, 1949, 24, fig. 19 below right?) and here at Los Nietos (*MadMit* 3, 1962, pl. 16a). On the other hand they are distinctly rare for instance in Etruria – so G. Camporeale, *Collezione alla Querce*, Florence 1970, 20, no. 3, pl. 2; *cf.* Shefton in *La Magna Grecia e il Lontano Occidente* (note 65 *supra*) 197. For the date of these dishes B. A. Sparkes & L. Talcott, *Black and Plain Pottery* (Athenian Agora XII, 1970) 1, 99f.

80. Enric Sanmartí-Grego & Rosa A. Santiago, La lettre grecque d'Emporion et son contexte archéologique, *RANarbon* 21, 1988, 3–17; *cf.* also Santiago, Comercio maritimo y epigrafia emporitana, in *Ravello,* 115–21.

81. Santiago (note 80 *supra*) 116.

82. Shefton 1982, 354f., 363 with map; *ibid.*, 349, fig. 4; *id.*, 1989, 212, n. 25. On the problems raised there note especially Martin Almagro Gorbea in *Magna Grecia e il Lontano Occidente* (note 65 *supra*) 340–50; also A. J. Dominguez, New Perspectives on the Greek Presence in the Iberian Peninsula, in J. M. Fossey (ed.), *Proceedings of the First International Congress on The Hellenic Diaspora*, Amsterdam 1991, 123–27 (with ample bibl.).

83. See note 75 *supra*.

84. *cf.* Rouillard, *Les Grecs* (note 75 *supra*) 356ff. esp. nn. 215–216. The work of Teresa Chapa is of importance here. For itinerant sculptors from Ampurias note Sanmartí's intervention in *La Magna Grecia e il Lontano Occidente* (note 65 *supra*) 383f.; contra: Almagro Gorbea, *ibid.*, 385f.

85. E.g. Dominguez Monedero, La escultura animalistica contestana como exponente del proceso de helenización del teritorio, *Arqueologia Espacial* (Coloquio sobre distribución y relaciones entre los asentiamientos), Teruel 1984

86. E. Langlotz, *Die kulturelle und künstlerische Hellenisierung der Küsten des Mittelmeers durch die Stadt Phokaia*, Cologne-Opladen 1966.

87. J. A. González Navarrete, *Escultura Iberica del Cerillo Blanco, Porcuna, Jaén*, Jaén 1987 – good illustrations by P. Witte, German Archaeological Institute, Madrid ("second quarter of 4th cent. BC"). I. Negruela, *Los monumentos escultorios Ibericos del Cerillo de Porcuna (Jaén)*, Madrid 1990 – further reconstitution ("first half of 5th cent. BC").

# Chapter 6

# The Foundation of Selinous:
# overpopulation or opportunities?

### Franco De Angelis

> "Colonisation, it is true, implies at all times a need for
> expansion, and under healthy conditions it is a sign that the
> population of the home-country is fast out-growing its
> productive capacity...." Gwynn (1918, 89)

In discussing the causes of ancient Greek colonisation, scholars have often cited overpopulation as a prime mover (*e.g.*, Bérard 1960, 60; Lepore 1969, 175–178; Graham 1982a, 157). Such a viewpoint has been especially prominent since Gwynn (1918) argued strongly in favour of it in a justly famous paper. Three quarters of a century on, enormous advances have needless to say been made not only in the quantity and quality of evidence available, but also in the variety of new questions being asked of the ancient world and the inter-disciplinary approaches that such novel inquiries encourage. Recent criticisms of the overpopulation theory must be set against this backdrop.[1] At its most basic level the opposition voiced demonstrates the dangers of making sweeping generalisations of the causes of a phenomenon both complex in nature and of great historical significance, although it would certainly be wrong to throw out overpopulation altogether (Gallant 1991, 136, for example, does not rule it out completely). Given the widespread explanatory force overpopulation has had till late, it should not be surprising to learn that this concept has spilled over into some modern interpretations of events in the new world of the Greek colonies, being called upon in particular to explain the foundation of sub-colonies. Sub-colonies were the colonies of colonies, and as a historical phenomenon sub-colonies have naturally elicited research into their origins. All too often, it has been assumed that the parameters leading to sub-colonisation were no different from those that led the Greeks to leave the homeland in the first place. In consequence, we are asked to believe that overpopulation was at the root of some of these sub-colonies, the Greeks having once again outstripped the available natural resources of their newly established homes. However, the critical difference, seldom made explicit or even noticed in such interpretations, is that in the new world of the colonies we are regularly dealing with larger and quite often better expanses of land and population levels which, in

87

their initial stages at least, are lower, an odd combination indeed for overpopulation.[2] Here, then, we have *a priori* grounds to suspect the causal significance attributed to overpopulation, thus permitting this version of the theory to be added to the list of growing dissension.

On the island of Sicily Megara Hyblaia's foundation of its sub-colony Selinous is one such instance where overpopulation has been regarded by some as the underlying factor (Fig. 6.1). The most recent statement of this thesis is typical of the state of affairs envisaged by its adherents: "Already in 628, pressed by overpopulation, the city sent out colonists to found Selinus; the city's chora was unable to provide the *basic necessities*" (Berger 1991, 132; my italics).[3] According to this view, Megara Hyblaia was compelled to establish a colony somewhere else on the island in order to trim off excess numbers unsupportable by natural conditions at home; colonisation merely served as the cure to a problem imposed by nature. But why is it that advocates of the overpopulation theory have made a special case for the sub-colonising activity of Megara Hyblaia, when other Greek sub-colonies on the island are viewed differently? The answer could well be due to a number of possible reasons. In addition to overpopulation being widely assumed as paramount in the causes of Greek colonisation, misconceptions surrounding the size of Megara Hyblaia's territory exist (Dunbabin 1948, 128, 301 has certainly caused some of the confusion); little attention, moreover, is generally paid to the study of population (the latter items being the two most important elements of the overpopulation formula). The difference may also be owed to the idea, largely warranted, of Megara Hyblaia's unimportance in Sicily, and hence its inability to control to any degree its own affairs (Berger [1991, 132], unsurprisingly, reduces the *polis* to this lowly position). Whatever the guiding reason(s), the soundness of such historical reconstruction is questionable. The arguments made above suggest that, at a purely theoretical level, there are good reasons for mistrusting the use of overpopulation as an explanatory tool in colonial contexts. In the absence of ancient literary sources, archaeology can act as a yardstick against which to measure the general validity of the overpopulation theory. Today, thanks to a century of archaeological exploration conducted at Megara Hyblaia by Italian and particularly French scholars, we are in a position to do so. If Megara Hyblaia was indeed suffering from overpopulation, resulting in the foundation of Selinous, the archaeology should certainly be able to detect this situation at the home end.

The intention of what follows is to make a contribution to the debate concerning Selinous' foundation by challenging the lingering view that overpopulation led Megara Hyblaia to found Selinous. To do so I will largely add the numbers to existing descriptions which claim that overpopulation was ailing Megara Hyblaia, for to make such an assertion, it must be pointed out, is in itself half of a quantified statement, implying conception of the quantities involved, though only without the accompanying numbers. Examination of the size and nature of Megara Hyblaia's territory as well as the carrying capacity and carried capacity of that territory will render most improbable the idea that overpopulation had anything to do with Selinous' foundation. Thereafter, by highlighting some internal developments at both Megara Hyblaia and Selinous, a reason for the sub-colony's creation is put forth. Before turning to these matters, we first need some relevant background.

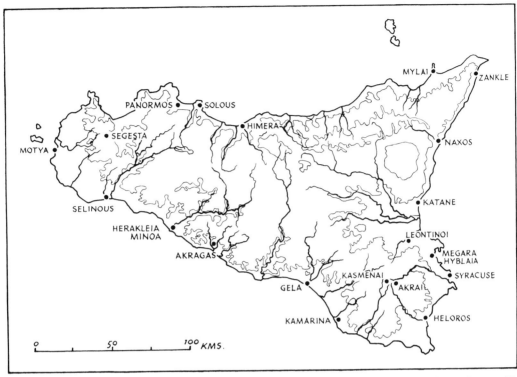

*Fig. 6.1 Ancient Sicily, showing major sites mentioned in the text (after Pugliese Carratelli 1986, loose fold-out map).*

## I. BEGINNINGS

The foundation of Selinous cannot be properly understood without knowing something of the foundation of its mother-city Megara Hyblaia, and in turn the two colonies must be placed in the wider context of Greek and non-Greek settlement in Sicily.

The first Greek colonies on the island were established on the east coast in the second half of the eighth century. Upon their arrival in this part of the island, the Greeks found almost everywhere a native culture living in small settlements and in the process of making the transition from bronze to iron (Bernabò Brea 1957, 136–174; S. Tusa 1983, 457–487). Relations with these natives varied from peaceful co-habitation to expulsion and even enslavement. Only three Greek states, namely Chalcis, Corinth, and Megara, were responsible for settlement of the east coast. Of the three, the Chalcidians were the earliest and most prolific colonisers who, through the establishment of a number of colonies (Naxos, Zankle, Leontinoi, Katane, and Mylai), laid claim to the whole north-east part of Sicily in two decades (Thuc. vi.3, vi.4.4–5; *cf.* Boardman 1980, 169–171; for updates of more recent research, see Wilson 1982, 90–93; 1988, 114, 117, 120–122). As the Chalcidians were busy in this area, Corinth was second to arrive on the scene, founding Syracuse in 734/3 (Thuc. vi.3; *cf.* Boardman 1980, 172–174; Wilson 1982, 86–87; 1988, 111–113). The Megarians followed a few years later, the last of the Greeks to come to eastern Sicily. The story told by Thucydides (vi.4.1) is that the Megarians experienced several trying moments before they settled down permanently. The original colonising party sent out from Greece was led by Lamis and landed at a place called Trotilon, usually identified with modern Brucoli (Manni 1981, 239) (Fig. 6.2). They were then invited by the Chalcidians of Leontinoi, founded a little earlier, to live together as citizens, yet were expelled shortly thereafter.[4] The Megarians retreated to the peninsula of Thapsos, where their oikist Lamis died. Even here, however, they were not immune, for the Megarians were again driven away, though by whom is this time not disclosed (Syracuse is the most likely candidate: Figueira 1985, 269; Graham 1988, 312). Homeless the Megarians were given a foothold on the mainland by the Sikel king Hyblon, and so began the ancient tradition of Megara Hyblaia's good relations with the natives. The end of these wanderings can be dated to 728/7.[5] By the time the Megarians arrived, therefore, their Greek predecessors had left slim pickings on the east coast from which to choose.

The next major wave of Greek colonisation in Sicily came in the seventh century. On this occasion settlement occurred further to the west of that of previous decades, in areas not touched by the first wave. Again, at almost every turn in their colonising quests, the Greeks met native Sicilians occupying the coasts and interior (Bernabò Brea 1957, 174–181; S. Tusa 1983, 487–495); however, unlike eastern Sicily, there was a third party already in place from the same time as the Greeks were settling the east coast (Thuc. vi.2.6), namely the Phoenicians, in the north-west coastal areas at Motya, Panormos, and Solous (a general sketch of the Phoenicians in Sicily is given by V. Tusa 1988). With one exception – Gela in 688/7 (Thuc. vi.4.3–4; *cf.* Boardman 1980, 177–178; Wilson 1982, 95–96; 1988, 129) – the second wave of Greek colonisation consisted of sub-colonies sent out from the nascent Greek cities of Sicily.[6] Syracuse sent out four colonies (Heloros, Akrai, Kasmenai, and Kamarina) to consolidate its hold of south-east Sicily all the way to the doorstep of the recently established Gela (Thuc. vi.5.2–3; *cf.* Boardman 1980, 185–186; Wilson 1982, 87–90; 1988, 114, 116). Towards the middle of the century the Chalcidians moved along the north coast and founded Himera (Thuc. vi.5.1; *cf.* Boardman 1980, 188; Wilson 1982, 99–100; 1988, 139–140). The foundation of Selinous formed part of this intense sub-colonising activity. According to Thucydides (vi.4.2), Megara Hyblaia, having sent for an oikist from the homeland, founded Selinous a century after it had itself come into existence – thus around 628/7. A second, slightly earlier foundation-date for Selinous of 651/0 is preserved in Diodorus (xiii.59.4). However, there is no need in becoming entangled in the massive debate over these latter two foundation-dates (see Wilson 1982, 101 for a possible solution); for our purposes it is important to note the wider context of Selinous' foundation which a minor chronological discrepancy affects not in the least. In any case, for the archaeological arguments to be advanced below, it is fine to target the third quarter of the seventh century (650–625), which accomodates both these foundation-dates, as the crucial period to bear in mind.

The ancient sources, therefore, are completely silent as to why Selinous was founded; as is customarily the case with the literary record for colonisation, only details of the basic act of colonisation have survived. Some scholars have assumed that overpopulation was behind Selinous' foundation (see note 3); we need to turn now to the archaeology of Megara Hyblaia to test that proposition.

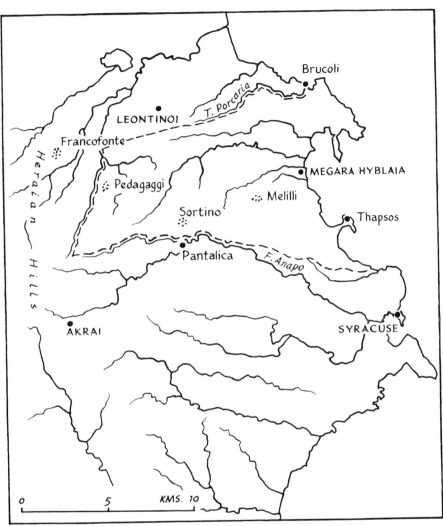

*Fig. 6.2 Megara Hyblaia and surrounding area, with maximum limits of the territory outlined (after Bernabò Brea 1968, 165).*

## II. THE SIZE AND NATURE OF MEGARA HYBLAIA'S TERRITORY

Megara Hyblaia's territory occupied an area almost triangular in shape (the best account of the territory is Vallet & Voza 1984; see also Vallet 1990, 93, 102; these accounts are followed below). As is usual with *polis* boundaries, especially those of earlier date, the ground on which such a picture is based derives from less direct and indirect sources; there is no direct documentary evidence giving details of the territory. Thus, although we are unable, on the one hand, to trace the exact history of Megara Hyblaia's territory, a general indication may, on the other, be gained by combining the archaeological, historical, and geographical clues at our disposal. The indications supplied by Megara Hyblaia's two Greek neighbours, Syracuse to the south-east and Leontinoi to the north-west (Fig. 6.2), are as good a place as any to begin the discussion.

Syracuse, for its part, laid claim to large tracts of the interior by establishing two sub-colonies, Akrai and Kasmenai, south of the river Anapos in 663 and 643 respectively (Thuc. vi.5.2). The military nature of these two outposts was driven home by Di Vita (1956, 181 note 21, 182, 193–194) and has been unanimously accepted since then. Syracusan expansion was direct in keeping, no doubt, with the colony's ambitions and its policy of enslaving the native Sikels to maintain control. In the environs of Akrai and Kasmenai, the frontier with Syracuse is relatively clear-cut, but south-east of Sortino the river Anapos takes a turn southwards in the direction of Syracuse; consequently, the dividing line is no longer as obvious (Fig. 6.2). The probable boundary may have extended to the Scala Greca, since the plain follows its natural course until the landscape gradually rises up to the limestone plateau of the Epipolai (the immense fortification of this area in later times lends credence to the idea that natural circumstances made it vulnerable). The actions of Leontinoi (and of many of the Chalcidian colonies of eastern Sicily in general) vis-à-vis natives and territorial expansion were once thought, in contrast with those of Syracuse, to have been rather more pacific (*e.g.*, Dunbabin 1948, 121; Vallet 1962), though recent archaeological work has upset such a view (see now Procelli 1989). In discussing Leontinoi's territorial ambitions, it must first be remembered that, of all the *poleis* founded in eastern Sicily, only Leontinoi was not established on the coast. The natural course for expansion was thus westwards, and it is in this direction that we find the Chalcidians at work (Fig. 6.2). Land was claimed by setting up outposts (Procelli 1989, 686), and cultural contacts with the natives proceeded up along the rivers and valleys on the west side of the Heraian hills, which formed a natural boundary with lands to the east. From an early date Leontinoi clearly exerted influence in this western region (a convenient, recent summary of the evidence is to be found in Domínguez 1989, 125–161). Moving away from the Heraian hills, there is no natural demarcation which could act as dividers from the foot of these hills to the south of Leontinoi (this area would make sense as the scene of the territorial dispute between Megara Hyblaia and Leontinoi in the *last* decade of the seventh century, as recorded in Polyaenus, v.47). A line may arbitrarily be drawn right through the middle of this region, stretching from the watercourses flowing in a north-south direction, in the hilly landscape west of Leontinoi, to the river Porcaria (probably the ancient Pantakyas). The latter watercourse is presumed to be roughly the line of separation, proceeding in the direction of the coast, because of Leontinoi's seemingly hostile reaction to the Megarians' first landing in Sicily at Trotilon above the river Pantakyas. Geography and the actions of Syracuse and Leontinoi thus enclosed Megara Hyblaia's territory in a sort of "pincer movement" (a situation illustrated by Drögemüller 1969, 39, fig. 7; *cf.* also Procelli 1989, 687).

Having laid out the probable south and north boundaries of Megara Hyblaia's territory, what about its western limit? We know that the territory had extended westwards at least as far as Melilli by the mid-seventh century, for stone was being quarried from here for use in the settlement (Vallet *et al.* 1976, 248–249). The greatest western extent of the territory cannot have continued beyond the Heraian hills. Thus Styella, the *polis'* outpost, which existed in at least the early fifth century, ought to be situated somewhere around here, perhaps at Pedaggagi

*Fig. 6.3 The topography of the landscape due west (c. 8 km.) of Megara Hyblaia; modern industry is visible along the coast.*

(Fig. 6.2), in an area undoubtedly belonging to Megara Hyblaia well before that date (Bernabò Brea 1968, 178–185 has illuminated this complex problem). There are two other points which could possibly suggest that this furthest extremity of the territory was in Megarian hands from an earlier date. The first is Bernabò Brea's (1968, 178) enticing theory that the Megarians ultimately inherited a good part of the kindgom of the Sikel king Hyblon with its capital probably at Pantalica (the inheritance would probably have been accomplished by the middle of the seventh century; see below), and, secondly, the Heraian hills may have been exploited for economic purposes at such an early date as well (De Angelis, in progress, ch. 5). Yet even without expounding this extra information – for both need additional research to be properly substantiated – it is clear that, at its greatest extent, Megara Hyblaia's territory measured something to the order of 20 km. by 20 km. (enclosing thereby an area of 400 km.²).[7] To all appearances the territory had attained this maximum size in the course of the seventh century. There is no good reason why Megara Hyblaia could not have gained access to this whole area within decades of its foundation; archaeology, history, and geography make this assertion reasonably certain.

The natural environment within these defined limits also requires comment. The bulk of south-east Sicily consists of Miocene limestone terraces. In the northern part of this vast area, the Miocene limestone is intercalated with and overlain by dark basaltic ash and lava of the same geological age. This volcanic stone forms the geological base of the area stretching from

*Fig. 6.4  A portion of Megara Hyblaia's territory around Villasmundo.*

Militello and Francofonte, in what was the territory of Leontinoi, to Sortino and Melilli, in
what was the territory of Megara Hyblaia (Vallet *et al.* 1976, 249). The limestone terraces
gradually descend to the sea as successive steps (Fig. 6.3). Most of the land in Megara
Hyblaia's territory is well under 600 m., with the 300–400 m. range being quite common
inland (Fig. 6.4). Along the coast the plains are long and rather narrow. The amount of arable
land potentially available would have been high given the nature of the topography, and it
would not be unreasonable to put that level at sixty percent (60%). This figure is derived from
information contained in the geographical handbook of the Admiralty Naval Intelligence
Division (1944–45, iii.30, fig. 7), Pollastri's (1948–49, i.198–200) extremely detailed post-WW
II assessment of the agricultural possibilities of Sicily, and the land-use survey published over
a decade after the appearance of Pollastri's work (Antonietti & Vanzetti 1961, 81, table 45).
These sources leave little doubt as to the general validity of the present estimate. The question
of soils is rather more difficult to assess, and I am hesitant to make other than general
statements concerning this aspect of the palaeoenvironment in view of the recent sophistication
of environmental archaeology. It is at least safe to say, however, that Megara Hyblaia's soils
were probably not wildly different from those of its neighbours because of the same climatic
conditions and parent material lying beneath the soils themselves. The fertile soils derived
from the volcanic rocks mentioned above would have been the same fertile soils that made
Leontinoi proverbially wealthy in antiquity. In more recent times, the lands of Megara

Hyblaia's former territory have been highly recommended for cereals, vines, olives, and fruit trees (Pollastri 1948–49, i.52), and there is no reason to think that it would have been otherwise in antiquity. There were also numerous watercourses, both on the surface and below, flowing throughout the land (the needs of modern industry have radically altered the ancient picture, *cf.* Vallet & Voza 1984, 27–28). On the plausible assumption that climate has not changed drastically since antiquity, rainfall would also have abundant and spread throughout the year at crucial moments of the growing season (Vallet & Voza 1984, 26).

It seems, therefore, that the environmental conditions necessary for agricultural success were not lacking in Megara Hyblaia's territory.

## III. THE CARRYING CAPACITY AND CARRIED CAPACITY OF MEGARA HYBLAIA'S TERRITORY

With some idea of the size and nature of Megara Hyblaia's territory, we must now turn our attention to calculating the agricultural productive capacity of the land, and then set this level against the needs of the community, to see whether overpopulation was really the problem.

### III.1. The Agricultural Capacity of the Territory
In gauging the number of people Megara Hyblaia's territory could have sustained, there are two types of calculations that can be made. The first is an older method and involves using wheat yields alone; the second, more recent calculations, on the other hand, take a wider view of the ancient diet. Both sets of calculations are useful theoretical tools which in no way profess to describe an actual situation at any one given time. Combination of these two sets of calculations will supply a rough idea of how many people could have been supported from the natural conditions just discussed.

### A. The First Set of Calculations
An interesting discussion on which to model the present one is that of Figueira (1981, 22–64) for the island of Aegina. According to Figueira's calculations, the island could only support some 4,000 people from its own resources, yet the estimated population of the *polis* in late archaic and early classical times approached 40,000 people (Figueira 1981, 26, 29–43). Thus, in order to meet basic subsistence requirements, huge amounts of grain had to be imported, though Aegina, as one of ancient Greece's foremost trading states, was in a position to make up the shortfall. The soundness of Figueira's basic framework is not in question, but there are two points which need to be briefly raised as a result of recent developments in the study of ancient Greek agriculture. First, doubts have been cast on whether biennial fallow – which Figueira (1981, 25) factored into his calculations – was as widely practised in antiquity as commonly accepted (Halstead 1987, 81–83; Garnsey 1988, 93–94; Gallant 1991, 52–56). As usage of the practice cannot be verified in the case of Megara Hyblaia, it is assumed to have taken place (it so happens that this assumption merely adds greater effect to the conclusions below). Secondly, Figueira (1981, 25) used 250 kg. of wheat as the annual quantity of consumption per person; however, this figure could be lowered to as much as 212 or 230 kg. in light of recent work which suggests a lower consumption level (Foxhall & Forbes 1982, 71; Gallant 1991, 67–68). The middle ground, that is 230 kg., is used here. What results are

obtained using the skeleton of Figueira's model?

About 60%, or 240 km.$^2$ (24,000 ha.), of Megara Hyblaia's territory consisted of arable land (Fig. 6.5). One-half, or 120 km.$^2$ (12,000 ha.), would probably have lain fallow in a year, with the other half put under cultivation. These 12,000 hectares could each have grown a maximum of 0.624 tonnes of grain, thus producing a total of 7,488 tonnes per annum. Of this total production (7,488 tonnes), one-fifth, or 1,497.6 tonnes, would have been set aside for the following year's seed, leaving 5,990.4 tonnes for consumption. From this amount we may immediately subtract 15%, or 898.56 tonnes, as waste, which leaves a consumable output of 5091.84 tonnes (or 5,091,840 kg.). Dividing the consumable output (5,091,840 kg.) by the figure for biological subsistence (230 kg. per person per annum) yields just over 22,000 as the number of people sustainable by Megara Hyblaia's territory, if pushed to its limit (as will become evident below, there is no need to make similar calculations using barley which produces higher yields).

### B. The Second Set of Calculations

A second, perhaps slightly more realistic way to proceed is not by cereals alone, since, although they made up anywhere between two-thirds and three-quarters of the ancient Greek diet (Gallant 1991, 68), it may be argued with reason that cereals, let alone wheat, are not wholly representative. Recent estimates suggest that a household of five would have required, during its lifecycle, somewhere between three and four hectares of land for subsistence (Osborne 1987, 46; Gallant 1991, 82). If we again assume that half the land was left fallow each year, we have 12,000 hectares of land for cultivation. At three to four hectares per household of five, Megara Hyblaia's territory could thus have supported 15,000–20,000 people.[9] This second set of calculations produces figures only slightly lower than the first.

### III.2. How many mouths to feed? Population and subsistence needs

Putting aside these production capacity figures for a moment, we must next address the question of community size and its dietary requirements. An estimate of Megara Hyblaia's population in the third quarter of the seventh century may be derived from settlement data alone: the number of early tombs presently known from the site is clearly not representative enough to be incorporated into the discussion (on the oldest tombs: Cébeillac-Gervasoni 1976–77, 589–590; for the number of archaic tombs, 1,500 in total: Gras 1985, 571). Fortunately, the settlement evidence is of quality high by any standard and of quantity largely unparalleled elsewhere (Vallet *et al.* 1976; *cf.* also Holloway 1991, 50–53). A nice selection of houses, built in stone from the first generation owing to the abundance of this material (Vallet & Voza 1984, 23–24), is available for the period of time of direct concern here. If all these houses are tallied up, by chronological period, and each assigned an estimated population, the result is at least 130–160 people by the third quarter of the seventh century (Table 6.1).[10] This figure, of course, cannot be taken literally as the population of Megara Hyblaia at this time because the houses uncovered come from an excavated area of about 2.25 hectares (Gras 1984–85, 802), and there are 61 hectares enclosed within the archaic city wall (Orsi & Cavallari 1890, 694 and note 3, 742; Vallet 1990, 18).[11] Needless to say, not all of these 61 hectares were given over to domestic use; public and religious architecture, streets

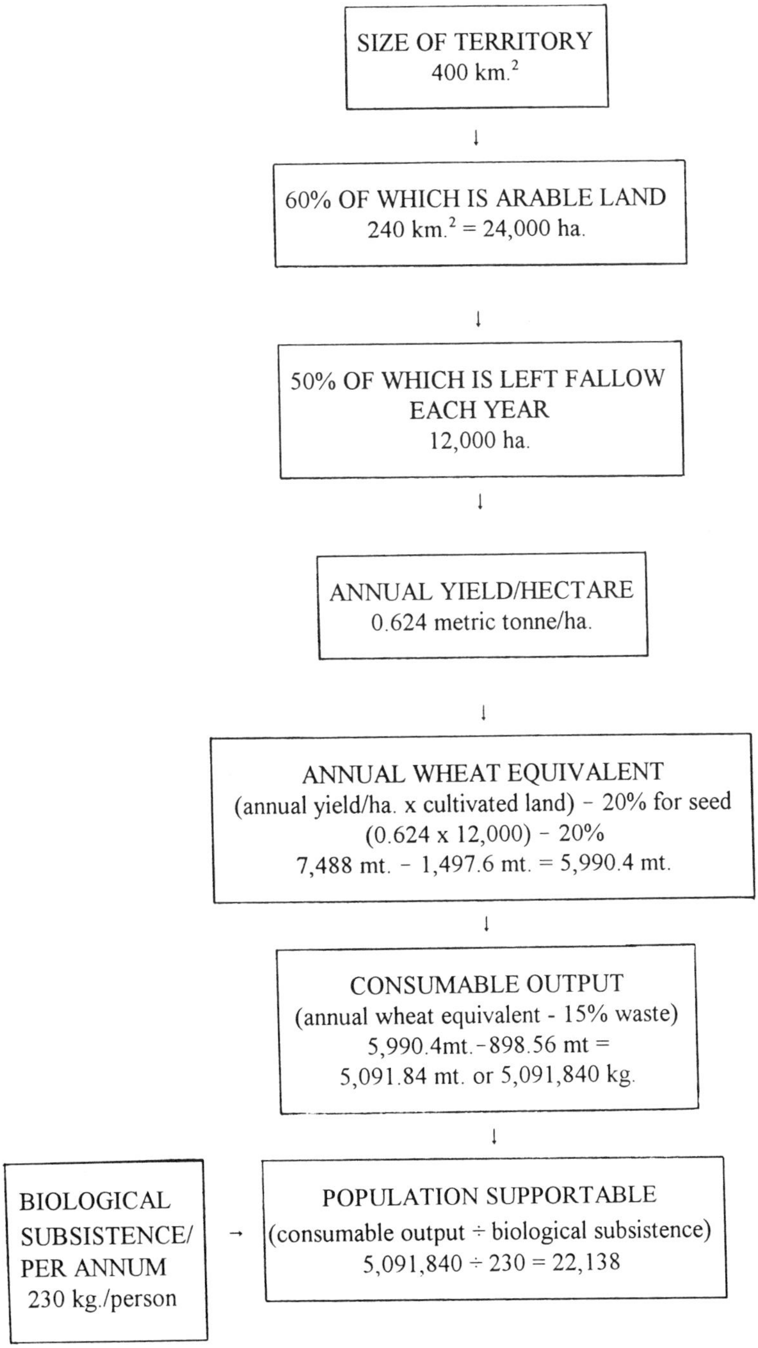

SIZE OF TERRITORY
400 km.$^2$

↓

60% OF WHICH IS ARABLE LAND
240 km.$^2$ = 24,000 ha.

↓

50% OF WHICH IS LEFT FALLOW
EACH YEAR
12,000 ha.

↓

ANNUAL YIELD/HECTARE
0.624 metric tonne/ha.

↓

ANNUAL WHEAT EQUIVALENT
(annual yield/ha. x cultivated land) – 20% for seed
(0.624 x 12,000) – 20%
7,488 mt. – 1,497.6 mt. = 5,990.4 mt.

↓

CONSUMABLE OUTPUT
(annual wheat equivalent - 15% waste)
5,990.4mt. – 898.56 mt =
5,091.84 mt. or 5,091,840 kg.

↓

BIOLOGICAL
SUBSISTENCE/
PER ANNUM
230 kg./person    →

POPULATION SUPPORTABLE
(consumable output ÷ biological subsistence)
5,091,840 ÷ 230 = 22,138

*Fig. 6.5 The agricultural capacity of Megara Hyblaia's territory (the first set of calculations).*

| DATE | NUMBER OF HOUSES | NUMBER OF POSSIBLE HOUSES | ESTIMATED POPULATION/UNIT | TOTAL ESTIMATED POPULATION |
|---|---|---|---|---|
| 1. 725-700 | 10 | 3 | 2 | 22  (+6)* |
| 2. 700-675 | 3 + 2 renovations | nil | 4 (2 per renovation) | 16  (+0) |
| 3. 675-650 | 5 | nil | 4 | 20  (+0) |
| 4. 700-650 | 10 + 3 renovations | 4 | 4 (2 per renovation) | 46  (+16) |
| 5. 650-625 | 1 + 1 renovation | 1 | 4 (2 per renovation) | 6  (+4) |
| 6. 625-600 | 12 | nil | 4 | 48  (+0) |
| 7. 650-600 | 6 + 3 renovations | 2 | 4 (2 per renovation) | 26  (+8) |
| 8. 700-600 | 2 | nil | 4 | 8  (+0) |

TOTAL: 172 (+34)*

*Table 6.1   The number of archaic houses (725–600 BC), by period, at Megara Hyblaia and their estimated population.  \*Number in parenthesis obtained by multiplying figure of number of houses (column 3) by that of estimated population/unit (column 4) to arrive at a potential population for each period; the figure 34 is the sum of these numbers.*

and other open spaces, and the agora also shared the intra-mural space.[12] At most between 30 and 40 hectares could ever have been used for habitation (De Angelis, in progress, ch. 2).[13] From the excavated area the people per hectare density observable there may be multiplied by the 30–40 hectare range to get an overall picture of population (Table 6.2).[14] At the time of Selinous' foundation, therefore, the *polis* centre of Megara Hyblaia was home to around 2,000 people, or, put in other terms, say 400 families at five people per household. Before this estimate can be accepted as final, the question of whether there were any people resident outside the city walls, in the territory of Megara Hyblaia, needs to be addressed.

The information relevant to answering such a question derives from excavations and surface reconnaissance carried out as part of various projects of exploration over the past century or so (as is generally the case in Sicily, no modern survey archaeology has ever been applied to the surrounding countryside). The most obvious place to start is with the natives who were living inside what was to be Megara Hyblaia's territory at the time of initial Megarian settlement. All material trace of these natives disappears from the countryside well before the time of Selinous' foundation (Vallet & Voza 1984, 57; a similar pattern has been noted for the native sites around nearby Leontinoi: Procelli 1989, 682). I am prepared to see some natives amongst the 2,000 people estimated for Megara Hyblaia's population (De Angelis, in progress, ch. 4; Domínguez 1989, 268–273 reaches the same conclusion, though by a different route; see also the "Excursus" below). Two other possible situations could account for dwindling native numbers. Some natives may have been enslaved by Syracuse to work that colony's lands, or some may have gone further inland to live with fellow natives, for the time being out of the grasp of Greeks. Whatever the case, there is no sign of natives sharing

| DATE | PEOPLE PER HECTARE | SETTLEMENT SIZE IN HECTARES | TOTAL ESTIMATED POPULATION |
|---|---|---|---|
| 1. 725-700 BC | 8 | 30-40 | 240-320* |
| 2. 700-675 BC | 28 | 30-40 | 840-1,120 |
| 3. 675-650 BC | 48 | 30-40 | 1,440-1,920 |
| 4. 650-625 BC | 57 | 30-40 | 1,710-2,280 |

*Table 6.2  Population estimates for Megara Hyblaia (725-625 BC). *The number in column 2 is multiplied by both those in column 3 to arrive at an estimated population range.*

Megara Hyblaia's territory; any one, or all, of the three possibilities suggested could easily explain the lack of native presence in the countryside. As to the Megarians, nothing indicates that they had set up a settlement of any kind outside the *polis* centre at this early date. Although farmers must surely have moved out to their fields on a seasonal basis at harvest time, it seems legitimate to conclude that not many more of Megara Hyblaia's citizens were living outside the nucleated settlement in the third quarter of the seventh century. We may thus take the above population estimate as being on the whole representative. Having made these remarks, what is the verdict regarding overpopulation?

On the first of the two calculations made above, Megara Hyblaia's territory could have sustained a little more than 22,000 people, and there were 2,000 or so mouths to feed; thus the overpopulation theory cannot stand. Much the same conclusion applies to the second calculations as well. A family of five needed between three and four hectares of land for subsistence. At 2,000 people, or 400 families, the Megarians would have used 1,200–1,600 hectares of land per annum for subsistence purposes around the time of Selinous' foundation, whereas 12,000 hectares of land were available, assuming another 12,000 hectares as laying fallow each year. In both calculations, Megara Hyblaia was using a fraction, say 10–15%, of the land it had at its disposal. The only conclusion that emerges, therefore, is that Megara Hyblaia was not suffering from overpopulation when the decision to found Selinous was made. Even if we arbitrarily cut the size of the territory in half, on the grounds that its full, later extent had not yet been consolidated at the time of Selinous' foundation, or on the grounds that only land of one to two hours' travel was exploited, and double, even triple, the estimated population, to make ample allowance for any miscalculations caused by blanks in the archaeological record, the same conclusion imposes itself: the Megarians could supply themselves with more than the "basic necessities" from the surrounding countryside. The distance between population size and land available is not close enough to warrant the term overpopulation.

*Excursus: land tenure at early Megara Hyblaia*
Much attention has been given above to the quantity of land available. In a discussion on overpopulation, something must be said about the nature of land ownership. For it could

rightly be objected that, despite the theoretical availability of land, this land may have been in the hands of a small group of colonial families, similar to the oligarchic regime of the *gamoroi* from nearby Syracuse. According to such a line of reasoning, a minority of rich landowners controlled the land, provoking the unprivileged to establish Selinous to acquire their own. Any argument to this effect is untenable, however. One of the most fascinating aspects of the early history of Megara Hyblaia revealed by the French excavations is the division of space which dates to the beginning of the colony; land was set aside for domestic, public, and religious use (Fig. 6.6). In this division of space the colonists, it seems, were each allotted a plot of land on which to build a house.[15] The substantial increase in population at Megara Hyblaia during the first half of the seventh century (see Table 6.2), which is probably in large part to be explained as the outcome of an influx of new settlers (De Angelis, in progress, ch. 4), witnessed the erection of more houses on other plots of land. It seems safe enough to infer that all the colonists, old and new, received an allotment of land in the town. In the *polis* the town could not have existed without the surrounding countryside, and, in order for both town and country to function as a unit, rural land division was also necessary. The best documented and oldest evidence for such rural land division comes from the archaic Greek colony of Metapontion in southern Italy, where actual traces have been found on the ground (see Carter 1990, 403 notes 3 & 4 for bibliography). The lack of similar evidence from Megara Hyblaia need not be distressing. As Boyd and Jameson (1981, 327) point out, "When it comes to the archaeological record the regular division of urban land for houses is conspicuous but in the Greek world only exceptionally does the countryside reveal its patterns. Nevertheless the link between the two is fundamental, and for both the same techniques of surveying and geometry would have been used." It is beyond dispute that the countryside around Megara Hyblaia was also partitioned in much the same way as is evident in the city (Vallet & Voza 1984, 58), thus also implying that the apparent, widespread personal ownership of land extended to there too at the time of Selinous' foundation. It seems doubtful, therefore, that land tenure could have been a problem which precipitated the foundation of Selinous; the "aristocracy of first settlers" principle appears not to have been in operation at Megara Hyblaia (Sartori [1980–81, 265–266] is thus probably not completely correct in stating that archaeology has revealed nothing of Megara Hyblaia's constitution). Consideration of some noteworthy internal matters at both Megara Hyblaia and Selinous strengthens this view.

## IV. SOME SUGGESTIVE INTERNAL DEVELOPMENTS AT MEGARA HYBLAIA AND SELINOUS

The foregoing case has shown the overpopulation argument advanced by some scholars to explain Selinous' foundation to be an ungrounded assumption. What, then, can be put in place of overpopulation as the reason(s) for Megara Hyblaia's colonising activity? An internal look highlighting developments at both Megara Hyblaia and Selinous suggests a possible context for the latter's foundation.

*IV.1. The Transformation of Megara Hyblaia: the* polis *materialises*
Besides the establishment of a sub-colony, the history of Megara Hyblaia in the third quarter of the seventh century witnessed another event of equal importance. At the very period to

which the ancient sources ascribe the foundation of Selinous, archaeology overwhelmingly indicates that Megara Hyblaia itself, the metropolis, was undertaking extensive building activity which was to transform the appearance of the city forever. As mentioned earlier, the division of newly acquired lands for different purposes was a major concern of the first-generation colonists; to facilitate the physical growth of the city, areas destined for domestic, public, and religious use had first to be delineated. Although it is certain that all these categories of space had been defined, in some shape or form, from the start, material signs of only domestic use initially appear, public and religious architecture being conspicuously absent. For roughly the first three generations of its existence, Megara Hyblaia consisted of houses with empty spaces between them and so resembled in appearance a large rural village. Beginning around 650, and continuing in archaeological terms for the next half-century, Megara Hyblaia was busy building.

No fewer than five monuments can be precisely dated to the crucial quarter-century (650–625) singled out earlier (Fig. 6.6). Two of these five monuments were small temples; one, of which only five blocks in two courses survive, was built in the south-east part of the agora (Vallet *et al.* 1976, 222–224). The other temple, it too in a bad state of preservation, was discovered north of the agora in block 16 (Vallet *et al.* 1976, 231–232). The remaining three monuments, all of them built in the agora area, are classifiable under the rubric of public architecture. A stoa marked off the northern limit of the agora (Vallet *et al.* 1976, 213). To the west of this stoa, a building, labelled a heroon by the excavators, stood at the north-west corner of the agora at the intersection of streets A and C1 (Vallet *et al.* 1976, 209–211; Bergquist 1992, 141–143 has recently expressed doubts concerning the heroon identification). The last of the public buildings, possibly the city's *bouleuterion* (so Gullini 1978, 433), is also datable to this period; it occupied the whole of block 10 in the south-west area of the agora (Vallet *et al.* 1976, 168–183, 188–193). In the following quarter-century (625–600) a second stoa and a third temple were built (Vallet *et al.* 1976, 218–220, 227–228), and to the 650–600 half-century, a period so defined because of insufficient diagnostic dating material, belong possibly another public building and yet another temple in block 17 (Vallet *et al.* 1976, 195, 239). There is also plenty of clear evidence indicating that the streets received kerb-stones which now materially defined them (Vallet *et al.* 1976, 351–365).

The mid-seventh century at Megara Hyblaia represents, therefore, a remarkable turning-point in the site's architectural history. Public and religious buildings made their first appearance, and other architectural additions were also made. Although building at Megara Hyblaia was to continue until the last decades of the *polis'* existence, it was not at all on the same scale as this first flurry of activity, which provided the backbone of the city's urban framework. The archaeological evidence abundantly proves that much time and effort was being invested in Megara Hyblaia when the decision to set up new life elsewhere on the island was made; civic pride and identity, manifesting itself in physical form, coincided with the foundation of Selinous.[16] The *polis* of Megara Hyblaia had clearly materialised in more than one sense of the word.[17]

## IV.2. The Big Thinker in the West: early Selinous

The actions of Selinous at the other end of Sicily may also yield insightful clues in establishing the intention of the sub-colony. Archaeology has shown that the evidence of seventh-century Megarian settlement at Selinous is spread over a very large area indeed; in fact, at Selinous' height in the fifth century, the city had grown to the size specified by its first settlers (Parisi Presicce 1984, 26; Di Vita 1990, 353). The area contained within the sanctuary of Demeter Malophoros in the west, temple E in the east, and the Manuzza hill in the north was taken control of already by the last quarter of the seventh century. As we have seen, the claiming of large tracts of the Sicilian landscape by Greek colonists was quite commonplace, but the two monuments just mentioned raise another issue. Early versions of the sanctuary of Demeter Malophoros and temple E, as well as some of the temples on the acropolis, were originally built in the last quarter of the seventh century (Parisi Presicce 1984, 25; Bergquist 1992, 119–120); the quick appearance of such monuments – with others following on their heels soon after – at this date may be regarded as a clear indication of the priorities of the first generation of Megarian colonists. The colonists' concern was to make their presence felt in this new homeland.

Selinous' ambitious activity in the *polis* centre was also paralleled in the countryside. Here, too, archaeology has thrown light on Selinous' big thinking. The discovery near Poggioreale in the 1950s of a dedication to Herakles, inscribed in the Selinountine alphabet, has been of utmost interest (Piraino 1959). On the basis of both the stele's letter-forms and the archaeological context in which it was found, the inscription is dated to the first half of the sixth century (Piraino 1959, 160–161). Additional archaeological investigations were encouraged by this find, and these have securely established Selinous' presence, in addition to the cult-place indicated by the inscription, in this area by the end of the seventh century (V. Tusa 1979, 49; Falsone & Leonard 1980–81, 937; *cf.* also de Polignac 1984, 95, 103; Domínguez 1989, 400–403). Thus, within decades of its foundation (just how many decades depends on the foundation-date accepted), Selinous had moved up the Belice Valley to around Poggioreale, that is, some 25–30 km. from the coast. Throughout its history Selinous continued to exhibit a preoccupation with territorial expansion and with maintaining its territorial integrity (de la Genière 1977, 255, 259, 264), gradually amassing a territory four to five times larger than that of its mother-city (Fig. 6.7; on the size of this territory, see Vallet 1990, 131).

## V. CONCLUSION

Why did Megara Hyblaia feel the need to colonise in the third quarter of the seventh century? The archaeology of that site makes overpopulation an unsatisfactory response to the question posed, for several reasons. At its greatest extent Megara Hyblaia's territory consisted of some 400 km.[2] of land, and there is every reason to believe that this maximum had more or less been attained by the end of the seventh century. The environmental conditions present in the exploitation area were no doubt highly amenable to agriculture, so excluding the possibility of colonisation being the result of any deficiency of nature. At the time of Selinous' foundation, approximately 2,000 people made their livelihood from this territory, there being considerably more land available for subsistence purposes than actually required by the community. We may confidently posit, moreover, that the division of land for domestic, public, and religious purposes clearly visible in Megara Hyblaia's *polis* centre also took place

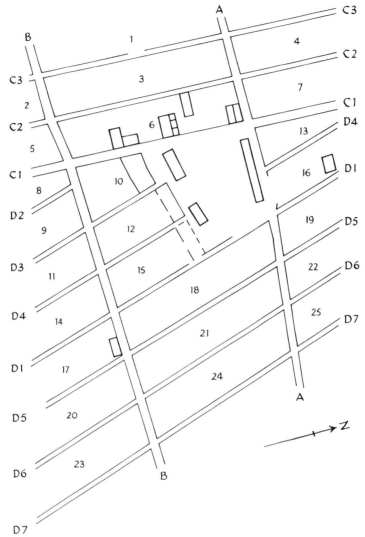

*Fig. 6.6  Plan of the area of the agora at Megara Hyblaia (after Vallet et al. 1976, fig. 57).*

in the countryside. By implication such a land distribution scheme would have guaranteed each family a plot of land outside the city on which to subsist. In view of these points it seems rather unlikely, therefore, that overpopulation was a pressing problem at Megara Hyblaia. The answer to the above question should be sought, rather, in the larger context of early colonial developments in Sicily.

   The settlement of Sicily by Greeks, it must be recalled, was achieved by four groups. The first colonies were established on the east coast by Chalcis, Corinth, and Megara in that order. Ancient tradition maintains that the Megarians encountered several obstacles in finding a place to settle, difficulties doubtless attributable to the fact that they had come last to a world largely controlled by other Greeks who were willing to fight, if necessary, to get their way. With so little room to manoeuvre, the Megarians accepted the land given to them by the native king Hyblon, and there, like their Greek neighbours, the Megarians attended to the urgent tasks of setting up life in a new world. A few generations later, the young Greek cities of Sicily once again became colonisers, sending out sub-colonies to different parts of the island. As part of this sub-colonising fervour, Megara Hyblaia struck out with Selinous to south-western Sicily, almost certainly the only area of the island unclaimed.[18] The urge to colonise came to Megara Hyblaia when the *polis* was enjoying a period of prosperity and a sense of community spirit, as the building programmes strongly suggest. In this moment of glory also came the realisation that, under present conditions, there were severe limitations to such success. Hemmed in between Syracuse and Leontinoi, Megara Hyblaia wanted more room, but simply could not have it in eastern Sicily: it was by then clear who the big controllers of land in this part of the island were destined to be, and Megara Hyblaia was not counted amongst them. Thus Selinous was founded mainly to acquire land, the main source of wealth and power in antiquity (Ste. Croix 1981, 120–133), to give the Megarians of Sicily a bigger rôle on the island, an opportunity not afforded to them in the first wave of colonisation (though never really spelled out, a by no means novel conclusion: Vallet *et al.* 1983, 150; Parisi Presicce 1984, 42). This desire seems to receive confirmation from Selinous' early and persistent preoccupation with expansion; never again were the Megarians allowing the territorial ambitions of others to get the better of them. The early appearance and especially later size of Selinous' monuments were also appropriate symbols of the big player status.

But what of other possible motives in founding Selinous? For instance, what about political unrest at Megara Hyblaia as a reason? Any such tension, at least on a very widespread scale, seems improbable in view of the collective well-being required for the extensive building and community actions operative at both Megara Hyblaia and Selinous at the time of, and after, the latter's foundation. Nor is there any hint in the archaeological and historical record of the period of such tension (De Angelis, in progress, ch. 4). What of trade, the antithesis to overpopulation in modern estimates of the causes of Greek colonisation? The foundation of Selinous *solely* for motives of trade appears doubtful, as some scholars have pointed out (de la Genière 1977, 255–256; Graham 1982b, 167; *cf.* also de la Genière 1978, 41–42). At the same time, however, the establishment of a sub-colony in south-western Sicily in close proximity to the Phoenicians, who largely traded for a living, and the native Elymians, who showed themselves, especially in later centuries (as in the case of Segesta), to be very receptive to Greek culture, placed the Megarians in an admirable position for additional economic success. If this idea of extra economic security is to be translated into the concept of trade, only then may we speak of trade as one of the Megarians' motives. The subject of trade also raises the question of the early prosperity of Selinous, a subject which has naturally attracted attention because of the site's monuments. The massive temple building at Selinous is unparalleled at Megara Hyblaia and at Megarian colonies elsewhere. If we work back from Selinous' rapid growth to its foundation, in order to search for any clues of the colonists' motives, the accumulation of a vast territory and the geographical positioning of the colony (perhaps in part imposed on the Megarians by the colonising activities of others) did indeed

*Fig. 6.7: The countryside around Herakleia Minoa, sub-colony of Selinous, looking in the direction of Selinous (too far out of sight), showing both nature and immensity of the territory.*

guarantee Selinous its success, but it is difficult to assign this ascendancy to a more precise origin.[19]

What this brief digression touching on other reasons for Selinous' foundation should make obvious is the complexity of sorting out in exact terms, from archaeological evidence alone, the primary from the secondary motives in colonisation, in so far as such a distinction is to begin with permissible. Although archaeology may furnish valuable clues of the internal workings of a society, it can, unfortunately, never replace – in the archaic period of Greek history where it is needed most – the individual thoughts and intentions that crossed the minds of those making the decision to colonise. I thus prefer, following the lead of various scholars over the past few decades (earlier references to be found in: de la Genière 1977, 252; de Polignac 1984, 94), to see the basic aim of Greek sub-colonisation in Sicily as being a "process of acquistion," involving the conquest of new lands and all the possibilities embedded in them.[20] In this reconstruction overpopulation finds no place. To come back to Gwynn, quoted at the outset, colonisation did indeed fulfil "a need for expansion", but the "healthy conditions" referred to by him need not only be brought into connection with overpopulation. In the third quarter of the seventh century, for instance, colonisation allowed the Megarians to take advantage of opportunities which initial settlement on the east coast did not completely satisfy and which, sooner or later, would have been seized by others, in the ever-growing competitive world of early Greek Sicily. "To colonize was, for the most part, a sign of vitality" (Figueira 1985, 275).

## ACKNOWLEDGEMENTS

I am most grateful to Dr R. G. Osborne, Prof. J. N. Coldstream, and Dr N. Spencer for their advice and comments on earlier drafts of this paper; their insights have greatly enriched the final product. Thanks are also due to the late Prof. G. Vallet, who kindly answered queries by letter and generously sent a copy of his joint monograph on the territory of Megara Hyblaia (Vallet & Voza 1984) in the months prior to his death. The final word of gratitude goes to Prof. J. Boardman.

## NOTES

1. A range of the angles from which the overpopulation theory has been attacked is as follows: Holloway (1981, 143–145): influenced by anthropological arguments ultimately derived from Esther Boserup's work (*cf.* Trigger 1989, 305, 320–321); Garnsey (1988, 113–114): discussing famine and food supply; Purcell (1990, 45–46): in a discussion on mobility, pointing out the demographic unlikelihood of overpopulation; Cawkwell (1992): re-examination of the demographic arguments, suggesting instead that climatic catastrophe was behind colonisation; Rihll (1993): emphasising colonisation as acquisition; Fossey (forthcoming): re-examines parts of Gwynn's article and looks at overpopulation in light of settlement data from Greece itself. No longer can the overpopulation theory, without some form of modification, maintain its previous, unassailable position in the face of such criticisms. Only Ruschenbusch (1991) has upheld the old view in recent times.

2. On the spatial dimensions of the West, Gras (1985, 414) sums it up correctly in his discussion of Phocaean population and colonisation: "L'Occident c'est, pour les Grecs, une autre notion de l'espace." Mertens (1990, 377), moreover, in a general discussion on colonial architecture, speaks of the "unrestricted availability of space." There is little doubt that the demographic element of early colonies was small (Di Vita [1990, 348] states the widely accepted view that no more than a few hundred were involved). The recent population estimates from Pithekoussai, however, are the exception (*cf.* Ridgway 1992, 101–103).

3. Berger is surely following the opinion of his illustrious mentor Asheri (1980, 113) who, while apparently accepting the size of the territory as set out in this work, nevertheless believes that overpopulation incited the Megarians to found Selinous. The overpopulation view is also shared by Faure (1978, 306, *cf.* also 48–49) and Domínguez (1989, 107, *cf.* also 363), with similar sentiments strongly implied by Waters (1974, 1, 7). For a view of the cause of Selinous' foundation prior to the appearance of Gwynn's (1918) article, see Orsi and Cavallari (1890, 695).

4. Polyaenus (v.5.1) defines closer this period of co-habitation as six months. In Polyaenus' amplified version of the story, the Megarians are asked to drive out the Sikels who also happened to be living at Leontinoi, since the Chalcidians could not themselves do so being bound by previous oaths.

5. This date is derived from Thucydides' statement that Megara Hyblaia survived for 245 years before being destroyed by Gelon of Syracuse. We must then turn to Herodotus (vii.156) to extrapolate the date of this destruction, and 483/2 is the most probable one; adding 245 years to the likely date of destruction yields an initial foundation-date of 728/7 (*cf.* Dunbabin 1948, 435)

6. In the first quarter of the sixth century Gela, too, became a sub-coloniser in Sicily, founding Akragas on the south coast roughly halfway between the mother-city and Selinous (*cf.* Boardman 1980, 187–188; Wilson 1982, 96–97; 1988, 126–128). The foundation of Akragas effectively brought to an end Greek colonisation in Sicily.

7. It is interesting to note that Megaris of Old Greece only had a slightly larger territory at 470 km.$^2$ (Legon 1981, 22).

8. The figure adopted (230 kg.) makes no distinction between adults and children, though the latter, of course, will have consumed less (*cf.* Gallant 1991, 62–75).

9. That is: 12,000 hectares of land ÷ 3 to 4 hectares of land per household = 4,000 to 3,000 "subsistence plots". We then multiply 3,000 to 4,000 "subsistence plots" by 5 people per plot, which yields 15,000 to 20,000 people supportable.

10. The population estimates of Table 6.1 are calculated in the following way. The 46 people of line 4 (700–650) were evenly distributed (*i.e.*, 23 each) to the two quarter-century phases within this fifty-year period. The same is done with the 26 people of line 7 (650–600), though in this case, of course, 13 people were assigned to each of the two quarter-century phases encompassed by this last fifty-year period. Then the 8 people of line 8 (700–600) were also evenly distributed (thus 2 each) to all four of the quarter-century phases within this one-hundred-year period. The "weighing" carried out on lines 4, 7, and 8 is perhaps the fairest and truest way of dealing with these data.

11. In the early seventh century, the city's cemeteries began to ring the site just outside the later city wall (itself built in the late sixth century), making it impossible for settlement to extend beyond these 61 hectares (*cf.* Cébeillac-Gervasoni 1975).

12. The recent archaeological attention given by Italian and Sicilian scholars to retrieving the earliest town plans of the Greek colonies has made it clear that intra-mural settlement was usually not very dense; rather, the *poleis* of this new world had a certain "garden city" (Murray 1993, 114) look to them.

13. Admittedly, we are being rather simplistic in saying that domestic settlement at Megara Hyblaia covered 30–40 hectares, but what we are aiming at is an absolute maximum. It is obvious, moreover, that Megara Hyblaia's city wall was big in comparision with its actual level of population (De Angelis, in progress, ch. 2).

14. The people per hectare densities of Table 6.2, based on the agora sample, should be seen only as close approximations which may legitimately be extended to the rest of the site. There is little use in quibbling about precision when it does not affect the overall argument.

15. The individual plots may initially have been equal in size, but the evidence is impressionistic. For the seventh century onwards, the French excavators believe that the lots of land were not all equal (Vallet *et al.* 1976, 302, 405). However, the evidence is admittedly meagre and on the whole ambiguous at that, and in any case plot sizes should not be judged merely by their dimensions, for external factors concealing any visible equality could be at work (see, for instance, Gras 1985, 414 for some possibilities).

16. Parisi Presicce's (1984, 57) unprovable idea that wealth of some kind acquired by the Megarians in western Sicily, before the foundation of Selinous, allowed this building activity to take place is unlikely because the initial appearance of major building programmes in the older colonies of the Greek west seems to have occurred, in the vast majority of cases, two or three generations after foundation.

17. If land was at a premium, as advocates of the overpopulation theory would have us believe, it is surely odd that the space taken up by the building programmes was not devoted to food production, certainly a more urgent matter to attend to in this crisis scenario.

18. It has often been wondered why the Megarians went so far to found their sub-colony. Part of the answer must be conditioned by the idea that central southern Sicily was already under the control of Gela (see, *e.g.*, Hulot & Fougères 1910, 76; Dunbabin 1948, 301; de la Genière 1977, 259–260). Although there is no unequivocal archaeological evidence to support the idea (Graham 1982b, 166), we must seriously entertain such a suggestion in view of Gela's early expansionistic ambitions, and the likelihood of its veracity has a knock-on effect on how we look at Megarian intentions in founding Selinous, such as questioning the spatial advantages the siting of the colony could bring to the trade argument (see below).

19. We must welcome the survey archaeology project of the territory of Selinous recently proposed by Marazzi and Tusa (1987, esp. 39–40) which has as one of its aims the intention of tackling, from an environmental viewpoint, the question of Selinous' rise to success. Such survey work would add a different, and indeed needed, dimension to the debate, whose parameters have remained relatively unchanged for quite a while (compare the picture which Hulot and Fougères [1910, 30–34] were able to formulate just after the turn of the century to that of today).

20. Although it has often been repeated that Sicily was for the ancients poor in mineral resources--so allowing us to dismiss the possibility that Selinous was founded for their exploitation – one must wonder whether the first colonists realised all the possibilities the landscape could contain. In this respect it might perhaps be better to speak in more general terms of the acquisition of natural resources as the settlers' aim.

## BIBLIOGRAPHY

ADMIRALTY NAVAL INTELLIGENCE DIVISION 1944–45: *Italy*, 4 vols. (*Geographical Handbook* B.R. 517, 517A–C; London).

ANTONIETTI, A. & VANZETTI, C. 1961: *Carta della utilizzazione del suolo d'Italia* (Milan, Feltrinelli).

ASHERI, D. 1980: La colonizzazione greca. In Gabba, E. & Vallet, G. (eds.), *La Sicilia antica, i/1. Indigeni, Fenici-Punici e Greci* (Naples, Società editrice storia di Napoli del Mezzogiorno continentale e della Sicilia), 89–142.

BÉRARD, J. 1960: *L'expansion et la colonisation grecques jusqu'aux guerres médiques* (Paris, Aubier).

BERGER, S. 1991: Great and Small Poleis in Sicily: Syracuse and Leontinoi. *Historia* 40, 129–142.

BERGQUIST, B. 1992: The Archaic Temenos in Western Greece: a survey and two inquiries. In Schachter, A. (ed.), *Le sanctuaire grec (Entretiens sur l'Antiquité Classique,* vol. 37; Geneva, Fondation Hardt), 109–152.

BERNABÒ BREA, L. 1957: *Sicily Before the Greeks* (London, Thames and Hudson).

BERNABÒ BREA, L. 1968: Il crepuscolo del re Hyblon: considerazioni sulla cronologia delle fondazioni di Leontinoi, Megara e Siracusa e sulla topografia della Megaride di Sicilia. *Parola del Passato* 23, 161–186.

BOARDMAN, J. 1980: *The Greeks Overseas*[3] (London, Thames and Hudson).

BOARDMAN, J. & HAMMOND, N. G. L. (eds.) 1982: *The Cambridge Ancient History*[2], iii/3: *the expansion of the Greek world, eighth to sixth centuries B.C.* (Cambridge, Cambridge U.P.).

BOYD, T. D. & JAMESON, M. H. 1981: Urban and Rural Land Division in Ancient Greece. *Hesperia* 50, 327–342.

CARTER, J. C. 1990: Metapontum – Land, Wealth, and Population. In Descoeudres 1990, 405-441.

CAWKWELL, G. L. 1992: Early Colonisation. *CQ* NS 42, 289–303.

CÉBEILLAC-GERVASONI, M. 1975: Les nécropoles de Mégara Hyblaea. *Kokalos* 21, 3–36.

CÉBEILLAC-GERVASONI, M. 1976–77: Une étude systématique sur les nécropoles de Mégara Hyblaea: l'example d'une partie de la nécropole méridionale. *Kokalos* 22–23, 587–597.

DE ANGELIS, F. in progress: The Evolution of Two Archaic Sicilian *Poleis*: Megara Hyblaia and Selinous (D. Phil. thesis, Oxford University).

DE LA GENIÈRE, J. 1977: Réflexions sur Sélinonte et l'Ouest sicilien. *CRAI* 251–264.

DE LA GENIÈRE, J. 1978: Ségeste et l'hellénisme. *MEFRA* 90, 33–49.

DESCOEUDRES, J.-P. (ed.) 1990: *Greek Colonists and Native Populations* (Oxford, Clarendon Press).

DI VITA, A. 1956: La penetrazione siracusana nella Sicilia sud-orientale alla luce delle più recenti scoperte archeologiche. *Kokalos* 2, 177–205.

DI VITA, A. 1990: Town Planning in the Greek Colonies of Sicily from the time of their Foundations to the Punic Wars. In Descoeudres 1990, 343–363.

DOMÍNGUEZ, A. J. 1989: *La Colonización Griega en Sicilia: Griegos, Indígenas y Púnicos en la Sicilia Arcaica: Interacción* (*BAR International Series* 549. i–ii; Oxford).

DRÖGEMÜLLER, H.-P. 1969: *Syrakus: zur Topographie und Geschichte einer griechischen Stadt* (*Gymnasium* Beiheft 6; Heidelberg).

DUNBABIN, T. J. 1948: *The Western Greeks: the history of Sicily and South Italy from the foundation of the Greek colonies to 480 B. C.* (Oxford, Clarendon Press).

FALSONE, G. & LEONARD, A. Jr. 1980–81: Quattro campagne di scavo a Castellazzo di Poggioreale. *Kokalos* 36–37, 931–972.

FAURE, P. 1978: *La vie quotidienne des colons grecs: de la Mer Noire à l'Atlantique au siècle de Pythagore VI^e siècle avant J.-C.* (Paris, Hachette).

FIGUEIRA, T. J. 1981: *Aegina: society and politics* (Salem, NH, Ayer).

FIGUEIRA, T. J. 1985: Chronological Table: archaic Megara, 800–500. In Figueira, T. J. & Nagy, G. (eds.), *Theognis of Megara: poetry and the* polis (Baltimore and London, The Johns Hopkins U.P.), 261–303.

FOSSEY, J. M. forthcoming: Some Parameters of Archaic Greek Emigration. Paper presented to the Sixth International Symposium on the Ancient History of the Black Sea Littoral, 22–29 September 1990 (Vani, Transcaucasian Georgia) (Paris).

FOXHALL, L. & FORBES, H. A. 1982: *Sitometreia:* the role of grain as a staple food in classical antiquity. *Chiron* 12, 41–90.

GALLANT, T. W. 1991: *Risk and Survival in Ancient Greece: reconstructing the rural domestic economy* (Cambridge, Polity Press).

GARNSEY, P. 1988: *Famine and Food Supply in the Graeco-Roman World: responses to risk and crisis* (Cambridge, Cambridge U.P.).

GRAHAM, A. J. 1982a: The Colonial Expansion of Greece. In Boardman & Hammond 1982, 83–162.

GRAHAM, A. J. 1982b: The Western Greeks. In Boardman & Hammond 1982, 163–195.

GRAHAM, A. J. 1988: Megara Hyblaea and the Sicels. In Lordkipanidze, O. (ed.), *Local Ethno-Political Entities of the Black Sea Area in the 7th–4th Centuries BC: materials of the 4th All-Union symposium dedicated to the problems of the ancient history of the Black Sea littoral. Tsqaltubo-Vani-1985* (Tbilisi, Metsniereba), 304–321.

GRAS, M. 1984–85: Ricerche sul pianoro meridionale dell'abitato di Megara Hyblaea. *Kokalos* 30–31, 801–804.

GRAS, M. 1985: *Trafics tyrrhéniens archaïques* (BEFAR vol. 258; Rome).

GULLINI, G. 1978: Documenti della cultura greca in Occidente durante il primo arcaismo (A proposito di Megara Hyblaea I). *Parola del Passato* 33, 427–469.

GWYNN, A. 1918: The Character of Greek Colonization. *JHS* 38, 88–123.

HALSTEAD, P. 1987: Traditional and Ancient Rural Economy in Mediterranean Europe: plus ça change? *JHS* 107, 77–87.

HOLLOWAY, R. R. 1981: *Italy and the Aegean 3000–700 B.C.* (*Publications d'histoire de l'art et de l'archéologie de l'université catholique de Louvain,* vol. 28; Louvain-La-Neuve).

HOLLOWAY, R. R. 1991: *The Archaeology of Ancient Sicily* (London and New York, Routledge).

HULOT, J. & FOUGÈRES, G. 1910: *Sélinonte: la ville, l'acropole et les temples* (Paris, Ch. Massin).

LEGON, R. P. 1981: *Megara: the political history of a Greek city-state to 336 B.C.* (Ithaca and London, Cornell U.P.).

LEPORE, E. 1969: Osservazioni sul rapporto tra fatti economici e fatti di colonizzazione in Occidente. *DdA* 3, 175–212.

MANNI, E. 1981: *Geografia fisica e politica della Sicilia antica* (*Kokalos* suppl. vol. 4; Rome).

MARAZZI, M. & TUSA, S. 1987: Selinunte e il suo territorio analisi storica e progetto di ricognizione. In *La preistoria in Sicilia* (*I Quaderni di Sicilia Archeologica* 1; Trapani), 39–109.

MERTENS, D. 1990: Some Principal Features of West Greek Colonial Architecture. In Descoeudres, 1990, 373–383.

MURRAY, O. 1993: *Early Greece*² (London, Fontana Press).

ORSI, P. & CAVALLARI, F. S. 1890: Megara Hyblaea: storia-topografia-necropoli e anathemata. *Monumenti Antichi* 1, 689–950.

OSBORNE, R. 1987: *Classical Landscape with Figures: the ancient Greek city and its countryside* (London, George Philip).

PARISI PRESICCE, C. 1984: La funzione delle aree sacre nell'organizzazione urbanistica primitiva delle colonie greche alla luce della scoperta di un nuovo santuario periferico di Selinunte. *Archeologia Classica* 36, 19–132.

PIRAINO, M. T. 1959: Iscrizione inedita da Poggioreale. *Kokalos* 5, 159–173.

POLIGNAC, F. de 1984: *La naissance de la cité grecque: cultes, espace et société VIII^e-VII^e -siècles avant J.-C.* (Paris, La Découverte).

POLLASTRI, F. 1948–49: *Sicilia: notizie e commenti ecologici di agricoltura siciliana,* 3 vols. in one (Palermo, Industrie Riunite Editoriali Siciliane).

PROCELLI, E. 1989: Aspetti e problemi dell'ellenizzazione calcidese nella Sicilia orientale. *MEFRA* 101, 679–689.

PUGLIESE CARRATELLI, G. (ed.) 1986: *Sikanie. Storia e civiltà della Sicilia greca²* (*Antica Madre* series vol. 8; Milan, Garzanti).

PURCELL, N. 1990: Mobility and the Polis. In Murray, O. & Price, S. (eds.), *The Greek City: from Homer to Alexander* (Oxford, Clarendon Press), 29–58.

RIDGWAY, D. 1992: *The First Western Greeks* (Cambridge, Cambridge U.P.).

RIHLL, T. 1993: War, Slavery, and Settlement in early Greece. In Rich, J. & Shipley, G. (eds.), *War and Society in the Greek World* (*Leicester-Nottingham Studies in Ancient Society,* vol. 4) (London and New York, Routledge), 77–107.

RUSCHENBUSCH, E. 1991: Übervölkerung in archaischer Zeit. *Historia* 40, 375–378.

SARTORI, F. 1980–81: Storia costituzionale della Sicilia antica. *Kokalos* 26–27, 263–291.

STE. CROIX, G. E. M. de 1981: *The Class Struggle in the Ancient Greek World: from the Archaic Age to the Arab conquests* (London, Duckworth).

TRIGGER, B. G. 1989: *A History of Archaeological Thought* (Cambridge, Cambridge U.P.).

TUSA, S. 1983: *La Sicilia nella preistoria* (Palermo, Sellerio).

TUSA, V. 1978: Materiali greci del'VIII e del VII secolo a. C. nella Sicilia Occidentale. In Rizza, G. (ed.), *Insediamenti coloniali greci in Sicilia nell'VIII e VII secolo a. C.: atti della 2ª riunione scientifica della scuola di perfezionamento in archeologia classica dell'Università di Catania (Siracusa, 24–26 novembre 1977)* (*CronASA* 17 [1980]; Catania), 47–51.

TUSA, V. 1988: Sicily. In Moscati, S. (ed.), *The Phoenicians* (Milan, Bompiani), 186–205.

VALLET, G. 1962: La colonisation chalcidienne et l'hellénisation de la Sicile orientale. *Kokalos* 8, 30–51.

VALLET, G. 1990: *Sicilia greca* (Palermo and Siracusa, Arnaldo Lombardi).

VALLET, G. & VOZA, G. 1984: *Dal neolitico all'era industriale nel territorio da Augusta a Siracusa* (Siracusa, Assessorato Regionale Beni Culturali e Ambientali e Pubblica Istruzione-Soprintendenza alle Antichità per la Sicilia Orientale).

VALLET, G., VILLARD, F. & AUBERSON, P. 1976: *Mégara Hyblaea, i: le quartier de l'agora archaïque* (*École française de Rome, Mélanges d'archéologie et d'histoire,* suppl. 1) (Rome).

VALLET, G., VILLARD, F. & AUBERSON, P. 1983: *Mégara Hyblaea, iii: guide des fouilles* (*École française de Rome, Mélanges d'archéologie et d'histoire,* suppl. 1) (Rome).

WATERS, K. H. 1974: The Rise and Decline of Some Greek Colonies in Sicily. *Ancient Society* 5, 1–19.

WILSON, R. J. A. 1982: Archaeology in Sicily, 1977–81. *AR for 1981–82,* 84–105.

WILSON, R. J. A. 1988: Archaeology in Sicily, 1982–87. *AR for 1987–88,* 105–150.

# Chapter 7

# Greek Penetration of the Black Sea

## Gocha R. Tsetskhladze

In 1948 R. Carpenter expressed his opinion that the Black Sea was closed to Greek sailors before *c*. 680 BC and only with the development of the first powerfully oared vessel – the pentekonter – were the Greeks able to pass through the Bosphorus, thus explaining why there is no archaeological evidence of colonization in the Pontus area before about 680 BC (Carpenter 1948). In response to this two articles appeared written by B. W. Labaree (1957) and A. J. Graham (1958), in which it was demonstrated that the Greeks were able to sail into the Black Sea. Graham based his thesis on information provided by ancient authors, to the effect that the first Greek colonies – Sinope and Trapezus – had been founded as early as the 8th century BC. The lack of archaeological proof for such early dates he explains by the fact that the region to the south of the Black Sea has not been investigated (Graham 1958, 31–3; *cf*. Cook R. 1946, 71–2, 84). Soon more general works appeared whose authors were more cautious in their approach to the question of the dating of the founding of the Greek colonies on the Black Sea, trying to bring together written sources and archaeology (Roebuck 1959, 116–24; Cook J. 1962, 53–9; Huxley 1966, 64–9, etc.).

In 1971 Graham (1971, 39) reasserted his original position, and he was supported by R. Drews (1976) who took Graham's ideas one stage further. The theory assumed its complete form in the Chapter on colonization by Graham in *CAH* in 1982 (*CAH*, 122–30, 160–2). Archaeologists had more confidence in archaeological material, placing the date of the founding of the first colonies on the Black Sea in the second half of the 7th century.[1]

In 1990 the controversy flared up again and the opposed views of historians and archaeologists were aired once more. Graham accepts the first date given for the founding of Sinope by the Milesians, before 756, as found in Ps.-Skymnus (986–97), and accepts 756 (1990, 52–4; *cf*. CAH, 122–3) as the foundation date for Trapezus, colony of Sinope (Xen. *An.* IV. 8. 22). In support of the appearance of Greeks in the Black Sea as early as the 8th century he calls attention to early pottery (Graham 1990, 53–4) alleged to have been found in Histria (the rim of an LG kotyle) (Graham 1990, 53; *cf*. Alexandrescu 1978a, 21, no. 15) identified by J. N. Coldstream as a Euboean copy of a Corinthian type dated to *c*. 750–720 BC (1968, 377, no. 8). Another vessel is allegedly from Berezan (Graham 1990, 53). It is a small Geometric hydria bought from a dealer (*cf*. Farmakovsky 1910, 227) called Attic or Atticizing by Coldstream (1968, 337, no. 7) and assigned by him to MG II (*c*. 800–760). Reference is also made to fragments of Cypriot "White Painted IV" ware from the Cypro-Archaic period

(c. 740–660) found at Histria and Berezan (Graham 1990, 53–4; *cf.* Alexandrescu 1978a, 63, no. 256; Demetrion 1978).

In response to this J. Boardman published a short but very detailed article, in which he clearly stated his purpose: "Whether there is any archaeological evidence for earlier [8th century] exploration or settlement is another matter, but Graham has pressed claims which, as I hope to show, cannot be upheld, since the dating of the pottery or its pedigree are either wrong or too dubious to be taken seriously, however tempting they may seem" (1991, 387). The author did, indeed, succeed in showing that the 'fact' that the vessel had been found in Berezan and in a tomb was merely the assertion of a dealer, while excavation of that site over many years had not produced any pottery earlier than the late 7th century. "In the circumstances such a dealer's provenance should not be taken seriously" (Boardman 1991, 387; for the same opinion, see: Vinogradov Y. G. 1989, 35, Note 13). Fragments allegedly originating from Histria, currently kept in the Museum of Classical Archaeology in Cambridge, were found in Al Mina, and it is possible "that an unlabelled fragment could move from one tray or box to another, in the course of an exercise in comparison of colonial pottery" (Boardman 1991, 387–8). This opinion was supported by Professor R. M. Cook of Cambridge, who catalogued the fragments in 1961, despite the fact that the fragments had been acquired in 1950. "It seemed to Cook improbable that an excavator [Mme Lambrino] who was also a pottery expert would have given away what was obviously the earliest piece from the site" (Boardman 1991, 387). Moreover, the Cypro-Archaic pottery is of the "Cypro-Archaic II" period, which may bring it well down into the 6th century (Boardman 1991, 389).[2]

After this it might have appeared that the questions concerned had all been clarified, but Graham, who considers that "it is bad method to prefer an archaeological *argumentum e silentio* to statements in literary sources" *(CAH,* 123), in December 1993 stressed in his paper in Washington entitled "Greek and Roman settlements on the Black Sea Coasts. Historical Background" that archaeologists were unable to agree amongst themselves over the chronology of pottery: while criticizing Boardman's article in *OJA*, he expressed his mistrust of archaeologists and once again repeated his opinion regarding the appearance of the Greeks in the Black Sea in the 8th century BC.[3] He agreed, however, that the Histria pottery should be disregarded, and implied that Boardman had "re-dated" the Cypriot pottery, which is not the case.

What lies behind this controversy? The answer is simple: written sources are contradictory and offer differing dates for the founding of one and the same Greek cities. The value of such information has long been exhausted. In archaeology the situation is far from ideal. No strict chronology for early Greek pottery has been elaborated; the Greek cities on the southern coasts of the Black Sea have not yet been investigated for a number of objective and subjective reasons. 'Western' scholars use, to a limited degree, the achievements and publications of new material from the excavations of the last decade undertaken by 'eastern' archaeologists. At the same time 'eastern' scholars have only had access to 'western' literature for the last three to five years.[4] Yet more important is the fact that in the archaeology of the Black Sea, owing to the limited range and character of the archaeological material now available, there are more questions being asked than answers being found. This region of the ancient world is today a hotbed of 'scholarly wars' in which virtually every scholar indulges his own subjective opinion. We are, at present, too far removed from the conclusion of a general academic cease-fire in this region.[5]

*Early and Precolonial Contacts*

The tribes that inhabited the Black Sea region had enjoyed some kind of contact with the Aegean world since the beginning of the second millenium BC. No Mycenaean pottery has been found along the Black Sea coast and finds at Masat, inland from Samsun (shoulder of an LH IIIA2 stirrup jar) (Mellink 1984, 445; 1985, 558; Mee 1978, 132–3), cannot be seen as penetration from the Black Sea: they are more likely to have made their way there overland (French 1982, with extensive bibliography on the problem).[6] Some Mycenaean-type objects are known from West and North-West Pontic areas: swords, spears and double axes of Mycenaean types (Bouzek 1985, 31–5, 41–6, 213–4; 1990, 13–5). Aegean swords have been found in Transcaucasia, gold roundels of the Shaft Graves period and double-axes (Bouzek 1985, 35, 46, 82). These finds do not demonstrate Mycenaean colonization of the Black Sea and are probably the result of royal trade (along the Danube and in the Transcaucasian region), which included, among the commodities, amber (Kilian 1990, 465).

Stone anchors of the second half of the second and beginning of the first millennia BC at many points on the Bulgarian coast (Ropotamo, Masalen Nos, Kaliakra, Sozopol, Nesebar) have given rise to the view that native Thracian chieftains sponsored sailing along the coast, both long before and after the Greek settlements.[7] Some scholars see these as a sign that Greek sailors penetrated as far as the Black Sea as early as the Late Bronze Age (Bouzek 1990, 13; *cf.* Nibbi 1993).

The eastern part of the Black Sea region, where Greek colonies appeared as early as the mid-6th century, provides material to justify the assumption that there were precolonial links in the 8th-7th centuries. This includes the so-called Caucasian bronze arc-shaped fibulae, which probably appeared there in the 8th century: Greek fibulae clearly played a large part in their evolution, giving rise to the emergence in the Caucasus of a local north-eastern variant, and it is evident that the Greek models must have made their way to the region along the southern coasts of the Black Sea (Bouzek 1983, 204–5; 1985, 153; 1990, 15; Voronov 1983). For a long time bronze figurines of a sleeping woman holding a child to her breast, from Samos (Jantzen 1972, 80–5) and Nigvziani (Mikeladze 1985, 59–62; 1990, 63–6), and small bronze bells from Samos, were believed to have been made in the Caucasus (Jantzen 1972, 80–5; Boardman 1980, 240–1). M. Voyatzis, however, has doubts about this and sees the figurine from Samos as being of local Greek origin (1992, 262–9). Clay figurines depicting two- and three-headed fantastic animals from Vani, dating from the 8th-7th centuries, are also of debatable origin. It is difficult to form a clear opinion: they could have been made under the influence of Luristan bronzes, or that of the Greek world, where they are known from the 8th-7th centuries on (Lordkipanidze 1991, 150–9, pl. 2a, b; Tolordava 1990, 243–7, 298–301).

It is unlikely that these early relations were of any regular kind (Buchholz 1983). It can be assumed, with a good deal of probability, that the Greeks knew the Black Sea as early as the 8th century BC. This is indicated both by archaeological material from Georgia, and by the first information about Pontus in Greek literature (Eumelus, fr. 2; Hesiod., *Theog.,*

337–340). Thus the 8th century appears to have been a time of exploration (Huxley 1990, 200).

Greek mythological tradition links the first contacts between the Greeks and the peoples of Pontus in the story of the Argonauts' voyage to Colchis in search of the Golden Fleece. Some scholars place this myth in the category of those that reflect history, and believe that the voyage took place before the Trojan War. They support this idea by reference to the fact that Homer mentions the myth (Lordkipanidze 1966, 9–18; 1986, 15–47; Urushadze 1980, 21–28, etc.).[8] They consider it to have been second only in its popularity to that of the Trojan War (Lordkipanidze 1979, 4), and they are even convinced that the "Journey of the Argonauts was a journey after gold!" (Lordkipanidze 1984, 43).

I should like to approach this myth[9] from the archaeologist's viewpoint, to determine whether or not it was so popular. It is unjustified from the methodological point of view to see the myth as a reflection of reality – this question is too delicate and complex (Brillante 1990; Sourvinou-Inwood 1987; Thomas E. 1976; Thomas C. 1993, etc.) – especially when we have it most fully presented only in Hellenistic poetry, when the Greeks were already well acquainted with Colchis.

Virtually all scholars, apart from the Georgians, maintain that the land of Aia, where the Golden Fleece was to be found, had no real geographical existence. For them, it is one of those fantastic countries at the edge of the world, which include the Isles of the Blessed, the Gardens of the Hesperides, the Island of Erytheia, the mythical Ethiopia, most of the countries visited by Odysseus, the Dionysiac Nysa, Plato's Atlantis, etc. With the growth of rationalism, attempts were made to identify all these places. Since Aia was imagined to lie somewhere in the North and at the same time in the East (closer to sunrise), it was finally identified with Colchis. The word *aia* is found in poetic speech signifying 'earth, country' – but, of course, a fabulous region must have borne a less abstract, more expressive proper name. Moreover, the *Odyssey* describes another locality with a very similar name, the island of Aiaie, where Aeetes' sister, the sorceress Circe, lived (Cook J. 1962, 52; Astour 1967, 283–8; Huxley 1969, 60–79; Boltunova 1976, etc.).

When did the identification of Aia with Colchis take place? Eumelus (c. 700) is the earliest witness to its localization in Colchis beside the River Phasis, which traditionally marked the eastern boundary of the known world. This identification points to the period of increasing exploration and colonization, when a New World was fitted to old perceptions. The identification was probably arbitrary. For Eumelus (fr. 2) the River Phasis was the eastern border of the known world, and in the myth of the Argonauts Aia was also the eastern kingdom. This identity probably became more credible only thanks to Herodotus (VII. 193) in the 5th century, when it was already known to the Greeks that Colchis, like the mythical Aia, was a 'gold-rich' country. It was then that the wealth of gold and the Golden Fleece merged together for the Greeks of Colchis, as a single concept and image.[10]

To determine whether the myth of the Argonauts was as widely popular as it is held to have been by Georgian scholars, we must turn to visual art.[11] In architectural sculpture the only scenes linked with the Argonauts are on the so-called Sicyonian Treasury at Delphi, of the second quarter of the 6th century (Ridgway B. 1966, 196–7; 1993, 341–2; Szeliga 1986; Griffin 1982, 92–119; *cf.* Voyatzis 1982, 32–3). These need not be explained with reference to the myth's popularity or to links with Colchis itself. Such travel myths found their first monumental expression in the western areas of colonization and in the great pan-Hellenic sanctuaries, especially Delphi, once the oracle assumed the role of leader of colonists (Ridgway B. 1991; Penglase 1994, 8).

Some twenty general scenes from the voyage have been found dating from the 5th-2nd centuries BC *(LIMC* 2, 593–7; Simon 1990, 227–9; Olmos 1990, 231–4). Jason was depicted 57 times. The early depictions date from around 600, as does that on a Corinthian vase. Most date from the 5th-4th centuries *(LIMC* 5, 630–7). Medea was more popular in Roman than Greek art. Only about ten depictions of her are known in Greek art and six on Etruscan vases. The early depictions on Etruscan vases date from 630–600, the early Greek ones from 530 BC, while the rest are of the 5th-4th centuries *(LIMC* 6, 388–95; Sourvinou-Inwood 1990).

Altogether approximately 93 depictions of subjects from the myth are known.[13] It must be judged poorly illustrated. Several vase paintings indicate versions of myths that are lost or almost lost in literature (Schefold 1992, 183–97). Jason does not seem to be a very common figure – he was an anti-hero (presented as such by Apollonius Rhodius), helpless *(LIMC* 5, 630). It was only thanks to Medea, a barbarian princess, that he was able to bring the Golden Fleece to Greece and, again thanks to her, become king of Corinth. Medea – a murderess with a tragic destiny from a barbarian world – was better known to the Greeks via tragedy (Kerenyi 1979, 20–40). The majority of the depictions are from the 5th century, which again serves to underline that Aia was probably then first identified with Colchis. So the myth could not reflect any voyage to the Black Sea allegedly undertaken by Greeks in the 13th century.[14] We frequently want to believe the myths of the Greeks more than they did themselves (Breamer 1987; Penglase 1994, 9–14; Henrichs 1987; Buxton 1994, 155–68).

Penetration of the Black Sea region by the Greeks began in the second half of the 7th century (Fig. 7.1 *overleaf*). This is linked in the main with the colonizing endeavours of Miletus, which was reputed to have possessed as many as 75 or even 90 colonies. In the words of Strabo: "the city [Miletus] is known to many, and mainly thanks to the large number of its colonies, since the whole of Pontus Euxinus, Propontis and many other places have been settled by Milesians" (XIV. 1. 6). What follows is a series of observations on some aspects of the three archaic stages of Milesian colonization.[15]

*The First Greek Colonies*
The question as to the identity of the first Greek colonies in the Black Sea is controversial. Some scholars have more faith in written sources (Graham 1958; *CAH*; Drews 1976), and others in archaeological ones (Boardman 1980, 242); the controversy focuses on Sinope. We have accounts by two ancient authors Eusebius and Pseudo-Skymnus. Most troublesome is the 756 foundation-date given by Eusebius (II. 81) for Trapezus and, by implication, a date thereabouts for Sinope, its mother city. Eusebius, however, dates the foundation of Sinope to the 37th Olympiad (631/630). Pseudo-Skymnus (941–952) mentions an earlier foundation of Sinope by Habrondas, which was destroyed by the Kimmerians, to be refounded later by two exiles from Miletus, Kretinus and Kous, when the Kimmerians were pillaging Asia. Some scholars consider that Sinope was founded in the first half of the 8th century BC by the Corinthians, others that it was founded by the second half of the 7th century, and a third group

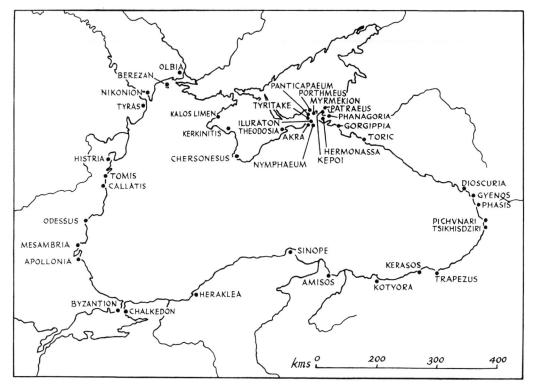

*Fig. 7.1  Map of the Black Sea showing major Greek cities.*

by the end of the 7th century, and so on (Hind 1988; Kacharava and Kvirkveliya 1991, 239–42).

Without dwelling on the Kimmerian advance into Asia I should like to draw attention to one point. Virtually all scholars refer to the account by Herodotus (I. 15; 104; 109) and hold that the Kimmerians used the Maeoto-Colchian (eastern) route. The second account, which deserves our confidence, is usually ignored, namely Strabo's (I. 3. 21). According to Strabo the Kimmerians advanced along the western shore of the Black Sea. Archaeological material supports this. The most important question is also controversial – identification of Kimmerian culture (Sulimirski 1960; Kvirkveliya 1985; Ivantchik 1993). Thus it is inappropriate to speak of two different Sinopes – Sinope I and Sinope II – in other words of the founding of Sinope in two stages: before and after the Kimmerian campaign. It is unlikely that one controversial issue will be resolved with the help of another.

Excavation at Sinope (modern Sinop), which occupies a peninsula site with a superb harbour, is complicated by the fact that it has since been built over. Smallscale excavations have unearthed a cemetery. The pottery from the graves is largely from East Greece with a little Corinthian. All pottery dates from the late-7th century to a little after 600 BC and the Phrygian pottery that has been found attests to close relations with the peoples of the interior.

The same can be said of Amisos (Samsun) (Akurgal and Budde 1956, 9; Boysal 1959; Hind 1964, 174–5; 1984, 95; Boardman 1980, 254–5).[16] We have no archaeological information about Trapezus. G. Huxley's recent study shows that "neither excavations nor Eusebian chronography confirm the notion of 8th-century settlement at Trapezus" (Huxley 1990, 200).[17]

Among the earliest Milesian colonies in the Black Sea region are Histria in the West and Berezan in the North. They were both founded on peninsulae, were well protected and had convenient harbours.[18] Written sources offer a variety of dates. For Histria it is 656/5 (Eusebius) and the end of the 7th century (Pseudo-Skymnus).

Excavation in Histria has yielded 36 items of Middle Wild Goat Class pottery, which go back to *c.* 630 BC, between the dates given by the literary sources. In any case, Histria appears to have been a fully viable centre at the end of the 7th century (Alexandrescu 1978a, 19; 1978b; Bouzek 1990, 21–5; Coja 1990, 160; Dmitriu and Alexandrescu 1973; Dupont 1983).

The settlement on Berezan, which was identified with Borysthenites (*cf.* Hdt. IV. 17; 24; 78)[19] is given a foundation date of 646/5 by Eusebius. The earliest examples of East Greek pottery found on the modern island of Berezan can be dated to the second quarter of the 7th century: they are, however, very few and scattered (fragments of kylikes with birds and geometric decoration) (Kopeikina 1973, 240). The bulk of the pottery dates from the second half of the 7th century. All the fragments were found in occupation deposits: L. Kopeikina provides the following numbers for fragments of different classes of archaic pottery from the 1962–79 excavations, sector G and the NW sector together: Wild Goat (Milesian, Clazomenian and North Ionian) – 1083; Fikellura – 200; Chiot – 123; Ionian banded-ware – 536; Clazomenian Black Figure – 43; Corinthian – 125; Attic Black-Figured – 552; Attic Red-Figured – 8 (Kopeikina 1986, 42). This pottery shows that the settlement was founded by the Milesians no later than the third quarter of the 7th century and possibly nearer the middle of it (Kopeikina 1979, 107).

The first settlers lived in dugouts or semi-dugouts. The 1989 excavation revealed a rectangular pit-shelter (no. 51) 3.8 x 5.0m and 1m deep. East Greek painted pottery dates this complex to the last quarter of the 7th century, making it the earliest reliably dated habitation area on the site (Treister and Vinogradov 1993, 539). An important find was a hoard of coins, which included coins of Miletus dating from the last third of the 7th century (Karyshkovskii and Lapin 1979).

The question as to the nature of the settlement on the modern island of Berezan is controversial. The scholars most likely to have resolved this problem consider that the settlement had been an *emporion* (Kopeikina 1979, 109; *cf.* Vinogradov Y. G. 1989, 60–62). This is borne out by the fact that in the 7th century the settlement did not have its own agricultural area – *chora*. Fragments of early pottery have been found deep in Berezan's hinterland (Nemirov, Trachtemirov, etc.) (Boardman 1980, 243–4).

The next city on the Black Sea that was founded in the 7th century BC, was Apollonia in Thrace. According to Pseudo-Skynmus (728–731) it was founded by the Milesians in 610. Part of the city had probably been built on an island (at the time of Strabo) and it had a convenient harbour. The earliest pottery dates from the late 7th century (Hind 1984, 72–3; 1993, 84–5). Archaeological dates from Histria, Berezan and Apollonia (as well as Byzantion) indicate that all these cities were founded in more or less the same period. For Apollonia, this would indicate that it was not founded as a port of call for ships on their way to Histria and Berezan, but as an *apoikia* in its own right (Isaac 1986, 243).

Thus, the first colonies on the Black Sea were founded by the Milesians in the second half of the 7th century (Sinope, possibly Trapezus, Histria, Berezan, Apollonia and Amisos). Most of the colonies in the Propontis were probably founded at that time as well (Malkin and Shmueli 1988). Originally, these were trading settlements (Histria, Berezan), being situated on peninsulas without their own *chora.* Apart from Greeks, the population would have included representatives of local tribes (the handmade pottery in Berezan) (Marchenko 1979; Kopeikina 1981). Apollo was worshipped: the Milesians sought advice in Didyma, the oracular sanctuary, the oracular of Apollo founded by Miletus and shared by all the Pontic colonies, according to which their god and protector was *Apollon Ietros* (Ehrhardt 1983, 145–7; Vinogradov Y. G. 1989, 30–1).

Discrepancies in the dating of the first colonies on the Black Sea in written sources are a major obstacle, but it would seem that archaeologists should have the last word. After all, the priority of archaeology over and against accounts by Thucydides, as regards the foundation dates of the Greek colonies in Sicily, has already been acknowledged (Snodgrass 1987, 53–60). Should not the same approach be adopted when it comes to the colonies around the Black Sea?

As usual, we are obliged to judge when the early colonies were founded on the basis of pottery finds: yet when it comes to determining dates, it emerges that the earliest pottery fragments are few in number. We have to decide whether to take into account the small number of samples, or even isolated finds, or to explain their presence in other ways (for example, that a vessel had been a family heirloom). The problem is as important as it is complex. The principle should be that when dates for foundations are being calculated, all early archaeological material should be taken into account, even isolated examples. A quantitative approach is evidently inappropriate here, since it can be assumed that the earliest artefacts are bound to be few in number. Indeed, the first group of settlers is unlikely to have been large. It is difficult to imagine that they would have set off on a long and extremely difficult voyage to foreign lands loaded with fragile tableware. Let us recall, for example, the story of the *apoikia* from Thera to Cyrene narrated by Herodotus (IV. 150–158): the settlers succeeded in consolidating their position in their new home only after grim and lengthy tribulations. It might also be added that the archaic levels in most sites are those most inaccessible for the archaeologist, and secondly that these levels are usually thin, indeed they are most likely to be almost non-existent (Kuznetsov 1991, 32–3).

In these circumstances it is difficult to expect that the earliest pottery could be abundant. Yet the approach to each site should be adapted to the specific conditions. If, for example, the earliest pottery from Berezan (several dozen fragments) gives Kopeikina grounds for dating the settlement to the third quarter of the 7th century, which enabled her to bring into line the archaeological material and the written sources, it may be that the situation is rather different in Olbia. Here all the archaic pottery was confined to the 6th century, with the exception of one sherd from the third quarter of the 7th century. Its presence can, however, perhaps be explained by the presence nearby of the earlier settlement of Berezan (Kuznetsov 1991, 33).

*The Second Stage*

At the beginning of the 6th century BC Miletus began extending its colonizing activity. In Berezan there appeared a new wave of settlers and stone buildings. This new population ushered in the gradual penetration by Greeks from Berezan of the mainland and the opening up of a *chora*. The earliest of these settlements within the *chora* were founded no later than the second quarter of the 6th century BC clustered on the left bank of the Berezan estuary and in the western part of the Dnieper-Bug estuary in the immediate vicinity of Berezan (Vinogradov 1989, 51). A similar situation is to be observed at Histria where the first city walls were built in 575 (Coja 1990, 159–60).

Apart from the extension of the colonies that had already been founded, new cities appeared. In the western part of Pontus, Tomis was founded, where the early pottery dates from the early 6th century (Bouzek 1990, 28; Hind 1993, 89). At this stage Olbia was also founded by the Milesians not far from Berezan. Only two fragments of pottery found there have been dated to the third quarter of the 7th century, while there is more dating from the first half of the 6th century (Korpusova 1987; Vinogradov Y. G. 1989, 36, Note 16). Its emergence can probably be placed earlier than the end of the first quarter of the 6th century BC, or later than the beginning of its second quarter (*cf.* Graham in *CAH*, 125–26 and Vinogradov Y. G. 1989, 36).[20] The bulk of the archaeological material and remains of buildings do not appear before the third quarter of the 6th century (Kryzhitskii and Otreshko 1986). Olbia then extended her zone of influence and founded rural settlements in the lower reaches of the River Bug. In the Archaic period Olbia's *chora* comprised 107 settlements (Kryzhitskii, Buiskikh and Otreshko 1990, 12–43).

Miletus by this time was beginning to settle new territories – the Taman and Kerch peninsulae. The earliest pottery is in the burial at Temir-Gora – an oinochoe belonging to the Vlasto group and dated to 635–625 (Korpusova 1980; Kopeikina 1972). In this area one Greek settlement had already been in existence, unfortunately not well known, the so-called '*Taganrog settlement*'. It has been totally destroyed by the sea. A collection of pottery from the sea-bed and the shore, not yet properly publishcd, allows us to assume that this settlement had already been in existence in the last third of the 7th century (Treister and Vinogradov 1993, 551, fig. 17). (It had probably played a similar role in the development of areas adjacent to it, as had Berezan). Excavations of the last 10–15 years make it possible to review the dates of the founding of many colonies in the Kimmerian Bosporus.

*Panticapaeum.* Mithridates Mount is dated to the last decades of the 7th century (Blavatskii 1964, 23), or to the beginning of the 6th century (Noonan 1973, 80). The pottery associated with the earlier date is slight. The rest, mainly Ionian, gives grounds for the first appearance of Greeks at *c.* 590–570. The first colonists lived in dugouts (Koshelenko and Kuznetsov 1990; Kuznetsov 1991, 33; Tolstikov 1992).

*Nymphaeum* was firmly dated to the second quarter of the 6th century, which might be narrowed down to approximately 580–570 BC (Kuznetsov 1991, 33).

*Theodosia* was usually held to have been founded in the second half of the 6th century, yet pottery of an earlier period has been found during excavation, which obliges us to consider an earlier date of *c.* 580–570 (Kuznetsov 1991, 33).

*Myrmekion* was founded in the second quarter of the 6th century. The first colonists there lived in dugouts (Vinogradov Y. A. 1992).

*Tyritake* produced material very similar to that found at Myrmekion, from which we assume
that the founding dates were also the same (Kuznetsov 1991, 33).

A similar, but evidently somewhat more complex situation is to be observed on the Asian side
of the Bosporus:

*Hermonassa* was a joint colony of Miletus and Mytilene. The early level of the city-site is
dated roughly to the second quarter of the 6th century (Kuznetsov 1991, 33).

*Kepoi.* Fairly numerous finds of pottery from previous and recent excavations give a date of
580–560 (Kuznetsov 1991a; 1992).[21]

*Patraeus* is usually dated to the second half of the 6th century: but appears to have been
founded somewhat earlier than the middle of the century, to judge by the pottery that has
been found (Koshelenko and Kuznetsov 1990).

Early Greek pottery was also found in the so-called *Tuzlian Cemetery* (not far from
Hermonassa) which belonged to some kind of Greek settlement. The settlement has been
destroyed by the sea, and the early pottery can be dated to 580–560 (Kuznetsov 1991, 32).

This means that there is every reason to assume that the first mass wave of Greek colonists
in the territory of the Kimmerian Bosporus arrived approximately during the period 580–560,
several decades earlier than had been proposed in most previous literature.

Within the territory of the European Bosporus, we see five centres of that date, and four
within the territory of the Asian Bosporus. All these cities were situated right on the coast and
had convenient harbours.

*The Third Stage of Greek Colonization*

The third stage of the Greek penetration of the Black Sea began after 560 BC, assumed a
particularly wide scale after the middle of the 6th century and lasted until approximately 530
BC, when Miletus, because of strong pressure from the Achaemenians, was obliged to
abandon its colonizing activity. This period is also characterized by the appearance of colonies
which were founded by people other than Milesians, but their number is small. New parts of
the Black Sea region (Colchis) were being opened up.

Heraklea was founded to the South of the Black Sea in 554 by Megarians and Boeotians
(Pseudo-Skynmus 968–975). Different written sources provide different kinds of information
about the founding of the city (Burstein 1976, 12–8). The city (modern Eregli) has never been
the subject of archaeological excavation: investigations of other parts of the Black Sea region
have shown, however, that Heraklea developed into a major trading centre of importance for
the whole of Pontus and that it even founded two of its own colonies – Callatis (in modern
Romania) and Chersonesus in the Crimea (see below) (Hind 1984, 75–6; Saprykin 1986,
52–69). Admittedly on the subject of the founding of Callatis there is information
(Ps.-Skynmus 761–64; *cf.* Strabo VII. 6. 1; XII. 3. 6) to the effect that it took place in the last
quarter of the 6th century BC, but archaeological excavations point to its having been founded
in the early 4th century (Hind 1984, 765; Isaac 1986, 261–5).

On the western shore of the Black Sea, Odessus was founded by the Milesians.
Pseudo-Skymnus even gives a date: "It is said to have been founded when Astyages ruled the
Medes" (748–49). This was *c.* 585–539. Excavation brought to light a thin archaic level and

three ritual pits of the middle/late 6th century. Pottery, including Corinthian and East Greek, rosette bowls and Fikellura ware, suggests that the city was founded a little before or after 560 (Hind 1984, 74; Isaac 1986, 254–5; Boardman 1980, 247).

Excavation has also shed light on many small settlements, which were situated right on the sea-shore. They probably appeared as a result of the extension of the Greek cities that had already been founded in the western part of the Black Sea region and had been part of their *chora* (Hind 1984, 72–7; Isaac 1986, 238–78).

To the North of the Black Sea, near Olbia and Berezan, major changes were taking place. Olbia was already a *polis:* the city itself and the *chora* were extensive and it had its own coinage.[22] Berezan had already become part of Olbia (Rusyaeva 1986; 1992; Kryzhitskii and Buiskikh 1989; Wasowicz 1975; Vinogradov Y. G. 1981; 1989)23. In the mid-6th century new cities appeared as well: Tyras, Nikonion and a large number of settlements (approximately 50) which, taken together, formed the *chora* of those cities (Treister and Vinogradov 1993, 531–9; Karyshkovskii and Kleyman 1985; Samoylova 1988; Sekerskaya 1989).

New cities also appeared within the Kimmerian Bosporus. The only colony that had not been founded by the Milesians was Phanagoria, an *apoikia* of the Teians. The written tradition (Arrian, *Byth.*, fr. 56 Roos) and archaeological material show that Phanagoria was founded around 542 (Koshelenko, Kruglikova and Dolgorukov 1984, 77).

It was also at this time that the city of Gorgippia (or to be precise, that Greek city which preceded Gorgippia – Sindica) was founded (Alekseeva 1991). To that period the founding of the small city of Toric – at the location of the modern town of Gelendzhik – was dated (Onaiko 1980). A large number of small centres of population grew up in the territory of the Asian Bosporus (approximately 30) (Abramov and Paromov 1993; Paromov 1990). In the territory of the European Bosporus, on the other hand, only a few small cities appeared: Akra, Porthmeus and Iluraton (Treister and Vinogradov 1993, 547).

On the Taman peninsula more than 30 sites relating to the period embracing the middle and the third quarter of the 6th century have been recorded (many of the cities and settlements are now under the sea). The majority of those centres of population is situated either right on the sea-shore (9 of them), or on the banks of deep straits or rivers of the Kuban. Unlike the situation obtaining in the second stage (when all the cities were situated only on the coasts), settlements had, by now, also appeared in the interior.

During the third stage of the colonization of Pontus, the Ionians began settling new territory – in Eastern Pontus (Colchis). We know very little about this process and for this reason the subject of the Greek colonization of Colchis nowadays appears the most controversial and difficult problem of Black Sea archaeology, and very far from a final solution. The controversy stems mainly from the fact that the Greek cities have been virtually ignored, so far, by those engaged in archaeological research.[24]

The names of the Greek cities are known from written sources. They are Phasis, Gyenos and Dioscuria. According to both the written tradition and archaeological evidence, the Greek cities were founded by Miletus in the middle of the 6th century (notwithstanding the existence of examples, few in number, of early Greek pottery in Colchis, dating from the second quarter of the 6th century) (Lordkipanidze 1983; 1985; 1991; 1991a; 1991b; Tsetskhladze 1992; 1993; 1994; 1994a–d).

Apart from the Greek cities, Hellenic settlements existed elsewhere in Colchis – at Pichvnari and Tsikhisdziri. Unfortunately, we know practically nothing about them because, to date, only Greek graves have been studied and not the settlements themselves. We know of the burial customs of the Greeks in Colchis, especially how they adapted their funeral practices to the local climatic and natural conditions. At the same time the Hellenization of the local population was quite strong. Study of these graves shows that there existed either a separate Greek settlement or quarter within the Colchian one (Pichvnari) or a mixed Ionian-Attic-Colchian settlement (Tsikhisdziri). The cults of Apollo and Demeter were practised in both places (Tsetskhladze 1994d) and the cult of Apollo Hegemon was the official cult of colonists in Phasis (Tsetskhladze 1994b).

A question which in recent years has been widely debated is the date of the foundation of Chersonesus in the Crimea. For a long time it was held that it was the only Dorian colony on the northern Pontic shore and had been founded by colonists from Heraklea Pontica in 422/21 (Saprykin 1986, 52–69, with bibliography). Yet during excavations at Chersonesus earlier material kept appearing, admittedly in small quantities: painted Ionian pottery, and black and red-figure pottery. Scholars put forward a variety of explanations for what had been, until recently, a question of isolated finds. Some had assumed this to be an indication that a trading station and Ionian settlement had come into being there as early as the 6th century BC; others that the Dorian colony had been preceded by a mooring for ships (Koshelenko *et al.* 1984, 15).

Renewed interest in this problem has resulted from the excavations undertaken in the Chersonesus Historical-Archaeological Reserve in the north-eastern part of the city-site, begun in 1976. On this part of the site many hundreds of objects from the Archaic period of various categories have been found: a large collection of Ionian and Corinthian vessels and Attic black-figure pottery, archaic amphorae and terracotta figurines, an Ionian ring, and cast Olbian coins. All this material dates from the last quarter of the 6th century and the 5th century BC (Vinogradov and Zolotarev 1990; Chtcheglov 1992, 214–20).

I shall consider some of the material which may help determine the date of the founding of Chersonesus: one black-figure lekane lid, of which 15 fragments have been preserved. The inner surface is painted. The outside is decorated with three friezes using silhouette technique. The lid dates from the third quarter of the 6th century BC and was made in a Boeotian (?) workshop (Vinogradov and Zolotarev 1990, 88).

At first glance such an early date for the lid of a painted Boeotian (?) lekane is difficult to associate with the main mass of archaic material found on the site. The dozens of pieces of Ionian and Attic pottery found date from the late 6th century and the beginning of the 5th century BC. The earliest archaeological level at Chersonesus is datable 25–30 years after the founding of the Dorian settlement in the first quarter of the 5th century BC.

This time-gap of a quarter of a century spans the period between the foundation and the appearance of the first burials (Zedgenidze and Savelya 1981; 1981a). In the northern part of the city over 100 burials of the late 5th and 4th centuries BC have been studied. The burials in other parts of the necropolis are also of this date. In the necropolis in the northern part of the city, however, scholars have identified five burials in amphorae used as funerary urns. Three were in amphorae from Samos dating from the very beginning of the 5th century, one in an amphora from Thasos and one in a proto-Thasian amphora of the very late 6th century BC. Thus the earliest burials appear to predate the founding of the settlement, just as the earliest settlement level does, by 25–30 years, i.e. by a single generation.

The excavations of the last decade also brought to light a series of 26 graffiti "ostraka" from amphorae and black-glaze pottery. They are inscriptions of male names, both with and without patronymics, and they date from some time during the 5th century. A comprehensive study of them (Y. G. Vinogradov) has shown that of the 26 "ostraka" containing 24 prosopographical units, the earliest two were executed in the Megarian alphabet dating back to 500–480 BC (Vinogradov and Zolotarev 1990, 103–9). Analysis of the remaining "ostraka" has shown that from the second quarter of the 5th century the names are written in a more legible Milesian alphabet, while the predominance of Dorian personal names is retained. The Dorians are represented by ten names, but four names on three "ostraka" bear strongly pronounced Ionic features.

The discovery of the "ostraka", dating from the 5th century BC, provided grounds for some scholars to suggest that a new colony was founded in the last quarter of the 6th century BC in the south-west of the Crimea jointly by Ionians from Sinope and Dorians from Heraklea (Vinogradov and Zolotarev 1990, 103–9). This hypothesis would appear premature since there is not yet adequate material for such a far-reaching conclusion. We can only say with confidence that at the site of Chersonesus, founded in 422–421 BC, there existed a large setlement which had been founded in the last quarter of the 6th century BC by Ionians. The question as to the status of the settlement still remains open, as does that regarding its relationship to the later city of Chersonesus. The city had probably been refounded by the Dorians from Heraklea Pontica.[25]

It had always been thought that the first houses at Chersonesus had been built of stone. New excavations in the third sector of the north-western part have, however, brought to light dwellings sunk into the rock. These were round or oval in shape with earthen floors, hearths and walls: those parts of the dugout protruding above earth were made of mud-brick. Amphorae have been found Herakleian, Mendean, etc., many of which bear stamps dating from the end of the 5th century BC. To this period also date the large quantity of fragments of black-glaze Attic and handmade pottery (Zolotarev 1990). This means that the dugout buildings are the earliest of the city, similar to those of Berezan, Olbia, Panticapaeum, Nymphaeum, etc. (Kryzhitskii 1982, 10–1). They were in use between the end of the 5th century and the first quarter of the 4th century BC. Around the middle of the 4th century BC stone buildings above ground were erected over the rock dugouts.[26]

*Conclusions: The Reasons for Colonization*

This highly complex problem has been argued over by scholars for more than 150 years.[27] The Greeks themselves tell us many times and in many ways that they were forced to leave home to search for a new place to live: they were unwilling colonists, driven from home by various disasters. Rarely is there explicit mention of commercial or agricultural benefits that must have lured the colonists to explore new sites. Instead, colonial narratives emphasize the negative factors – natural, political, personal and physical – that encouraged the colonists to leave their homeland (Dougherty 1993, 16–8).

I shall not dwell in detail on all the points in this controversy (Kocybala 1978, 126–36). They can be summarized in the words of J. Fine: "Greek colonization of the Black Sea region was of great importance for subsequent Greek history. A huge area, rich in metals, timber, grain, fish and many other products, was thus opened to a Greek world, whose resources in raw materials and food products were inadequate for the constantly growing population. The necessity to pay for those imports stimulated the activity of Greek craftsmen – especially the potters and metal-workers" (1983, 81).

Most scholars, following C. Roebuck (1959, 116–30), consider that the main reason behind colonization of the Black Sea was interest in the metal of the southern and eastern parts and the grain of the North. Recent studies have shown that these regions, in particular the southern coast, were not all that rich in metal and alternative reasons for colonization have to be sought (Jesus 1978; *cf.* Treister 1988; 1992). A. Shcheglov (Chtcheglov) in his highly detailed analysis of the available written, archaeological and palaeobotanical sources connected with the grain trade in the Black Sea region, ended with the conclusion that the real picture did not match the generally accepted view of a large-scale and well regulated Graeco-Scythian grain trade in the 7th-5th centuries and later: "Such trade was a myth that evolved in the minds of modern scholars". He draws a convincing conclusion that, if we accept as probable that grain was exported from Greek centres along the north coast of the Black Sea in the 7th-5th centuries, then it could have been grain that was grown in the *chora* of those cities rather than acquired from the population of the steppe and wooded steppe zones. In any case, the export of grain from any centre on the north coast of the Black Sea could not have been a permanent or regular phenomenon that continued without interruption and always on a significant scale (Chtcheglov 1990; *cf.* Noonan 1973a).

The reasons for colonization were never exclusively agrarian, or commercial, or connected with the need for metals on the one hand, or with over-population on the other. There was a whole range of reasons. Each mother-city had its own reasons for sending out colonies (Blavatskii, Koshelenko and Kruglikova 1979). First, it is important to analyse the metropolis and the reasons that might have *obliged* the Greeks to emigrate, and then look for reasons in the region where the colonies had been founded – natural resources and local conditions (Koshelenko and Kuznetsov 1992). This is the appropriate order in which to approach this question rather than to start with the natural resources.

Virtually all the colonies in the Black Sea region were founded by Miletus.[28] What compelled Milesians to seek their fortune beyond the confines of Ionia, which became involved in the colonization process later than the other cities of homeland Greece? We must remember that the Ionian *poleis* were situated in favourable geographical conditions and possessed large expanses of fertile land (Hdt. I. 142). Herodotus refers to Miletus as "the pearl of Ionia" (V. 28).

At the end of the 8th century the Ionian *poleis* began advancing deep into the mainland, enlarging their territory. Miletus pushed back its boundaries up the river valley twenty or thirty miles (Cook J. 1968, 35). Expansion of this kind was typical of the other Ionian *poleis.* After the Mermnad dynasty had been established (c. 675), clashes began between Lydia and the Greeks (Dandamaev 1989, 20–4). The next Lydian dynasty, that of the Gyges, continued to pursue a hostile policy and its campaigns against Miletus and other cities (Hdt. I. 14–15).

Particularly unfortunate was the outcome of the war waged by Alyattes against Miletus (Hdt. I. 16–18). His successor Croesus was known for his hostile stance towards most Greek cities (Hdt. 1. 26–28).

The purpose of Lydia's aggression was to seize agricultural land (Hdt. I. 73). The main result of the Graeco-Lydian wars was the curtailing of the possessions of the Ionian *poleis*, including Miletus. The expansion of Lydia's territory led to a restructuring of the economy and foreign policy of the Ionian *poleis*. When extension of land became out of the question (and existing possessions had been reduced) the Ionians began to search for overseas colonies, and trade was to become one of their major activities (Cook J. 1962, 50; Akurgal 1962, 373). Miletus' loss of part of its *chora* led to a grim struggle within the *polis* itself (Hdt. V. 28–29) (Jeffery 1976, 214). The very existence of part of the civilian population was under threat when discussion was underway as to how existing land ought be redistributed. One of the most radical solutions was emigration. At that time there was only one region that had not yet been colonized by other Greek cities – the Black Sea – and it was precisely towards Pontus that Miletus looked.

The Milesian colonies appeared after the middle of the 7th century, when Lydia had already begun its expansion. This is the first stage of Greek penetration of the Black Sea. Miletus founded only seven settlements – on its northern, southern and western coasts. They were all small and situated on islands or peninsulae. Most probably they were designed to serve as bases for future reconnaissance. Their purpose was to collect information about those lands and to examine possibilities for further colonizing. Cautiously, they sought to forge relations with the local population of Scythians, Thracians etc. In the 7th century few imports are to be found on the native sites: relations clearly expanded rapidly in the 6th century.

The long struggle for land between Miletus and Lydia always led to losses for Miletus. It came to an end at the beginning of the 6th century when Miletus was obliged to accept a treaty that reduced its possessions (Hdt. 1. 25). This led to an internal crisis and one of the methods used to resolve it was emigration. New waves of emigrants set off for the shores of Pontus. This is the second stage of the Greek colonization of the Black Sea.

The crisis in Miletus ended for a time and relations between Lydia and Greece were friendly, with Lydia coming under the influence of Greek culture (Dandamaev 1989, 21–2; Hanfmann 1978). The flowering of Miletus was not to last for long. In the middle of the 6th century disaster struck again: this time dealt by the Persian king, who began to conquer the Greek cities of Asia Minor (Dandamaev 1989, 23–8). Once again the Ionians were obliged to send off new colonies to Pontus. This is the third stage of the colonization of the Black Sea. The written sources make it quite clear, for example, that the Phocaeans and Teans were fleeing so as to avoid Persian conquest and enslavement: the Teans founded Abdera in Thrace (Hdt. 1. 168–169) and Phanagoria in the Kimmerian Bosporus about 542 (Arrian, *Byth.,* fr. 56 Roos). This did not mark the end of forced emigration. After the Ionians had been defeated in their revolt against the Persians, in the first quarter of the 5th century, they were obliged once again to flee from their native cities (a fourth stage of colonization).[29]

The constant armed incursions by the Lydian kings against the Greek cities of Asia Minor, on which they embarked not long before the end of the 7th century, had the most disastrous consequences for the Greeks. Their cities had been founded in geographically advantageous locations and, unlike the *poleis* of mainland Greece, did not suffer from a shortage of fertile land. Now they were not only robbed of a chance to extend their territory but had also lost part of their *chora*. To make matters worse, some of the cities had been seized and destroyed by the Lydians. Such was the fate of Smyrna, for example (Hdt. I. 16). Trial and tribulation were also to be the lot of Miletus, whose lands were laid waste over the course of many years. Similar examples could be cited in relation to other *poleis*. All this gave rise to a crisis in Ionia, a crisis which was reflected in a shortage of the very means of subsistence, above all a shortage of land. Each *polis* sought its own solution. One involved extension of trading so as to obtain food, but trade could not compensate for the losses resulting from incessant hostilities. Trade alone was not enough to feed a substantial section of the hungry (if not starving) population, which, in addition, was threatened by death or slavery. There is no doubt that at critical moments in their history many Ionian *poleis* had to resolve to take the one remaining step open to them which could provide a fundamental solution to their problem – to leave their homeland and settle elsewhere.

As G. Koshelenko and V. Kuznetsov observed: "An important consideration here was that the Ionian *polis,* as a result of all this, had to lower itself one or more steps beneath the level of culture which it would have achieved by the time the struggle against Lydia began, or later. Consequently, the Ionian Greeks were obliged not only to endure economic losses and, as a result, live in conditions of growing social tension in the cities, but also renounce the level of prosperity and culture (in the broad sense of the term) to which they were accustomed. This meant that the very principles underlying the existence of the *polis* were under threat. By setting up their *apoikiai* the Greeks not only delivered themselves from physical destruction and slavery, from economic and social problems, but also endeavoured to return to their earlier way of life and civilization befitting a *polis*" (1992, 24–5).

## ACKNOWLEDGMENTS

I am extremely grateful to Professor Sir John Boardman for his comments and advice. I am very proud to have been his first East European pupil. I consider this a real honour and it is with great pleasure that I dedicate this essay to my Teacher, who has done so much for me since I first arrived in Oxford. I should like to thank Professor G. Koshelenko (my former Ph. D. supervisor in Moscow) for his support while I was writing this paper and for the new information he supplied me with about excavations on the north coast of the Black Sea. Dr J. Hind's publications in *AR* of reports about new discoveries on the Black Sea are always a helpful guide to what has been done. I am grateful to Mrs K. Judelson and Dr J. F. Hargrave for their assistance in the preparation of the text. Finally, I should like to express my thanks to my mentors and friends in Oxford (Professor F. Millar and Dr O. Murray) and to the many people who attended this lecture in the Ruskin Lecture Theatre of the Ashmolean Museum, Oxford (1 March, 1994).

## NOTES

1. The cautious position of the archaeologists is voiced: Boardman 1980, 238–55.
2. J. Boardman's main conclusion at the end of this article reflects the actual situation as we understand it

which exists today on this question and the differences of opinion between archaeologists and historians: "Archaeologists will welcome secure evidence for the discovery of Geometric Greek material on Black Sea shores and will join historians in speculation about how it arrived there, in the hands of Greeks or of others. But we are still waiting, and patience is no lesser archaeological virtue than discretion" (Boardman 1991, 389).

3. This paper was given at a workshop entitled "Greek and Roman Settlements on the Black Sea" held at the 95th Annual Meeting of the Archaeological Institute of America, Washington D.C., December 1993. The papers given at this workshop are to be published: G. R. Tsetskhladze (Ed.), *Greek and Roman Settlements on the Black Sea Coast* (Issue no. 1 of the series: G. R. Tsetskhladze (Ed.), *Colloquenda Pontica*, Bradford, Loid Publishing), Bradford, 1994.

4. In recent years the archaeology of the Black Sea has become very popular in the West and in America. General articles on the excavations in the Black Sea region have long been traditional in *AR* (for: 1962–63; 1971–72; 1983–84; 1990–91; 1992–93). A similar practice was begun by *AJA* (see: 97 (1993), 521–63); *RÉA* is to publish my article on recent excavations in the eastern part of the Black Sea region (with review of the literature) in 1994. Professor W. Schuller (Konstanz) and Professor P. Lévêque (Besançon) are publishing not only separate articles in the *Xenia* series and in *DHA*, but also books devoted to specific regions and cities on the Black Sea. Professor J. Fossey (Montreal) and Mr. A. Caratzas (Publisher, New York) have inaugurated a series of monographs on the Black Sea. Recently, two special journals were set up - *Das Schwarzes Meer* and *Ancient Civilizations from Scythia to Siberia* (Leiden, E. J. Brill) [The first issue of this journal appeared when the present volume was already in press. For this reason I was unable to make use of the articles and new material published in it] - and a new series was launched entitled *Colloquenda Pontica* (Bradford, Ed. G. R. Tsetskhladze). J. Hind is preparing a Chapter on the colonization of the Black Sea for a collection of articles on colonization (Leiden, E. J. Brill, Ed. I. Malkin). Reviews of new research have also been published: J. Irmscher and D. Schelow (Eds.), *Griechische Städte und einheimische Völker des Schwarzmeergebietes* (Berlin 1961); H. Heinen (Ed.), *Die Geschichte des Altertums in Spiegel der sowjetischen Forschung* (Darmstadt 1980), 341–402; *Les Villes grecques de la Mer Noire. Olbia, Panticapée, Chersonèse* (Les Dossiers d'Archéologie, 188, Décembre 1993. No. 88, 1984 was devoted to the archaeology of the eastern Black Sea region). At the present time we are threatened by the pleasant danger of an explosion of information on Black Sea archaeology. In order to help scholars and students a bibliographical reference manual is being compiled (J. Fossey and G. R. Tsetskhladze, *Bibliography of the Archaeology of the Black Sea,* McGill University, Montreal (Classical Archaeology and History Companions)). The following general books on the subject have ben published: M. Koromila (Ed.), *The Greeks in the Black Sea from the Bronze Age to the Early Twentieth Century* (Athens 1991) and J. Bouzek, *Studies of Greek Pottery in the Black Sea Area* (Prague 1990) (See: Reviews on Bouzek by J. Hind in *JHS* 113 (1993), 230–1 and by J. Boardman in *Gnomon*, 65. 6 (1993), 564–5). New general books are being prepared: G. R. Tsetskhladze, *Greeks in the Black Sea* and *Romans in the Black Sea* (London and New York, Routledge). See also: B. Isaac, *The Greek Settlements in Thrace until the Macedonian Conquest* (Leiden, E. J. Brill 1986). An important review of the literature has been published by T. Sulimirski, "Greek Colonization and the Early Iron Age East of the Volga", *BIA* 11 (1973), 1–40. For a review of new literature on the northern coast of the Black Sea (1980–1989), see: A. A. Maslennikov and A. E. Medovichev (Eds.), *Problems of the History and Culture of the Northern Black Sea Region in Classical Antiquity* (Moscow 1991) (in Russian); A. Wasowicz, "Les Grecs dans le Pont: de Nouvelles Monographies", *DHA* 17.2 (1991), 127–32; B. Nadel, "The Euxine Pontos as seen by the Greeks", *DHA* 17.2 (1991), 115–26.

5. This "academic war" has become all the more intense as a result of nationalist emotions. (See: P. L. Kohl and G. R. Tsetskhladze, "Nationalism, Politics and the Practice of Archaeology in the Caucasus", P. L. Kohl and C. Fawcett (Eds. ), *Nationalism, Politics and the Practice of Archaeology,* Cambridge, U. P. 1995 forthcoming).

6. Some scholars assume that Balkan-Anatolian connections existed in the Late Chalcolithic period (see: L.

Thissen, "New Insights in Balkan-Anatolian connections in the Late Chalcolithic: Old Evidence from the Turkish Black Sea littoral", *Anatolian Studies* 43 (1993), 207–37).

7. There is an extensive literature devoted to these stone anchors: H. Frost, Stone Anchors as Clues to Bronze Age Trade Routes, *Thracia Pontica* I (1982), 280–9; K. Porojanov, Les relations entre les colonies grecques et les états thraces du littoral occidental de la Mer Noire VII$^e$-V$^e$ s. av. n. è. *Thracia Pontica* III (1986), 158–65; J. Hind, Archaeology of the Greek and Barbarian Peoples around the Black Sea (1982–1992), *AR* for 1992–93, 84; M. Lazarov, La Navigacion le long du Littoral Thrace du Pont Euxin avant la colonization grecque, *Dritter Internationaler Thrakologischer Kongress*, Vol. II (Sofia 1984), 63–8; K. Porogeanov, Navigation et Commerce de la population du Littoral Européen de la Mer Noire de la Thrace ancienne avec les peuples de la Mediterranée Orientale (XVI-XII s. av. n. è.), *Idem*, 69–75, etc.

8. After the expedition of T. Severin to test the credibility of the voyage of the Argonauts to Colchis, these authors refer to that voyage as the "new Argonauts" and adhere more firmly than ever to their opinion that the myth reflects reality (see: T. Severin, *The Jason Voyage. The Quest for the Golden Fleece* (London 1985)). Moreover, some distinguished Georgian archaeologists consider the opinion of Severin (a traveller not a scholar) the absolute last word on this problem, quoting him as a mantra, e.g. D. Khakhutaishvili: "The leader of the expedition of the new Argonauts, Tim Severin, after acquainting himself with the city-site and the collection of finds in Kobuleti, commented: 'At last everything fell into place. Without doubt this was the final confirmation of the legend of Jason, the detail which no-one could invent after the event - neither Apollonius Rhodius, nor other authors who wrote about the Golden Fleece. . . *Every detail of the legend found its archaeological confirmation* (my italics). What had seemed to us to be no more than an old fairy-tale at the beginning of the "Jason Voyage" suddenly emerged as reality in Georgia, 1,500 miles from the starting point at Iolkos (Volos)'" (D. Khakhutaishvili, Les sites archéologiques sur les terres submersibles des fleuves Tcholoki et Otchkamouri, in *Le Pont-Euxin*, 210).

9. The literature on the myth of the Argonauts is enormous. For recent studies with exhaustive bibliographies, see: *Apollonius of Rhodes. Argonautica. Book III.* Edited by R. L. Hunter (Cambridge 1989), 1–43; T. Gautz, *Early Greek Myth. A Guide to literary and Artistic Sources* (Baltimore and London 1993), 340–73; R. Hunter, *The Argonautica of Apollonius. Literary Studies* (Cambridge 1993).

10. In Colchis burials of the local nobility contain an abundance of golden jewellery of the 5th century (Lordkipanidze 1979, 85–100).

11. On the depiction of mythological subjects in art, see: J. Boardman, Herakles, Theseus and Amazons, in D. Kurtz and B. Sparkes (Eds.), *The Eye of Grcece* (Cambridge 1982), 2–28; *ibid.*, Herakles, in E. Bohr and W. Martin (Eds.), *Studien zur Mythologie und Vasenmalerei* (Mainz 1986), 127–32; T. H. Carpenter, *Art and Myth in Ancient Greece* (London 1990); H. A. Shapiro, *Myth into Art. Poet and Painter in Classical Greece* (London and New York 1994).

12. I wish to express my thanks to Professor J. Neils for her help and hospitality, and for discussing the question of the depiction of the myth of the Argonauts in Greek art during my visit to Cleveland (5–6 January, 1994).

13. I should like to thank Dr T. Mannack and Ms M. Mendonca of the Beazley Archive, Oxford University for their help.

14. The myths connected with the other part of the Black Sea region were more famous in Greek visual art and literature (*LIMC* 1, 586–653; *LIMC* 5, 713–26; J. Neils, The Group of the Negro Alabastra: A Study in Motif Transferal, *Antike Kunst,* 1980, 23.1, 13–23; M. F. Vos, *Scythian Archers in Archaic Attic Vase-Painting* (Groningen 1963), 66–9, 93–127; J. Henderson, Timeo Danaos: Amazons in Early Greek Art and Pottery, in S. Goldhill and R. Osborne (Eds.), *Art and Text in Ancient Greek Culture* (Cambridge 1994), 85–137; M. V. Skrzhinskaya, *Ancient Greek Folk-lore and Literature about the Northern Black Sea Region* (Kiev 1991), 11–72 (in Russian); F. V. Shelov-Kovedyaeav, A Berezan Hymn to the Island and Achilles, *VDI* 3 (1990), 49–62; G. Hedreen, The Cult of Achilles in the Euxine, *Hesperia* 60 (1991), 313–30).

15. For the stage of the activity of the Greek settlers in the Black Sea, and in particular the northern part of the region, see: V. P. Yailenko, Archaic Greece, in E. S. Golubtsova, L. P. Marinovich *et al.* (Eds.), *Ancient Greece,* Vol. 1 (Moscow 1983), 140–1 (in Russian); G. A. Koshelenko and V. D. Kuznetsov, The Greek Colonization of the Bosporus (in Connection with Certain General Problems of Colonization), in G. A. Koshelenko (Ed.), *Essays on the Archaeology and History of the Bosporus* (Moscow 1992), 6–28 (in Russian).

16. About some late 7th century East Greek pottery from Amisos, see: Hind 1984, 96; 1993, 110.

17. We know nothing about other Milesian colonies in the southern part of the Black Sea region: Kerasos, Kotyora, Tios and Sesamos.

18. Their modern geographical location (Berezan, for instance, is an island) does not correspond to their ancient one (See: N. Panin, Black Sea Coastline Changes in the last 1,000 Years. A new attempt at identifying the Danube mouth as described by the Ancients, *Dacia* 27 (1983), 175–84; B. Dimitrov and A. Orachev, The Harbour System along the West Pontic coast (II–I millennia BC), *Arkheologiya* 1 (1982, Sofia), 1–11; M. V. Agbunov, Classical Archaeology and Palaegeography, *KSIA* 191 (1987), 3–6; I. V. Bruyako and V. A. Karpov, Ancient Geography and Fluctuations of the Sea Levels, *VDI* 2 (1992), 87–97). On underwater archaeological investigations, see: G. Gamkrelidze, Hydroarchaeology in the Georgian Republic (the Colchian Littoral), *The International Journal of Nautical Archaeology* 21.2 (1992), 101–9; A. V. Okorokov, Development of Underwater Archaeological Investigations in Russia and the Former Soviet Union, *The International Journal of Nautical Archaeology* 22.3 (1993), 267–73; J. C. Neville, Opportunities and Challenges in the Black Sea, *The INA Quarterly* 20.3 (1993), 12–6.

19. This question is a focus of intense controversy (See: Kocybala 1978, 182–4; Vinogradov Y. G. 1989, 26–31). The book by S. Solovev (present Director of the State Hermitage's Berezan Archaeological Expedition) about archaic Berezan is currently being prepared for publication as a supplementary volume to the Journal *Colloquenda Pontica.*

20. Closed vessels of the Late Wild Goat Type, Ionian kylikes and cups, painted cups from Chios (See: Kuznetsov 1991, 33).

21. It should be noted that V. D. Kuznetsov is the pioneer among Russian archaeologists in using the 'new' terminology, classification and dating for early Greek pottery, which have been generally accepted in 'western' archaeological literature for the last 25 years. Together with P. Dupont he is preparing a book about early Greek pottery on the northern coast of the Black Sea.

22. Virtually all large cities in the Black Sea region began to mint their own coins. See: P. O. Karyshkovskii, *Coins of Olbia* (Kiev 1988), 27–55 (in Russian); V. A. Anokhin, *Coin Circulation in the Bosporan Kingdom* (Kiev 1986), 5–30 (in Russian) (For a critique of many of the conclusions this author draws, see: N. A. Frolova, The Problems of Minting Coins in the Bosporus, *VDI* 2 (1988), 12 2–43); M. J. Price, *Sylloge Nummorum Graecorum, Vol. IX, The British Museum, Part 1: The Black Sea* (London 1993), etc..

23. The cities on the west coast of the Black Sea also turned into large cities. See: Schuller 1985, 9–28; Alexandrescu and Schuller 1990, 9–102. (This book also provides a bibliography on Histria and the region on pp. 285–308).

24. On recent archaeological investigations in Georgia, see: D. D. Kacharava, Archaeological Investigations on the Eastern Black Sea Littoral, 1970–80, *AR* for 1983–84, 98–101; *ibid.*, Archaeology in Georgia, 1980–1990, *AR* for 1990–91, 78–86; Tsetskhladze 1994a. For a bibliography of Georgian archaeological literature, 1976–86, see: D. Kacharava and V. Tolordava, La Colchide antique. Bibliographie, *DHA* 13 (1987), 275–312.

25. A. A. Zedgenidze fiercely opposes any suggestions to the effect that Chersonesus was founded earlier (Zedgenidze 1993). V. Kuznetsov holds that it *is* necessary to set the foundation of the early settlement still further back in time and he suggests the second quarter of the 6th century BC as a probable date (Kuznetsov 1991, 36, note 42). Recently, the special article devoted to the lekana from Chersonesus was published. M. Zolotarev confirms his previous identification of this vase as of Boeotian origin (M. I. Zolotarev, A Boeotian Lekanis from Chersonesus, *Ancient Civilisations from Scythia to Siberia* 1(1), 1994,

112–17). J. Boardman, however, has doubts about its Boeotian origin and thinks that "The Chersonesus vase may be Attic, but the double frieze of animals upon it recalls also the black figure lekanai of Thasos" (J. Boardman, Olbia and Berezan: the Early Pottery, in G. R. Tsetskhladze (Ed.) *Greek Colonization of the Black Sea, Historia* supplementary volume, forthcoming).

26. Until recently scholars knew nothing about colonial activity on the part of Olbia itself. Now it is clear that Olbia founded its own settlements in the north-western Crimea in the 5th century (which area became part of *chora* of Chersonesus from the 4th century). This hypothesis was put forward for the first time by A. N. Shcheglov (Chtcheglov) in 1985. Gradually it has been borne out by archaeology and has come to be generally accepted (See: A. N. Shcheglov, Un établissement rural en Crimée: Panskoje I (fouilles de 1969–1985), *DHA* 13 (1987), 244–7; Y. G. Vinogradov, Olbiopolithes in north-western Tauric, in Y. G. Vinogradov (Ed.), *The Ancient Black Sea Region* (Odessa 1990), 51–64 (in Russian); Y. G. Vinogradov and A. N. Shcheglov, The Formation of the Territory of the Chersonesus State, in E. S. Golubtsova (Ed.), *Hellenism: Economics, Politics and Culture* (Moscow 1990), 313–4 (in Russian); Chtcheglov 1992, 236–48).

27. For the latest works on this subject, see: Graham in *CAH*, 157–9; Snodgrass 1980, 32, 38, 40–2, 119–21; Ridgway D. 1990; Cawkwell 1992; Hopper 1976, 83–108; Murray 1993, 102–23. The most detailed work is still: Gwynn 1918.

28. According to calculations by N. Ehrhardt the number of Milesian settlements reached approximately seventy, which is close to the number given by Seneca *(Consol. ad. Helv. matr.* VII.2). See also: Graham 1983, 98–117.

29. The fourth stage of colonization was not on such a large scale as the previous three. Only three major cities were founded: Mesambria in the West (Hdt. VI. 33; Pseudo-Skynmus, 737–742) – the archaeological material dates only from the Hellenistic period (Hind 1984, 73–4)); Kerkinitis and Kalos-Limen in Crimea (V. A. Kutaisov, *The Ancient City of Kerkinitis* (Kiev 1990), 141, in Russian). The Athenians, whose interest in the Black Sea began as early as the 6th century, included Pontus in their empire from the middle of the 5th century (Bouzek 1989; 1990, 51–2; 1994, 241–3). Moreover, Greek cities in both the European and Asian parts of the Kimmerian Bosporus united in 480 BC as one state, which came to be known as the Bosporan Kingdom with its capital at Panticapaeum (Gajdukevich 1971, 32–49; Shelov-Kovedyaev 1984, 63–78).

## ABBREVIATIONS

*GCNP*: J.-P. Descoeudres (Ed.) *Greek Colonists and Native Populations.* Proceedings of the First Australian Congress of Classical Archaeology held in honour of Emeritus Professor A. D. Trendall (Oxford, U. P. 1990).

*INA*: Institute of Nautical Archaeology.

*KSIA*: Kratkiye Soobshcheniya Instituta Arkheologii Akademii Nauk SSSR (Short Bulletins of the Institute of the Institute of Archaeology, Academy of Sciences of the USSR), Moscow (in Russian).

*Le Pont-Euxin*: O. Lordkipanidzé and P. Lévêque (Eds.), *Le Pont-Euxin vu par les Grecs. Sources écrites et archéologie.* Symposium de Vani (Colchide), septembre-octobre 1987 (Paris 1990).

*SA*: Sovetskaya Arkheologiya (Soviet Archaeology), Moscow (in Russian with summaries in French and English).

*Tskhaltubo 1977*: O. D. Lordkipanidze (Ed.), *Problems of Greek Colonization of the Northern and Eastern Black Sea Littoral.* Materials of the 1st All-Union Symposium on the Ancient History of the Black Sea Littoral (Tbilisi 1979).

*Tskhaltubo 1979*: O. D. Lordkipanidze (Ed.), *The Demographic Situation in in the Black Sea Littoral in the Period of Great Greek Colonization.* Materials of the 2nd All-Union Symposium on the Ancient History of the Black Sea Littoral (Tbilisi 1981)

*Tskhaltubo-Vani 1985*: O. D. Lordkipanidze (Ed.), *Local Ethno-political Entities of the Black Sea Area in the*

7th-4th cents. BC. Materials of the 4th All-Union Symposium on the Ancient History of the Black Sea littoral (Tbilisi 1988).

*Vani 1987*: O. D. Lordkipanidze (Ed.), *The Black Sea Littoral in the 7th-5th cents. BC: Literary Sources and Archaeology (Problems of Authenticity)*. Materials of the 5th International Symposium on the Ancient History of the Black Sea Littoral (Tbilisi 1990).

*VDI*: Vestnik Drevnei Istorii (Journal of Ancient History), Moscow (in Russian with summaries in English).

## BIBLIOGRAPHY

ABRAMOV, A. P. and PAROMOV, Y. M. 1993: Archaic Settlements of the Taman Peninsula. In Y. M. Paromov (Ed.), *Bosporan Collection* 2, 70–6 (in Russian).

AKURGAL, E. A. 1962: The Early Period and the Golden Age of Ionia. *AJA* 66, 369–79.

AKURGAL, E. A. and BUDDE, L. 1956: *Vorläufiger Bericht über die Ausgrabungen in Sinope* (Ankara).

ALEKSEEVA, E. M. 1991: *Greek Colonization of the North-Western Caucasus* (Moscow) (in Russian).

ALEXANDRESCU, P. 1978a: *La céramique de l'époque Archaique et Classique (VII$^e$-IV$^e$ s.).* (Bucuresti and Paris) (Histria IV).

ALEXANDRESCU, P. 1978b: La céramique de Grèce de l'est dans les cites pontiques. *Les céramiques de la Grèce de l'est et leur diffusion en occident* (Paris and Naples), 52–61.

ALEXANDRESCU, P. and SCHULLER, W. 1990 (Eds.): *Histria* (Konstanz, Xenia, ht. 25).

ASTOUR, M. C. 1967: *Hellenosemitica* (Leiden).

BLAVATSKII, V. D. 1964: *Panticapaeum* (Moscow) (in Russian).

BLAVATSKII, V. D., KOSHELENKO, G. A. and KRUGLIKOVA, I. T. 1979: The *Polis* and the Migration of the Greeks. In *Tskhaltubo 1977*, 7–29 (in Russian).

BOARDMAN, J. 1980: *The Greeks Overseas$^3$* (London).

BOARDMAN, J. 1991: Early Greek Pottery on Black Sea Sites? *OJA* 10 (3), 387–9.

BOLTUNOVA, A. I. 1976: The Argonauts and Colchis. *Bulletin of the Academy of Sciences of the Georgian SSR: History and Archaeology, Series 3*, 37–41 (in Russian).

BOUZEK, J. 1983: The Caucasus and Europe and the Cimmerian Problem. *Acta Musei Nationalis Pragae* 27 (4), 177–232.

BOUZEK, J. 1985: *The Aegean, Anatolia and Europe: Cultural Interrelations in the Second Millenium BC* (Göteborg and Prague).

BOUZEK, J. 1989: Athènes et la Mer Noire. *BCH* 113, 249–59.

BOUZEK, J. 1990: *Studies of Greek Pottery in the Black Sea Area* (Prague).

BOUZEK, J. 1994: The Distribution of Greek Painted Pottery in the Mediterranean and in the Black Sea Region. A Comparison. *OJA* 13 (2), 241–3.

BOYSAL, J. 1959: Uber die älteren Funde von Sinope und die Kolonizationsfrage. *AA* 1/4, 8–9.

BREMMER, J. 1987 (Ed.): *Interpretations of Greek Mythology* (London and Sydney).

BREMMER, J. 1987: What is a Greek Myth? In *J. Bremmer 1987*, 1–9.

BRILLANTE, C. 1990: History and Historical Interpretation of Myth. In *Edmunds 1990*, 91–138.

BUCHHOLZ, H.-G. 1983: Doppelaxte und die Frage der Balkanbeziehungen des ägäischen Kulturkreises. In A. G. Poulter (Ed.), *Ancient Bulgaria: Papers presented to the International Symposium on the Ancient History and Archaeology of Bulgaria, University of Nottingham, 1981*, Part I (Nottingham), 54–5.

BURSTEIN, S. 1976: *Outpost of Hellenism: The Emergence of Heraclea* (Berkeley).

BUXTOR, R. 1994: *Imaginary Greece. The Context of Mythology* (Cambridge, U. P.).

CAH 1982: Vol. 3, Part 3, second edition.

CARPENTER, R. 1948: The Greek Penetration of the Black Sea. *AJA* 52, 1–10.

CARPENTER, T. H. 1990: *Art and Myth in Ancient Greece* (London).

CAWKWELL, G. L. 1992: Early Colonization. *CQ* 42 (2), 289–303.

CHTCHEGLOV, A. A. 1990: Le commerce du blé dans le Pont Septentrional (second moitié du VII$^e$–V$^e$

siècle). In *Le Pont-Euxin,* 141–59.

CHTCHEGLOV, A. A. 1992: *Polis et Chora* (Paris).

COJA, M. 1990: Greek Colonists and Native Populations in Dobruja (Moesia Inferior): The Archaeological Evidence. In *GCNP,* 157–68.

COLDSTREAM, J. N. 1968: *Greek Geometric Pottery* (London).

COOK, J. M. 1962: *The Greeks in Ionia and the East* (London).

COOK, R. M. 1946: Ionia and Greece in the 8th-7th cents BC. *JHS* 66, 67–98.

DANDAMAEV, M. A. 1989: *A Political History of the Achaemenid Empire* (Translation by W. J. Vogelsang) (Leiden).

DEMETRION, A. 1978: Die Datierung der Periode Cypro-Archaisch nach Fundzusammenhängen mit griechischer Keramik. *AA,* 12–25.

DIMITRIU, S. and ALEXANDRESCU, P. 1973: L'importation de la céramique attique dans les colonies du Pont-Euxin avant les guerres médiques. *RA* 1, 23–38.

DOUGHERTY, C. 1993: *The Poetics of Colonization. From City to Text in Archaic Greece* (Oxford).

DREWS, R. 1976: The Earliest Greek Settlements on the Black Sea. *JHS* 96, 18–31.

DUPONT, P. 1983: Classification et determination de provenance des céramiques grecques orientales archaiques d'Istros. *Dacia* 27, 19–23.

EDMUNDS, L. 1990 (Ed.): *Approaches to Greek Myth* (Baltimore and London).

EHRHARDT, N. 1983: *Milet und seine Kolonien* (Frankfurt).

FARMAKOVSKY, B. V. 1910: Archäologische Funde im Jahre 1909: Russland. *AA,* 195–244.

FINE, J. V. A. 1983: *The Ancient Greeks. A Critical History* (Cambridge, Mass. and London).

FRENCH, D. H. 1982: Mycenaeans in the Black Sea? *Thracia Pontica* I, 19–30.

GAJDUKEVICH, V. E. 1971: *Das Bosporanische Reich* (Berlin).

GRAHAM, A. J. 1958: The Date of the Greek Penetration of the Black Sea. *BICS* 5, 25–42.

GRAHAM, A. J. 1971: Patterns in Early Greek Colonization. *JHS* 91, 35–47.

GRAHAM, A. J. 1983: *Colony and Mother City in Ancient Greece*² (Chicago, Ares).

GRAHAM, A. J. 1990: Pre-Colonial Contacts: Questions and Problems. In *GCNP,* 45–60.

GRIFFIN, A. 1982: *Sikyon* (Oxford, U. P.).

GWYNN, A. 1918: The Character of Greek Colonization. *JHS* 38, 88–123.

HANFMANN, G. M. A. 1978: Lydian Relations with Ionia and Persia. In *The Proceedings of the Tenth International Congress of Classical Archaeology* (Ankara), 23–35.

HENRICHS, A. 1987: Three Approaches to Greek Mythography. In *J. Bremmer 1987,* 242–77.

HIND, J. 1964: Sites of Ancient Cities to the South of the Black Sea. *SA* 3, 172–87.

HIND, J. 1984: Greek and Barbarian Peoples on the Shores of the Black Sea. *AR* for 1983–84, 71–97.

HIND, J. 1988: The Colonization of Sinope and the South-Eastern Black Sea Area. In *Tskhaltubo-Vani 1985,* 207–23.

HIND, J. 1993: Archaeology of the Greeks and Barbarian Peoples around the Black Sea (1982–1992). *AR* for 1992–93, 82–112.

HOPPER, R. J. 1976: *The Early Greeks* (New York).

HUXLEY, G. L. 1966: *The Early Ionians* (London).

HUXLEY, G. L. 1969: *Greek Epic Poetry* (London).

HUXLEY, G. L. 1990: Eusebius on the Foundation of Trapezus. In *Vani 1987,* 198–201.

ISAAC, B. 1986: *The Greek Settlement in Thrace until the Macedonian Conquest* (Leiden).

IVANTCHIK, A. I. 1993: *Les Cimmériens au Proche-Orient* (Göttingen).

JANTZEN, U. 1972: *Ägyptische und orientalische Bronzen aus dem Heraion von Samos* (Bonn).

JEFFERY, L. H. 1976: *Archaic Greece, The City-States c. 700–500 BC* (New York).

JESUS, P. De 1978: Metal Resources in Ancient Anatolia. *Anatolian Studies* 28, 97–102.

KACHARAVA, D. D. and KVIRKVELIYA, G. T. 1991: *The Ancient Cities and Settlements of the Black Sea Littoral* (Tbilisi) (in Russian).

KARYSHKOVSKII, P. O. and KLEYMAN, I. G. 1985: *The Ancient City of Tyras* (Kiev) (in Russian).

KARYSHKOVSKII, P. O. and LAPIN, V. V. 1979: Coin Hoard of the Age of Greek Colonization Found in Berezan in 1975. In *Tskhaltubo 1977*, 105–6 (in Russian).

KERENYI, K. 1979: *Goddesses of Sun and Moon* (Dallas).

KILIAN, K. 1990: Mycenaean Colonization: Norm and Variety. In *GCNP*, 445–67.

KOCYBALA, A. K. 1978: *Greek Colonization of the North Shore of the Black Sea in the Archaic Period.* Unpublished Ph. D. thesis, University of Pennsylvania (Philadelphia).

KOPEIKINA, L. V. 1972: Painted Rhodian-Ionian Oinochoe from Temir-Gora. *VDI* 1, 147–59.

KOPEIKINA, L. V. 1973: Earliest Example of the Greek Painted Pottery from Berezan. *SA* 2, 240–4.

KOPEIKINA, L. V. 1979: Special Features of the Development of the Berezan Settlement in Connection with the Course of the Colonization Process. In *Tskhaltubo 1977*, 106–31 (in Russian).

KOPEIKINA, L. V. 1981: Elements of a Local Character in the Culture of the Berezan Setlement of the Archaic Period. In *Tskhaltubo 1979*, 163–74 (in Russian).

KOPEIKINA, L. V. 1986: Archaic Painted Pottery from the Greek Settlements of the Lower Bug and Dnieper Basins as a Source Material for the Study of Trade and Cultural Contacts. *Archaeological Collection of the State Hermitage Museum* 27, 27–47 (in Russian).

KORPUSOVA, V. 1980: A Rhodian-Ionian Painted Oinochoe from the Crimea. *VDI* 2, 98–104.

KORPUSOVA, V. 1987: East Greek and Corinthian Pottery. In S. D. Kryzhitskii (Ed.), *The Culture of the Population of Olbia and its Environs in the Archaic Period* (Kiev), 35–56 (in Russian).

KOSHELENKO, G. A. 1992 (Ed.): *Essays on the Archaeology and History of the Bosporus* (Moscow) (in Russian).

KOSHELENKO, G. A. and KUZNETSOV, V. D. 1990: La Colonization grecque du Bosphore Cimmérien. In *Le Pont-Euxin*, 67–84.

KOSHELENKO, G. A. and KUZNETSOV, V. D. 1992: The Greek Colonization of the Bosporus (in connection with certain general problems of colonization). In *G. A. Koshelenko 1992*, 6–28.

KRYZHITSKII, S. D. 1982: *Dwelling Houses of the Ancient Cities of the Northern Black Sea Littoral* (Kiev) (in Russian).

KRYZHITSKII, S. D. and OTRESHKO, V. P. 1986: On the Problem of the Formation of the *Polis* of Olbia. In *A. S. Rusyaeva 1986*, 5–17 (in Russian).

KRYZHITSKII, S. D., BUISKIKH. S. B. *et al.* 1989: *The Agricultural Environs of Olbia* (Kiev) (in Russian).

KRYZHITSKII, S. D., BUISKIKH, S. B. and OTRESHKO, V. M. 1990: *Ancient Settlements in the Lower Reaches of the Bug (An Archaeological Map)* (Kiev) (in Russian).

KUZNETSOV, V. D. 1991: Early *Apoikiai* in the Northern Black Sea Region. *KSIA* 204, 31–7.

KUZNETSOV, V. D. 1991a: Kepoi: Ionian Pottery. *SA* 4, 36–52.

KUZNETSOV, V. D. 1992: Excavations at Kepoi, 1984–1989. In *G. A. Koshelenko 1992*, 28–45.

KVIRKVELIYA, G. T. 1985: On the Question of the Possibility of the Kimmerians Having Used the Maeoto-Colchian Route. In O. D. Lordkipanidze (Ed.), *Questions of the Archaeology of Georgia* III (Tbilisi), 111–22 (in Georgian).

LABAREE, B. W. 1957: How the Greeks Sailed into the Black Sea. *AJA* 61, 29–33.

LORDKIPANIDZE, O. D. 1966: *The Ancient World and Colchis from 600 to 200 BC* (Tbilisi) (in Georgian).

LORDKIPANIDZE, O. D. 1979: *Ancient Colchis* (Tbilisi) (in Russian).

LORDKIPANIDZE, O. D. 1983: The Graeco-Roman World and Ancient Georgia (Colchis and Iberia). In *Modes de contacts et processus de transformation dans les société anciennes* (Pisa and Rome), 123–44.

LORDKIPANIDZE, O. D. 1984: *Temple-City of Colchis* (Moscow) (in Russian).

LORDKIPANIDZE, O. D. 1985: *Das alte Kolchis und seine Beziehungen zur griechischen Welt vom 6. zum 4. Jh. v. Chr.* (Konstanz, Xenia, ht. 14).

LORDKIPANIDZE, O. D. 1986: *Argonautica and Ancient Colchis* (Tbilisi) (in Georgian).

LORDKIPANIDZE, O. D. 1991: Vani: An Ancient City of Colchis. *Greek, Roman and Byzantine Studies* 32 (2), 151–95.

LORDKIPANIDZE, O. D. 1991a: The Greeks in Colchis. In M. Koromila (Ed.), *The Greeks in the Black Sea* (Athens), 190–7.

LORDKIPANIDZE, O. D. 1991b: *Archäologie in Georgien* (Weinheim).

MALKIN, I. and SHMUELI, N. 1988: "The City of the Blind" and The Founding of Byzantium. *Mediterranean Historical Review* 3 (1), 21–36.

MARCHENKO, K. K. 1979: Interaction of the Hellenic and Barbarian Elements in the Lower Reaches of the Bug in the 7th-5th cents. BC. In *Tskhaltubo 1977,* 130–8 (in Russian).

MEE, C. 1978: Aegean Trade and Settlement in Anatolia in the Second Millennium BC. *Anatolian Studies* 28, 132–3.

MELLINK, M. J. 1984: Archaeology in Anatolia. *AJA* 88, 441–59.

MELLINK, M. J. 1985: Archaeology in Anatolia. *AJA* 89, 547–67.

MIKELADZE, T. K. 1985: *Colchian Burial-grounds from the Early Iron Age* (Tbilisi) (in Georgian).

MIKELADZE, T. K. 1990: *On the Archaeology of Colchis* (Tbilisi) (in Russian).

MURRAY, O. 1993: *Early Greece*[2] (London).

NIBBI, A. 1993: Stone Anchors: The Evidence Reassessed. *The Mariner's Mirror* 79 (1, February), 5–26.

NOONAN, T. S. 1973: The Origin of the Greek Colony at Panticapaeum. *AJA* 77, 77–81.

NOONAN, T. S. 1973a: The Grain Trade of the Northern Black Sea in Antiquity. *AJP* 94 (3), 231–42.

OLMOS, R. 1990: About the Attic Red-figure Crater with a Colchian Subject (Appendix to Professor E. Simon's paper). In *Le Pont-Euxin*, 231–4.

ONAIKO, N. A. 1980: *Archaic Toric. An Ancient City in North-east Pontus* (Moscow) (in Russian).

PAROMOV, Y. M. 1990: Intervention sur la péninsula de Taman. In *Le Pont-Euxin,* 161–4.

PENGLASE, C. 1994: *Greek Myths and Mesopotamia. Parallels and Influence in the Homeric Hymns and Hesiod* (London and New York).

RIDGWAY, B. S. 1966: Notes on the Development of the Greek Frieze. *Hesperia* 35, 188–204.

RIDGWAY, B. S. 1991: Archaic Architectural Sculpture and Travel Myths. *DHA* 17 (2), 95–112.

RIDGWAY, B. S. 1993: *The Archaic Style in Greek Sculpture*[2] (Chicago, Ares).

RIDGWAY, D. 1990: The First Western Greeks and their Neighbours, 1935–1985. In *GCNP*, 61–72.

ROEBUCK, C. 1959: *Ionian Trade and Colonization* (New York).

RUSYAEVA, A. S. 1986 (Ed.): *Olbia and its Environs* (Kiev) (in Russian).

RUSYAEVA, A. S. 1992: *Religions and Cults of Olbia* (Kiev) (in Russian).

SAMOYLOVA, T. I. 1988: *Tyras in the VI-I cents. BC* (Kiev) (in Russian).

SAPRYKIN, S. Y. 1986: *Heraklea Pontica and Chersonesus Tauric* (Moscow) (in Russian).

SCHEFOLD, K. 1992: *Gods and Heroes in Late Archaic Art* (Cambridge, U. P.).

SCHULLER, W. 1985 (Ed.): *Die bulgarische Schwarzmeerküste im Altertum.* (Konstanz, Xenia, ht. 16).

SEKERSKAYA, N. M. 1989: *Ancient Nikonion and its Environs in the VI-IV cents. BC* (Kiev) (in Russian).

SHAPIRO, H. A. 1994: *Myth and Art. Poet and Painter in Classical Greece* (London and New York).

SHELOV-KOVEDYAEV, F. V. 1985: *History of the Bosporus in the 6th-4th cents. BC* (Ancient States in the Territory of the USSR – 1984) (Moscow) (in Russian).

SIMON, E. 1990: Un cratère en cloche d'époque classique à sujet colchidien. In *Le Pont-Euxin,* 227–9.

SNODGRASS, A. M. 1980: *Archaic Greece. The Age of Experience* (Berkeley and Los Angeles).

SNODGRASS, A. M. 1987: *An Archaeology of Greece* (Berkeley, Los Angeles and Oxford).

SOURVINOU-INWOOD, C. 1987: Myth as History. The Previous Owners of the Delphic Oracle. In *Bremmer 1987,* 215–41.

SOURVINOU-INWOOD, C. 1990: Myth as History in Images: Theseus and Medea as a Case Study. In *Edmunds 1990,* 395–445.

SULIMIRSKY, T. 1960: The Cimmerian Problem. *BIA* 2, 45–64.

SZELIGA, G. N. 1986: The Composition of the Argo Metopes from the Monopteros at Delphi. *AJA* 90, 297–305.

THOMAS, C. G. 1993: *Myth Becomes History. Pre-Classical Greece* (Claremont).

THOMAS, E. 1976: *Mythos und Geschichte* (Köln).

TOLORDAVA, V. 1990: Un complexe culturel des VIIIᵉ-VIIᵉ siècles à Vani. In *Le Pont-Euxin,* 243–7, 298–301.

TOLSTIKOV, V. P. 1992: Panticapaeum – Capital of the Bosporus. In *G. A. Koshelenko 1992,* 45–99.

TREISTER, M. J. 1988: The Role of Metals in the Age of Greek Colonization. *VDI* 1, 17–42.

TREISTER, M. J. 1992: Trade in Metals in the Greek World. From the Archaic to the Hellenistic Epoch. *Bulletin of the Metals Museum* 18 (11), 29–43.

TREISTER, M. J. and VINOGRADOV, Y. G. 1993: Archaeology of the Northern Coast of the Black Sea. *AJA* 97, 521–63.

TSETSKHLADZE, G. R. 1992: Greek Colonization of the Eastern Black Sea Littoral (Colchis). *DHA* 18.2, 213–58.

TSETSKHLADZE, G. R. 1993: On the Numismatics of Colchis: the Classical Archaeologist's Perspective. *DHA* 19.1, 233–56.

TSETSKHLADZE, G. R. 1994: Colchians, Greeks and Achaemenians in the 7th-5th cents. BC: A Critical Look. *Klio* 76 (forthcoming).

TSETSKHLADZE, G. R. 1994a: Archaeological Investigations in Georgia in the Last Ten Years and Some Problems of the Ancient History of the Eastern Black Sea Region. *RÉA* 3/4 (forthcoming).

TSETSKHLADZE, G. R. 1994b: The Phiale Mesomphalos from the Kuban (Northern Caucasus). *OJA* 13 (2), 199–215.

TSETSKHLADZE, G. R. 1994c: *Die Griechen in Kolchis: historische-archäologische Abhandlung* (Berlin).

TSETSKHLADZE, G. R. 1994d: *Pichvnari and its Environs (6th cent. BC – 4th cent. AD)* (Paris).

URUSHADZE, A. V. 1980: The Land of the Sorceress Medea. In R. Gordeziani and A. Urushadze (Eds.), *The Caucasus and the Mediterranean* (Tbilisi), 21–8 (in Russian).

VINOGRADOV, Y. A. 1992: Myrmekion. In *G. A. Koshelenko 1992,* 99–120.

VINOGRADOV, Y. G. 1981: *Olbia* (Konstanz, Xenia, ht. 1).

VINOGRADOV, Y. G. 1989: *The Political History of the Polis of Olbia, VII-I cents. BC* (Moscow) (in Russian)

VINOGRADOV, Y. G. and ZOLOTAREV, M. I. 1990: La Chersonèse de la fin de l'archaisme. In *Le Pont-Euxin,* 85–119.

VORONOV, Y. N. 1983: Caucasian Arc-shaped Fibulae of the Early Bronze Age. *KSIA* 176, 29–33.

VOYATZIS, M. 1982: *Frühe Argonautenbilder* (Wurzburg).

VOYATZIS, M. 1992: Votive Riders Seated Side-saddle at Early Greek Sanctuaries. *BSA* 87, 259–79.

WASOWICZ, A. 1975: *Olbia Pontique et son territoire* (Paris).

ZEDGENIDZE, A. A. 1993: On the Earlier Date of Khersones Tavrichesky Foundation. *Russian Archaeology* 3, 50–6 (in Russian).

ZEDGENIDZE, A. A. and SAVELYA, O. Y. 1981: The Chersonesus Necropolis of the 5th-4th cents. BC as a Source for the Study of the Ethnic and Social Composition of the City's Population. In *Tskhaltubo 1979,* 191–203 (in Russian).

ZEDGENIDZE, A. A. and SAVELYA, O. Y. 1981a: Necropolis of Chersonesus of the 5th–4th cents. BC. *KSIA* 168, 3–9.

ZOLOTAREV, M. I. 1990: Concerning the Initial Stage of Construction in Ancient Chersonesus. *Arkheologia* 3 (Kiev), 68–75 (in Ukrainian).

# Chapter 8

# Settlement for Trade and Land in North Africa: problems of identity

## John Boardman

North Africa offers an especially interesting field in which to study the motivation for Greek presence overseas, whether colonial in the narrower sense of the word or not, of its effects on both Greeks and native populations, of the organisation and reinforcement of settlements, and of problems of identity which might or might not be solved from archaeological evidence alone. At one extreme we have Naucratis, an *emporion*, or port-of-trade in modern terms, but which was a Greek town with Greek temples and magistrates and even called a *polis* in later days; and at the other a more conventional colonising area in Cyrenaica which can be judged on much the same terms as Sicily and South Italy, but with a very different origin, in the Cyclades rather than the better known colonising cities of Greece (Fig. 8.1).

I want to make a few remarks first on the general problems of identity, though they will recur. We know that Greek goods travelled with ships and merchants who were not always or perhaps even often of the same origin as the goods they carried and sold. The mercantile role of non-producing states like Aegina is the obvious instance. Farther off, the merchants and ships need not even be Greek. In the classical period Phoenician ships took Athenian pottery to their stations in Morocco and their native neigbours, as Pseudo-Scylax (112) records, and excavation has revealed: an interesting reflection both on who carries what, and on the value of Athenian pottery as a trade commodity since it accompanies what must be regarded as luxury goods from Egypt. As a result, it has been argued that the identification of source of pottery (for it is usually pottery, inevitably) in a colony, need reflect not at all on the origins of either the merchants or the colonists. I presume that an exception would be made for whatever the colonists brought with them and anything accompanying new settlers, which would surely have been what they were used to at home, whether or not it had been locally produced. The question is whether there is a continuing interest kept up by trade, in whoever's hands.

Political and religious relationships between colony and mother city have been explored, as by Graham and Malkin[1], but the commercial depend on analysis of the archaeological evidence. Much in the rest of this paper will tend to demonstrate that the commercial links were to some degree maintained or determined by colonial origins, though there might of course be exceptional circumstances, of antagonism or decline at home, that could break the links. For the moment I would only observe one fairly simple way of testing the hypothesis.

Whatever we think of the value of literary sources for early colonisation, I imagine there would be no doubting the truth of their assertions that Euboeans were busy on Ischia and in Campania, at Cumae. The pottery of the first generations of the colonies is of an overwhelming Euboean character, with the strong admixture of Corinthian that is attested both in home Euboean preferences – they did a lot of imitation – and in the apparent early Corinthian interest in the west, although their own colonising activity was to be more southerly. The point is well made by Coldstream earlier in this volume. Syracuse, by the same token, is historically a Corinthian settlement, and the pottery there is, for the first generations, overwhelmingly Corinthian. At a different scale, the disproportionate amount of Laconian pottery at Tarentum compared with its appearance at other western colonies (which is the important factor) can only reflect the city's origins in Sparta, though the city was much at the mercy too of the commercial success of Corinthian and Attic pottery. Examples can readily be multiplied, especially for the Milesian colonies in the Black Sea. Given the very strong marketing value of some wares in the Archaic period for all markets (first Corinthian, then Attic) it is remarkable that even this degree of preferential trade can be observed. The continuing commercial demand was clearly met in the colonies, whoever the carriers might have been, and we might do wrong to assume that they must always have been folk with no familial or civic or commercial connections with producers and customers, at least in the colonising and early Archaic period. The customer remained as important a factor in trade as producer and carrier, which does not seem an unreasonable proposition; indeed it should go without saying.

This observation, incidentally, goes a long way to answering the suggestion made by Snodgrass in this volume, that the composition of early colonies was not exclusively, or even largely, drawn from the nominal colonising state, but from various Greek cities. Further considerations which make this view improbable are the fact that inscriptions and graffiti from colonies are fairly homogeneous and give no grounds to support the idea that there was present any substantial community drawn from other areas of Greece; and the same, I believe, is indicated by what can be judged from the names of the colonial inhabitants. Colonies were by no means bound to the apron-strings of their mother city, but links there were. Although colonies were often no less conscious of and influenced by their neighbours, Greeks or otherwise, it is often observable that in matters such as burial customs, however much they may differ from home, they generally remain more like their mother cities than like those of other colonies of different origin.

We start our main quest in Egypt. Leaving aside the Bronze Age, there is nothing whatever to suggest any serious Greek presence in Egypt before the mid-7th century, although Greeks were aware of Egyptian products, as we shall see; then, texts tell us that their presence was the result of Egyptian interest in Greeks, in Psammetichos I's employment of East Greek and Carian mercenaries. We do well to recall that for many years before this Egypt had been to various degrees under the thumb of Assyria, and owed its new independence largely to the effects of the Babylonian threat to Assyrian power at home.[2] Travelling mercenaries are not to be expected to carry decorated Greek pottery or stimulate trade until they are allowed to settle down. But this is what happens. Various sources attest this and we are by no means dependent only on Herodotus. But we are told that the mercenaries were allowed to settle, and it seems that the merchant Kolaios from Samos was trading with Egypt not late in Psammetichos' reign (Hdt. IV.15.2).

The crucial site is of course Naucratis, and I sketch briefly its early archaeological history, in parts depending heavily on Astrid Möller's study of the site, soon to be published (Oxford University Press). Naucratis is placed on the east bank of the Canopic branch of the Nile, the only one that could admit large ships to any distance. The earliest part of the site seems to be at the south, and the earliest event is represented by a broad and deep burnt stratum. It seems likely though not certain that the only pottery associated with it is Greek, and it may well be that cautious suggestions that the Greeks settled in or beside an existing Egyptian town are wrong, and that the Greeks could have been the first to live there, at least in any numbers. There is much wood in the burnt stratum and wood is scarce in the Delta where construction is mainly in mudbrick. Could this have been a quayside or from ships (Astrid Möller's suggestion)? Two feet or so above the burning come floors of the sanctuary of Aphrodite, which seems the earliest at Naucratis. The pottery is mainly from Chios and includes fine votives, so the sanctuary may be a Chian foundation, not mentioned by Herodotus. Nearby, at the same level, is a faience factory making scarabs and various faience trinkets and vases.

All this is rather odd. How many sanctuaries of Aphrodite of any importance can be identified in the Greek world so early; and why this production of egyptianising faience? At this point a red herring emerges of whale-like proportions. There was a temple of a so-called 'foreign Aphrodite' at Memphis, where there was also a so-called Tyrian camp (Hdt. II.112). The Aphrodite of Memphis is patently the eastern goddess Astarte who had a long residence in Egypt, since the XVIII Dynasty.[3] And egyptianising faience is deemed a speciality of Phoenician workshops. And texts tell of Egyptians using or commissioning Phoenician ships. But there are no Phoenician inscriptions in inscription-rich Naucratis,[4] no certainly Phoenician objects; the new Egyptian fleet seems to have been composed of Greek biremes and pentekonters (of Samos) and manned by Greeks,[5] and the Naucratite faience production is not only easily distinguishable from the Phoenician, but its distribution, from Italy and beyond to the Black Sea, excludes Phoenicia, Syria and Mesopotamia.[6] It does include parts of the Punic world, but not areas like Sardinia which were being more directly supplied from the homeland than from Carthage. This was decidedly not the direction which Naucratis faced. It is very likely that a faience factory was started by the Greeks at Naucratis, producing Greco-Egyptian scarabs, because there had been similar production since the late eighth century in Rhodes. There was, as it were, continuance of the Rhodian production in the land of the scarab and faience itself, once access and settlement were established. The Rhodian production of faience other than scarabs also had a wholly Greek distribution, not to Phoenician areas east or west (Webb 1978). The Rhodian and Naucratite factories seem parallel but distinct phenomena from Phoenician egyptianising faience.[7] So, at Naucratis at least, we are relatively if not completely free of Phoenicians, however unfashionable such a conclusion may appear. Austin (1970, 28) observed that the Egyptians seem to have confined Greek mercantile activity to the west Delta, Phoenician to the east. The distinction between Greco-Egyptian and Phoenicio-Egyptian production is perhaps one that needs closer observation.[8] There may have been more direct links between east Greece (Samos, Rhodes) and Egypt at an early date, not wholly dependent on Phoenician trade or traders, or at best partly promoted by Greek interest in a

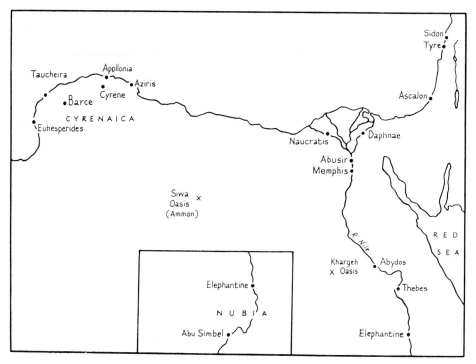

*Fig. 8.1  Cyrenaica and Egypt.*

locally phoenicianised Cyprus which had also long enjoyed direct relations with Egypt, not dependent on coastwise traffic.

   But we are indeed dealing with a period in which there are many foreigners in Egypt, and we should dwell on this a moment since it highlights the relative role of the Greeks. We have to retrace our steps to long before Naucratis. Through the first half of the seventh century Egypt, under its Ethiopian Dynasty, was subject to the Assyrians, and Egyptian Thebes itself was sacked in 663. The Assyrians retired to look after the threat from Babylon, and the new, Saïte Dynasty in Egypt, under Psammetichos I, was the one to invite Greek and Carian mercenaries. Soon afterwards they are allowed to settle. Psammetichos' successors were protective of the Phoenicians and no doubt their presence at Memphis is early, soon followed by settlements of Jews, eventually as far away as Elephantine on the borders of Nubia. There were Phoenician soldiers beside Greeks scratching graffiti at Abu-Simbel on Psammetichos II's expedition in 593/2. But the Greeks had bagged Naucratis, and after the big fire, built an Aphrodite temple and started local industry. Their livelihood seems to have depended on trade with home rather than local land, and this is, it seems to me, the only respect in which the town was unlike any normal colony: otherwise all Greek, with its own temple.[9] Aphrodite was soon followed by Apollo, Hera, Zeus and the Dioskouroi in the northern part of the town, most of them mentioned and probably rightly attributed to their founding states by Herodotus (II.178). This is another less than usual colonial feature – the number of different states involved in the town, their presence dictated by commercial interest, not prompted by land-hunger or the like. The rich finds, especially of pottery, throughout the Archaic period, match in their sources very closely indeed the states alleged by Herodotus to have been active there (*GO*, 121-5). Without Herodotus we would have deduced a very similar list from the finds and inscriptions alone. They are dominantly east Greek with the mainland represented only by mercantile Aegina. While the original motive for settlement derived from the activity of mercenaries, it obviously soon developed into one exclusively for the support of trade. The model for such enterprise could easily have been Al Mina in north Syria, on the river Orontes, visited by the same East Greeks throughout the seventh century, and very likely the home of a number of them (Boardman 1990).

Herodotus (I.30; II.16; 169) brings us to King Amasis and what he did to and for Naucratis. His predecessor Apries had a brief anti-Greek interlude in an invasion of Cyrenaica, which was repulsed. He then seems to have used Greeks and Greek ships against Amasis. He and his Greeks were soundly defeated by Amasis at Momemphis in what seems to be Amasis' first regnal year, 570. Contemporary sources, Egyptian and Babylonian, help us here more than anything Herodotus wrote over a century later, since it is clear that he conflated events and put a heavily pro-Amasis, pro-Greek slant on his tale. Fortunately we have a fine red granite stele of Amasis describing events; unfortunately it was used as a threshold in a Cairo palace and is badly defaced. And fortunately we have Nebuchadrezzar's cuneiform account of relevant activities from the Babylonian side.[10] So we now have Apries, with *his* Greeks, defeated at Momemphis near Naucratis in 570; his escape to return with a fleet and a Babylonian invading army in 567, facing Amasis who was supported by Greeks from Cyrenaica. Apries and the Babylonians are defeated; Apries is killed. But when Amasis had come to the throne three years earlier it was in an atmosphere of profound anti-Greek feeling. It is against this background that we have to read Herodotus' record of what Amasis did for Naucratis, since in his day the Greeks of Naucratis were doing very well and had nothing to complain about except, no doubt, taxes, and were able to remember how Amasis became more indulgent of the Greeks with time. Amasis may even have come to need the Greeks but was not going to let them run wild again. They were to be pinned down in Naucratis, allowed to trade only through Naucratis, and obliged to set up a form of administration, the *prostatai* of the port, who would presumably have been answerable to the Egyptian king. Amasis was being restrictive rather than beneficent, whatever it might have looked like a century later. This is certainly the view of Egyptologists, who are less likely to be mesmerised by Herodotus than many of us. He does, however, seem to imply (II. 179) that Amasis' restrictions had been removed by his day, no doubt by the Persians.

The evidence that Greeks were there long before Amasis is overwhelming; Herodotus' words do not contradict this, and the archaeology is emphatic. Indeed it provides an important fixed point for traditional chronology and in no way upsets it, as some have tried to argue. The decisive element in this is in Herodotus' account of Amasis allowing the creation of a joint Greek sanctuary, the Hellenion, shared by several states. It is clearly identified on the ground from pottery labelled "to the gods of the Greeks", as it were package dedications (Hogarth *et al.* 1898/9, 55–6; 1905, 116–8). On conventional dating, which is thereby confirmed, the earliest pottery is no earlier than the reign of Amasis, and is appreciably later than the earliest from the site overall, which we can place well before 600, near to 630. So Herodotus' association of Amasis with the Hellenion is acceptable. But consider the Hellenion and these strange dedications. Surely this is the first time that a degree of joint worship of Olympians, as the gods of the Greeks, is admitted by Greeks and foreigners. The gods' identities were determined by the different divine allegiances of the participating states. Some few years later another centre for joint worship was created, the sanctuary of the Twelve Gods in Athens, but here identities were determined by the more artificial divine genealogies.[11]

There are many problems about chronology, names and Herodotus where Naucratis is concerned. I do think the information he received about its early history was very garbled. He tells us (II. 134–5) about the courtesan Rhodopis who was owned by Sappho's brother and who made a dedication at Delphi. The inscription of the dedication seems to have been found and belongs to the last third of the sixth century, around or after 530 on usual dating (very much later, of course, on any revised dating).[12] Herodotus says she was contemporary with Amasis, which puts her in the second third of the century. But Sappho, and no doubt her eldest brother, were dead by about 570, to judge from literary sources, and so belong to the first third of the century; and the girl she mentions as involved with him is a Doricha not Rhodopis.[13] No doubt they were the same, as Strabo (XVII.1.33) and others have thought, but Sappho's brother must have been trading with Naucratis well before Amasis. I have no answers to this dilemma and we are left to assume that the pubescent Doricha was an old man's darling and survived to be a rich old Madame.

Naucratis may not have been a colony in the ordinary sense of the word, but it was in some respects something far more important: a joint settlement by Greeks overseas, organised like a Greek city with its own temples as well as one joint sanctuary, and run by a joint Greek administration, albeit with rules of trade dictated by the Egyptian king. It was peaceful and prospered, indifferent to the interstate rivalries at home, bound firmly by a common interest in trade with the foreigner, in a word, in making money.

We move along the coast now to Cyrenaica. The shoreline is not especially hospitable and not at all indented, a feature which has been thought an almost necessary prerequisite for busy colonising (see Snodgrass, earlier in this volume[14]). Going west along the coast the first decent area answering this alleged need is around Carthage, where the Phoenicians stopped to settle. But there are some potential harbours, and in places open anchorages sheltered by sunken fossil dunes offshore (*Tocra*, I, 3; II, 3, n.1). It was easy to sail across from Crete, a trip for all I know still undertaken by Cretan sponge-fishers, as it was in pre-Gadaffi days. It might seem to be the natural route west from Egypt and a good alternative for Phoenicians to one taking them past Greek islands, although prevailing winds and currents were against them.[15] Kolaios, at least, a trader with Egypt, was alleged to have found himself passing the coast of Cyrenaica en route to Spain (Hdt. IV.152). We must assume that at the time of colonisation this was a coast at least occasionally sailed by Phoenicians to Carthage and beyond, but totally neglected by them until they came to Carthage, which probably appealed as a forward base for trade as well as providing a good life.

The essence of Herodotus' account (IV.150–58) of the colonisation of the Libyan coast is likely to be correct since there would seem to be no particular motivation in anyone inventing it; and this despite the fact that he offers two versions, one Theran, one Cyrenean. The

Therans had suffered a drought. They learnt from Cretans, fellow Dorians, that Libya was potentially exploitable. Here there might indeed be a Phoenician element since it was said to have been a man of Itanos, east Crete, that led them, a purple person, *porphureos*, no doubt a dealer, called Korobios. The name is not otherwise known to us, but not therefore some sort of memory of a local sea god, which scholars used to believe. I wonder whether the name is a hellenised version of a Phoenician.[16] One tradition has Itanos founded by a son of Phoinix, and it certainly had eastern associations. The general situation is one that recalls the *Odyssey*, not so far off in date – recall the Phoenician vessel moored off Crete in Book XIII (256–86) – and of Odysseus in Book XIV (285–313), in Egypt, pretending to be a Cretan, and taken from Egypt by a Phoenician, ostensibly to Libya. Can these be episodes that have the early colonising of Libya as a background, providing it with some sort of heroic precedent?

This was the Theran version; the Cyreneans had a more fancy tale of intrigue in Crete and the stammerer Battos, which has no bearing here, whether historical or not. And there is the fourth-century Oath of the Founders inscription which, whatever the antiquity of much of its content, does not disagree in essentials with what Herodotos records.[17]

The Therans went first to an island called Platea, one of those in the Gulf of Bomba. Here they were visited by the Samian Kolaios, en route west, an indication that it was not only Phoenicians that used this route but any Greeks who had dealings with Egypt and found cause to go west and poach in Phoenician waters. The colonists moved on to the coast at Aziris for a few years. The site is identified and pottery has been found which, on conventional dating, belongs to the right years (conventionally 637–631) – a further vindication of our chronology. A few years at Aziris were followed by the Greeks being guided up on to the plateau and the foundation of the ideal colonial site at Cyrene (Boardman 1967).[18]

The whole quest was strictly motivated by search for land, only incidentally guided by the navigational expertise of Korobios, and momentarily crossed by the path of another merchant, the Samian Kolaios: as clear a contrast with Naucratis as could be wished. It did not take long, however, for the pastures and fields of the plateau to yield a profitable surplus for trade and for Cyrene to wax as rich as many of the Greek cities of Italy and Sicily; secure from threat by land, except for a brief intervention from Egypt, and apparently unaffected by a sea-lane from the Levant past its coast. Cyrene was up on the plateau, but excavation and survey have shown that its port at Apollonia, and, to the west, the towns at what was later called Ptolemais, at Taucheira and at Euesperides (now Benghazi) were founded within less than a generation of Cyrene, and almost certainly from Cyrene itself (Boardman 1967). This was consolidation of Greek hold on a fertile coastal plain, not trade prospection. It is possible to read Herodotus to mean that there was a gap of over half a century between the foundation of Cyrene and other settlements in Libya, but the archaeological evidence makes it very clear that this cannot possibly be the case since the earliest pottery from all sites, two of them very well excavated (Cyrene and Tocra), is so very similar; so either Herodotus is wrong, or historians have misread him, and all he (IV. 159) is saying is that there was division, *anadasmos*, of the Libyans' land in the Cyrene area in the days of Battos II. At any rate, there could hardly have been question of Cyrene's *anadasmos* of land a hundred miles or more away.

One of the sites, Taucheira, modern Tocra, has given us rich votive deposits from a sanctuary of Demeter, running from its foundation soon after Cyrene, in about 620, to near the end of the sixth century. In passing, and with a mind to what has just been said about the sea-lane and its Phoenician shipping, it may be noted that at Tocra the only possible intimation of this is one scarab, which is ordinary Egyptian, and a gold crescent, which could be Phoenician but need not be (*Tocra* I, pls. 104–5, nos. 3, 92). There is nothing even to link it clearly to Greek activity at Naucratis. But I do not wish to dwell particularly on Cyrenaica as a colonising area, rather than use the excavations at Tocra to explore a more general problem that arises in study of colonial foundations and especially problems of identity and its significance.

Tocra is a big site, walled and heavily occupied down to the Arab invasions. A chance seashore find of complete Archaic Greek vases led to a call for excavation and the British School at Athens was called in. What was found were the stratified deposits of a sanctuary of Demeter, running mainly from the later seventh to the end of the sixth century BC, lying behind what appeared to be a sea wall. No other substantial structures of the Greek period were uncovered, though the sanctuary went on in use through the Classical and Hellenistic periods. The finds to be associated with these periods must be largely elsewhere but there was a very substantial range of the early deposits. They were in sand and on a sea shore which is rapidly receding. The unity of the deposit is indicated by the way in which the pottery, though much fragmented and with fragments wide scattered in the excavated area, nevertheless made up for the most part into complete or near complete vases. This is a circumstance worth dwelling on a moment since it may suggest a way of determining how complete such deposits might be. In this case it seemed that there was little from these deposits that had crept far away from the area. Contrast the Athenian Acropolis where very few even nearly whole vases were found, and many an exquisite large vase is known from only a single fragment. Is it possible that something might be deduced about the size of a whole original assemblage on the basis of statistics about the proportion of pieces recovered complete or completable, the half-complete, the one-fragment vases, or some such approximate measure of relative survival? I am advised, however, by those who know the statistical techniques, that in this case it is probably better just to make an intelligent guess.

The range of finds was notable. I do not dwell on them here, but rather wish to consider the material in terms of the simple statistics that it generates, to see whether they can demonstrate anything of value to our understanding of the history of early colonies. The assumptions are made that our dating is broadly correct, our identification of the sources of pottery are broadly correct, and that we have established some sort of expected relationship between source and colony that goes beyond the accidents of trade.

At Tocra there were three main levels in a deposit which appears to have been almost completely explored, and all the pottery was kept and counted. The periods of each level seem to be of somewhat different lengths, in the proportions of 6:5:9, and in creating proportional statistics adjustments were made to allow for these differences. The results showed a pattern that made good sense; they are displayed in Fig. 8.2. Corinthian imports declined slightly while Attic increased, which is the general pattern for Mediterranean trade in the most popular decorated wares. The slight increase in Laconian and decrease in Chian also matches general patterns of trade, whoever the carriers might have been. The notable increase of Rhodian,

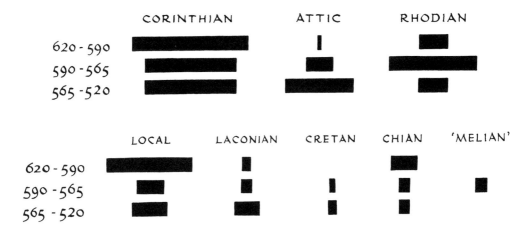

*Fig. 8.2 Proportions of pottery from the Archaic deposits at Tocra.*

however, in the middle level, of about 590 to 565, corresponds to a period in which texts indicate that there was positive encouragement of immigration to Cyrene, and the *anadasmos* of land to which I have already referred. In Cyrene this resulted in a new constitution and status for incoming islanders, from Rhodes. This could well be enough to explain the increase in Rhodian pottery, since the fortunes of the various Cyrenaican colonies seem to have been fairly closely linked.

This use of statistics was questioned by the late Professor Stucchi, excavator at Cyrene.[19] They can be defended, but I want to use the occasion to consider the problems all such statistical comparisons must face, but which are seldom faced squarely. He compared quantities and, correctly, proportions of material from Tocra, from the Agora excavations at Cyrene, and from the American excavations at the Demeter sanctuary outside the walls of Cyrene. The material is of comparable range in date and source, but there the resemblance ends. The Agora material comes from series of excavations over many years, is considerable but scrappy and in no way represents even a fair sample of any one major deposit. The Demeter material more closely resembles that from Tocra, but is also very scrappy and well strewn, so that much depends on the accident of survival of batches in the areas dug, while much must have disappeared into the ravine around the city. The Tocra material, by comparison, came from compact, apparently undisturbed deposits, and a very large proportion made up into complete or near complete vases, which suggests a measure of totality, although there is always the possibility that at one or another occasion votive material was taken to be buried somewhere outside the area dug. The Cyrene Agora material is little published but Stucchi had access to the storerooms. The Cyrene Demeter material is all published except the Corinthian (and the Attic was only published after Stucchi wrote). The Tocra material is all published. The lesson of this is that the nature of the site, excavation, completeness of material and publication all have to be taken into account, but seldom are.

Given this degree of non-comparability the results are still, to my mind, not so disparate that the exercise of comparing them is worthless. I tabulate Stucchi's figures for Tocra and the Cyrene Agora in Table 8.1 (he expressed them discursively); he could not include Cyrene Demeter since the proportion of the whole represented by Attic, Corinthian and local was not known. Each column ought to add up to 100% but in fact the first one adds up to 90%. The moral: always check other people's mathematics. But, even given the 10% discrepancy, there are certainly differences between the tables. They do not, however, seem to me to discredit the exercise. The similarities are more impressive than not, given the range of differences there might have been in sources and numbers. They are certainly more like each other than comparable tables from any other pair of western colonies could be. So they mean something, and there might of course be other reasons for the discrepancies.

For example. The Cyrene Rhodian probably includes many of the striped so-called Ionian cups which at Tocra were carefully distributed among their various non-Rhodian sources by John Hayes. How much black glaze you count rather depends on how diligent and skilful you are in mending the undecorated fragments. The amount of Corinthian at Tocra is at any rate remarkable, as is its very poor quality, and I had suggested that Tocra, at the end of the trading run along the coast, may have had more than its fair share of unpopular shapes.[20] Certainly, the record of the Corinthian shapes found is very puzzling in terms of votive or domestic material at any other Greek site, especially the number of plates, not a very popular shape at the best of times though with a record as votive pottery in some places, such as the Acropolis at Athens. At Tocra it looks much more as though special cult purposes, for dedication at least, were served by local production rather than from deliberate choice of whatever imported pottery was available, the range of which may not have been determined by cult needs, or even domestic needs, but more on the accidents of cargo composition.

Stucchi went on to make further statistical comparison between the sites in terms of the lesser imported wares (not Corinthian and Attic) and was again perplexed by the results. But his mathematics are no less perplexing and I do not consider them in detail. They still, to my eyes, broadly correspond, or at least more with each other than with any non-Cyrenaican complex, and the points of difficulty tend again to be whether you include Attic black glaze with the rest, and an allegedly heavy proportion of Laconian at Cyrene Demeter, which is, I think, no real problem. More impressive are other finds there which tend to emphasise the likeness of import experience at the Cyrenaican sites.

In pottery this relates especially to the Cretan pottery, which seems to come to Cyrenaica only; and the so-called Melian, which represents the continuing island interest – we recall that the original colonists came from Thera. It is the same island interest which must account for the presence of so many of the so-called island gems at Cyrene.[21] These are certainly products of one of the islands, probably Melos, which was Dorian like Thera. Their distribution is otherwise wide but scrappy, except for dozens in Melos and, unsurprisingly, several in Crete. All this simply goes to reinforce the view that imports to colonies can reflect continuing links with sources of colonists and are not simply accounted for by the vagaries of trade conducted by others. There is not that much linked to Thera itself except for some jewellery and a plate at Tocra,[22] but we know so little of distinctively Theran products in the relevant period.

All this, and the matter of other Chapters in this volume, should demonstrate well enough

|  | TOCRA | CYRENE |
|---|---|---|
| Local | 1.84 | 2.27 |
| Rhodian | 13.57 | 25.56 |
| Black glaze | 8.04 | 21.02 |
| Chian | 3.52 | 6.8 |
| East Greek other | 5.26 | 5.68 |
| Cretan | 0.99 | 2.27 |
| Laconian | 5.68 | 6.81 |
| Corinthian | 38.45 | 10.22 |
| Attic | 12.67 | 19.31 |
|  | 90.02 | 99.94 |

*Table 8.1 Percentages of Archaic pottery found at Tocra and at Cyrene Agora (after Stucchi, see n. 17).*

how wrong it would be to regard the phenomenon of Greeks travelling and settling overseas as any sort of unified colonising movement which can be reduced to simple factors of intention, hunger for land or raw materials, exploration, treatment of native peoples, trade – haphazard or otherwise, dependence on following or leading Phoenicians. And that attempts so to define it are more likely to obscure important issues that differ considerably from place to place and effectively resist being set in any unified pattern of behaviour. A major problem has been the tendency to regard local problems and solutions as in some significant way explaining the whole, and the subject has been more than a little bedevilled in recent years by considerations which are barely academic at all but concerned to give voice to other contemporary preoccupations. At least, I think, we have stopped thinking that the archaeology has to be adjusted to the texts, and have learned that the question *why* an ancient author has said something is of equal or prior importance to *what* he appears to be saying. We should probably trust relative archaeological chronology more than detailed relative chronologies derived from one or more written sources, while acknowledging that absolute chronology must depend ultimately on written sources, but preferably not of a hundred years and more after the event, and preferably not Greek at all.

## ABBREVIATIONS

*Cyrene:*  D.White (ed.), *The extra-mural sanctuary of Demeter and Persephone at Cyrene I–IV.* Philadelphia 1984–90).
*GO:*  J. Boardman, *The Greeks Overseas³* (London 1980)
*Tocra:*  J.Boardman and J.Hayes, *Excavations at Tocra,* 1963–1965 I (1966), II (1973). London.

## NOTES

1. A. J. Graham, *Colony and Mother City in Ancient Greece* (Manchester 1971); I. Malkin, *Religion and Colonization in Ancient Greece* (Leiden 1987).
2. For the fortunes of the countries of the Levant in this period, see: CAH III².2 (1991), Chapters 24–7 on Assyria and Babylonia (A. K. Grayson, J. Oates, D. J. Wiseman), Chapters 29–31 on Israel and Judah (T. C. Mitchell), Chapter 32 on Phoenicia (W. Culican), Chapter 35 on Egypt (T. G. H. James). And for the Greeks in the Near East and Egypt, T. F. R. G. Braun in CAH III². 3 (1982), Chapter 36a,b.  For the relations between Egypt and Phoenicia, J. Leclant in W. A. Ward (ed.), *The role of the Phoenicians in the Interactions of Mediterranean Civilizations* (Beirut 1968), 9–31. For the archaeology of the Greeks in these areas and basic references which are not repeated in this paper, see: *GO*, Chapters 3, 4.
3. J. Leclant, *Syria* 37 (1960), 3–8.
4. Hogarth *et al.* 1905, 118, mentions an amphora neck fragment painted with the Phoenician letter *shin* (basically a zigzag); it seems unpublished.
5. Necho II sent a Phoenician expedition round Africa at the end of the seventh century (Hdt. IV. 42). On the composition of his war fleet, however, see: James 1991, 720–2; Lloyd 1975, 33–8, and "Were Necho's triremes Phoenician?", in *JHS* 95 (1975), 45–61. Herodotus (II. 154) saw docks at the Camps where Psammetichos had stationed the Greek and Carian mercenaries.
6. I am indebted to Andrée Gorton for information about these. A version of her thesis on egyptianising faience and glass scarabs in the Mediterranean world is being prepared for publication.
7. G. Hölbl (*Beziehungen der ägyptischer Kultur zu Altitalien* (Leiden 1979) 208–14) finds subject differences in the scarabs though the techniques are identical, but may underestimate the differences occasioned by date, the Rhodian being earlier, many much earlier, than Naucratis.
8. For the relevance of this to identification of the faience scarabs on Ischia (and the easterners who may have been there) see my forthcoming paper in a volume dedicated to Giorgio Buchner (*AION* 16).
9. We have to assume that the livelihood of the Greeks in early Naucratis depended wholly on their trade and that they were not given land to farm, such as the Greeks on Ischia were able to acquire (see Coldstream's article in this volume).
10. For accounts of these documents, see: D. J. Wiseman, *The Chronicles of the Chaldaean Kings* (London 1956) 12, 26, 29f. , 94; E. Edel, Amasis und Nebukadrezzar II, in *Göttinger Miszellen* 29 (1978), 13–20; A. Leahy, *Journal of Egyptian Archaeology* 74 (1988), 183–99; A. B. Lloyd, *Historia* 37 (1988), 40–1 and Lloyd 1988, 178–80; James 1991, 734–6; A. T. Reyes, *Archaic Cyprus* (Oxford 1994), 72–6.
11. There was a Hellenistic "Hellenion" at Memphis: Lloyd 1976, 224.
12. L. H. Jeffery, *The Local Scripts of Archaic Greece* (Oxford 1961, 1990), 102.
13. Doricha would have been her 'real' Thracian name, Rhodopis (rosy-faced) her working name.
14. The attractions of irregular coastline (as of offshore islands) is at least as much a matter of the availability of anchorages and river-mouths with valleys and access inland, as the multiplicity of local connections. Thucydides' account of Phoenician preferences around Sicily (VI.2) simply records conditions for most colonising ventures.
15. On problems of passage along this coast, see: M. G. Fulford in *Libyan Studies* 20 (1989), 169–192.
16. Sebastian Brock tells me there is no plausible Semitic name. The *QRB* root means "offer".
17. A. J. Graham, *JHS* 80 (1960), 94–111.
18. The early pottery from Euesperides has now been published by M. Vickers and D. W. J. Gill in *Libyan*

*Studies* 17 (1986), 97–108.

19. "Die archäischen griechischen Vasen und die Kyrenaika: Importe, Imitationen und Einflüsse – ein Uberblick", in H. A. G. Brijder (ed.), *Ancient Greek and Related Pottery* (Amsterdam 1984), 139–43. He publishes (fig. 1) a fragment from Aziris which he seems to imply is too early for a site occupied from 637 to 631 and assigns to Coldstream's Group II (675–640); but at Emporio this type with a plain band below the bird panel is of Deposit III (630–600): J. Boardman, *Greek Emporio* (London 1967), 133. At any rate, only if it were a century earlier might there be something to be explained.

20. "Reflections on the Greek Pottery Trade with Tocra", in F. F. Gadallah (ed. ), *Libya in History* (Tripoli 1968), 89–91.

21. For the finds at Cyrene Demeter, see: *Cyrene*. For the island gems, S. Lowenstam in *Cyrene* III (1987), 10–13. For comparisons of the pottery with Tocra, G. P. Schaus in *Cyrene* II (1985), 102–7. *Idem* in *Scripta Mediterranea* 1 (1980), 21–6, suggests that Cyrene and Tocra were approached by different routes, but sources may well have been the same and there was surely coastwise traffic too.

22. *Tocra* I, pl.104, no. 1; Boardman (1967), pl.61.1–2

## BIBLIOGRAPHY

AUSTIN, M. M. 1970: *Greece and Egypt in the Archaic Age.* (Cambridge).

BOARDMAN, J. 1967: Evidence for the dating of Greek settlements in Cyrenaica. *BSA* 61, 149–56.

BOARDMAN, J. 1990: Al Mina and History. *OJA* 9, 169–190.

HOGARTH, D. G. *et al.* 1898/9: Excavations at Naukratis. *BSA* 5, 26–97.

HOGARTH, D. G. *et al.* 1905: Excavations at Naukratis. *JHS* 25, 105–36.

JAMES, T. G. H. 1991: Egypt: the XXV and XXVI Dynasties. *CAH* III$^2$.2, 677–747.

LLOYD, A. B. 1975, 1976, 1988: *Herodotus Book II.* Introduction; Commentary 1–98; Commentary 99–182 (Leiden).

WEBB, V. 1978: *Archaic Greek Faience* (Warminster).